Gods of Men

Rise of the Wolf

BY

Philip Remus

Rise of the Wolf

Gods of Men, Volume 3

Philip Remus

Published by Sword of Damocles, 2022.

RISE OF THE WOLF

First edition. November 10, 2022.

ISBN: 979-8230933700

Written by Philip Remus.

For Ukraine.

Notes to the reader:

With regard to the Spartan hippeis (cavalry). This book does not cover the period when mounted cavalry was reintroduced as fighting units in Sparta. At Sparta, the hippeis were crack hoplite infantry, of which there were 300, and often referred to simply as the 300 and sometimes the Dioskouri, (the sons of Zeus) Castor and Pollux. To distinguish these horseless cavalries from the hippeis of other belligerent states, who were mounted cavalry, I have called the hippeis of Sparta the Dioskouri in this book, singular, Dioskouros.

I hope you enjoy reading these novels.

Remus.

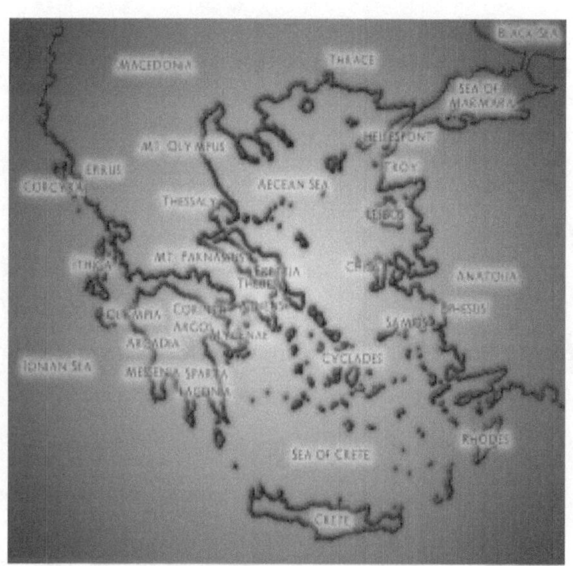
MACEDONIA
THRACE
SEA OF MARMARA
HELLESPONT
TROY
EPIRUS
AEGEAN SEA
THESSALY
MT. PARNASSUS
ANATOLIA
SAMOS
ARGOS
ARCADIA
IONIAN SEA
CYCLADES
RHODES
SEA OF CRETE
CRETE

PART ONE

Shadow War

And the Pythia said:

"Oh! Thou great Lykurgos, who comes to my beautiful dwelling, Dear to Apollo, and to all who sit within the halls of Olympus. Whether to hail thee a god I know not, or only a mortal, But my hope is strong that a god thou wilt prove...

Delphic Oracle, 7th Century BCE

PROLOGUE

Potidaea, Chalcidice Peninsula

Diosthyos/December

Eponymous Year of Isanor, 430 BC

Archestratus stood on the pale rocky peninsula, unperturbed by the pouring rain pelting him, spattering his face as he looked down at the six war triremes blockading the narrow channel, blocking the enemy's vital supply route and so completing the siege.

The Corinthians tried to break the siege to relieve the city, but his forces repulsed them, and two Corinthian triremes were broken and listing on their keels where they had come to rest after being rammed, in the shallows close to the shore, their decks washed by the waves.

There was a stillness in the air, an uncomfortable calm. His fleet of over a hundred triremes rested at anchor, or were drawn up onto the beaches along the Toronaic Gulf to his left. Hundreds of sailors were on the beach, and a city of tents sprawled up into the hills, adjoining the army camp around Potidaea, now walled up like a tomb, and the Potidaeans and Corinthians within were starving to death.

He wasn't without his own problems of course. The plague was sweeping through his army and the inclement weather and there had been dissent in the ranks too. Stirrings of mutiny. Archestratus soon got on top of the problem, ordering the ringleaders to be arrested and he sentenced them to an exemplary death by means of crucifixion. Ten of them in all, now hanging from X-shaped wooden crucifixes just beyond the camp up on a hill for all to see the fate of those in his army who would ferment mutiny.

There were the Macedons too, who had made several hit and run cavalry attacks on his patrols and supply lines. Athens might command the sea, but they were far from secure on land.

'What did Athens have to say?' asked Phanomachus, as he came up behind him, holding his cloak around himself against the wet and cold wind sweeping in from the Thermaic Gulf.

'What do they ever say? They want us to settle the siege quickly. The citizens are in uproar because of the cost of keeping a navy and an army here. While we swim in shit, they complain about money.'

'It's only a matter of time now, Archestratus,' Phanomachus said. 'Things are so dire, they've even started eating one another,' he added.

Archestratus turned slowly to his colleague.

'One of our spotters saw some soldiers butchering a dead woman and dividing her flesh to cook and eat,' Phanomachus explained.

Archestratus felt sick to his stomach at the thought of it. How desperate a man must be to turn to such a low and base practice. He felt a twinge of empathy for them; but this was war, and war has no room for soft hearts.

'We lost another five men to plague during the night. And three men are reported to have deserted. I've sent men out to find them and bring them back.' Cold rain dripped from his hair and drizzled down his neck. 'Why are you standing out here in the cold and wet, Archestratus? Come back to the villa where it's warm and dry, man, or you'll catch your death.'

'You go. I'll be there soon.'

Phanomachus stared at him for a long moment.

It had been two years since they arrived. Two long and bloody years, ravaged by war and plague, not to mention the weather, from the mosquito infested marshes in the sweltering summer, to the snow, rain and mud in the winter. It was having an effect on the army and Archestratus had never seen morale so low, nor such fear in the men as they had of the plague, which had killed scores of them and scores more were so sick they couldn't fight. It had taken all the persuasive powers of the three generals, and a pledge of a larger share of the plunder once the city fell, to maintain order – as well as ten crucifixions.

It had been raining for five days solid and the camp had become into a mire of cold slippery mud and it hampered everything and made everyone utterly miserable. The tents in the camp flooded and there was a problem with rats getting at the food supplies and into the tents of the men. There was only one man who seemed immune from it all, and that was Socrates, who set the best example to his men, enduring every misery the gods threw at them without a single complaint. He was something of a hero too, after rescuing Alcibiades from certain death during the fighting last year. He could drink Dionysos under the table too and appear as soba as an abstinent, Archestratus had never seen a man drink as much wine and remain steady afoot as Socrates, nor indeed with such a constitution as to spite even the hardiest of men, even against the cruellest of the weather.

*

Archestratus could hear the rain pelting the roof tiles, loud and annoying, like a million fingers drumming all at once, and beyond the noise of the rain, he could hear the shouts and clattering of soldiers, miserable with their lot, eager for rest and longing for home.

Hestiodoros had gone to the walls of Potidaea to meet one of their heralds who had come out of the city and called for a meeting with the generals.

Phanomachus, Xenophon* and Hestiodoros decided that it may look too eager for all three to go, so Hestiodoros went alone, playing it down. If they wanted to negotiate, he didn't want to give any ideas that Athens was in either a generous or desperate situation, despite the clear hardships the Athenian army was suffering. However much they suffered, it paled when compared to how much they were suffering in Potidaea.

Hestiodoros, cruel swine he was, went to meet them with a leg of mutton that he intended to eat in front of them as they made their requests, whatever they might be?

Phanomachus looked into the solitary flame of the lamp on his table, its light coruscating against the cracked plaster walls of the old villa he had occupied for nearly two years, just beyond the siege line. It served as a perfect headquarters and accommodation for his officers.

The news Xenophon brought with him when he arrived from Athens suggested that Pericles was under a great deal of pressure himself from the hardliners like that rabble-rouser Cleon, who had a big mouth and much to say about Pericles and none of it favourable. Cleon was totally opposed to Pericles's defensive war policy, he wanted to press an offensive war, a war of conquest.

Cleon hated the Spartans with every fibre of his being. He hated aristocrats too. Xenophon told him that Cleon's voice was getting louder and Pericles was rapidly losing support, in no small part due to this siege and the vast sums of money it was costing.

What would they have him do? Even with siege engines, the walls of Potidaea would not yield, such was their thickness. They had done battle at the beginning, but seeing they were up against a superior force, the Potidaeans retreated behind their walls and Phanomachus ordered the city to be put under siege. He told Pericles it would be a long affair. He told him it would cost a great deal of money. But the order stood, "deliver unto Athens that belligerent city by any and all means."

Phanomachus and built long high wooden walls with palisades around Potidaea, and the Potidaeans likewise built wooden walls to counter those of Athens to further obstruct any attempt by

Phanomachus to attack. They served no purpose; Phanomachus had no intentions of wasting men and resources by assaulting the city. He'd starve them out instead. His own army was kept well supplied by sea, which Athens dominated.

The siege was biting and at night, they could hear the wailing and crying of the grief stricken and starving Potidaeans. All they needed to do was hold on a little while longer, another month at most...

Xenophon, seated at another table eating was watching Phanomachus, writing on papyrus; Phanomachus was a prolific writer, Xenophon often wondered just what he wrote about, beyond responding to Pericles's dispatches and writing to his wife.

Cold air blew in as General Hestiodoros returned. Xenophon and Phanomachus looked at him. He was soaked through to the skin and water dripped from the hem of his cloak onto the stone floor where it formed a puddle. 'They want to discuss terms,' he said as he removed his rain spattered helmet and handed it to one servant and took a cup of wine from another. 'They said they'd send their representatives tomorrow.'

This was it, thought Phanomachus. *Finally*. 'How did they seem to you?' he asked.

'Defeated. They've endured all they can. The situation is dire in that city. The gods have deserted them and they're in utter despair.'

Phanomachus nodded his head.

'What more did the Potidaeans say?' asked Xenophon.

'Nothing more. They asked for a truce for their representatives to come and negotiate terms of their surrender. Nothing more did they offer. Upon my word, I told them, none among them or their representatives shall come to harm, and we are willing to receive them honourably into our camp, and the time was agreed for two hours after dawn, whereupon they turned about and went back into the city.'

It was the next day, and the Athenian army mustered in their best order to show the Potidaeans that they were still in their best condition, and those hoplites who had fallen sick with the plague were sent back behind the Athenian lines out of sight.

Four Potidaean aristocrats came to their headquarters, where they were greeted by the three generals, and to further salt the wounds of the Potidaeans, Xenophon had a long table set with a bounty of food. He knew the value of the psychological impact this would have on the hungry delegation, and he was right, they looked at the food as if about to pounce on it like a pack of wild dogs, but they kept their composure, the siege had not quite robbed them of their dignity.

Like a panel of judges, Phanomachus, Xenophon and Hestiodoros sat at another long table, while the Potidaean delegation stood before them like felons, their fates and the fate of their city now firmly in the hands of the Athenians, for the shadow of Death was over Potidaea now, and before noon, terms were agreed on very generous terms.

The generals allowed the Potidaeans with their wives and children, along with some auxiliary soldiers to leave the city and go anywhere they wanted to in freedom. Each woman was allowed to take two garments, each man a single garment, as well as a minimum amount of money to see them through to safe territory.

* ***Not to be confused with the writer and student of Socrates.***

ONE

Sparta

Gamelion/January

429 BCE

Agesilaos and his friends were hiding in the groves watching Lysander, sitting on the riverbank.

Tisamenos frowned. 'What's he doing? Why's he just sitting there?'

'Maybe he's waiting for somebody?' Agapitos whispered back speculatively.

'D'you think he saw us following him?' Tisamenos asked.

'I don't see how,' said Agesilaos. They had followed him all the way from Karystos, keeping themselves well-hidden up in the wooded hills, moving swift and light of foot. How could he possibly know? He made no gesture, he didn't so much as look in their direction, keeping his eyes on the road ahead of him. They were sneaky and crafty Mister Foxes, and no mistake.

'What should we do?' Tisamenos whispered, crouched between Agesilaos and Agapetos with his hands resting over their shoulders. 'Should we wait and see?' That would be his preference. Rather pull on a wolf's whiskers than provoke a Dioskouros. But something told him that Agesilaos had something else in mind. Agesilaos had made several attempts to bring himself to Lysander's attention, none of them had succeeded. But that was before Agesilaos's *phauaxir*,* a boy has a different status once he completes his fox time. It is a tradition that reaches far back into history, which was as meaningful then as it is today, for a youth cannot enter the *ephebeion** before completing the fox time, to kill the child in himself and awaken the man. So it is, upon entering the *ephebeion*, he was no longer a child, yet not a man either, but something in between.

The young prince was calculating in his moves. If Lysander was ever going to court him to be his Hearer, now was the time to make his move, and he needed to impress Lysander, fail in that and Lysander will reject him.

'You two go back, no point all of us getting our arses kicked. I'm going to show him I'm worthy of a lesson and creep up on him and take him by surprise.'

His friends looked alarmed at him.

'*A Dioskouros*! *Have you lost your mind*?' Tisamenos exclaimed in horror. 'Broken limbs and smashed up faces, that's where that foolishness leads.'

'At best, he'll give you a beating and send you on your way,' agreed Agapetos, looking warily at Agesilaos. 'My brother's a Dioskouros and he never wastes an opportunity to give a kid a good kicking. And you'd never get anywhere near him before he knew you were there.'

'Your brother is mean and cruel,' said Agesilaos. 'Lysander isn't like that.'

'I say you should happen by. Make it a happenstance. Bid him good day and see what happens.'

Agesilaos laughed. 'By the gods. He's a man, not a monster.'

'Says you.'

Agapetos reached and grabbed Agesilaos's wrist. 'I'm coming with you. If he beats one, he must beat two, that way it won't be so bad for either of us.'

'Me too,' said Tisamenos. 'Victory or death,' he said.

Agesilaos looked fondly at them. 'You're my best friends, and I love you both. But this is something I must do alone. Go back, whatever he does, he won't kill me. Now go, or it won't work.'

'Then don't be too keen. Play it calm,' said Agapetos who was wiser than his years.

Agesilaos limped down the hillside through the grove, descending to the river, Tisamenos and Agapitos warily watching. For as far back as they could remember, Agesilaos had dreamed of becoming Lysander's Hearer one day. They knew he would be utterly crushed if Lysander rejected him, which they thought he might well do, especially on account of his lame foot. But he was a prince, and that had to serve some advantage, and it was well known that Lysander and Crown Prince Agis were friends.

Lysander sat on the riverbank with his back to Agesilaos, not moving, apparently staring into the valley to the distant Parnon Mountains.

Agesilaos quietly approached Lysander, limping on his lame left foot, his hands under his tunic clasped in front of himself.

'Are your two friends not joining us?' said Lysander without looking round at him.

Agesilaos stopped dead in the grass and gulped. Did he have eyes in the back of his head? 'I sent them back, Dioskouros.'

'Then why are they still hiding in the bushes like a couple of thigh-flashers?'

Agesilaos looked over his shoulder up to the bushes they had been hiding behind. Both of them were too well hidden to be seen from here.

Still Lysander did not turn to look at him. 'Why have you been following me? Do you practice the arts of the *krypteia*,* or the worm, sneaking through the grass? You're not very good at it, Prince Agesilaos.'

Agesilaos gulped again, but his mouth was so dry, he gulped nothing but air. His heart quickened. He had singularly failed to impress him. He saw his dreams drifting away before his eyes. The glory tarnished to shame.

'Do you have nothing to say?' Lysander pressed quietly, still refusing to turn to him.

'I'll do better next time, Dioskouros.'

Lysander suddenly rose to his feet – Agesilaos took a nervous step back, his body stiffening with fear of a beating. Lysander turned to him levelling his penetrating green eyes on Agesilaos. 'Next time? What makes you think there'll be a next time?'

Agesilaos knew one thing of warriors, they admire courage and persistence. 'How else will I learn?'

'*Hmm.*' Lysander looked up to the bushes where Agapetos and Tisamenos were hiding. 'And your friends, they decided better of it, did they?'

'No. But I didn't want them here,' he said.

Lysander raised a brow. He knew full well what was going on here. 'Is that so? And why's that, little prince?'

Agesilaos shrugged his shoulders, feeling his face flush and his heart quicken, his body shifting nervously.

Once it became clear that he was too shy to say, Lysander turned away again and looked across the valley without speaking another work.

Agesilaos's heart sank to the grass at his feet. He was rejected by the only man he ever wanted to Inspire him. 'Forgive me for interrupting your meditations, Dioskouros Lysander.' He turned to walk away.

'I wasn't meditating,' said Lysander. 'I was waiting for three foolish mister foxes who thought they could get the better of me. Now call your friends down, and I'll hear what they have to say about this,' he said in a tone that implied seriousness.

Agesilaos raised his hand and beckoned his friends.

Agapetos and Tisamenos both stood up. They picked their way down the hill towards them, their faces tight with worry, convinced they were about to get a beating.

**"Fox Time". A tradition of right of passage for boys to be sent out into the wilderness to survive a period of months, possibly longer, alone to fend for himself against all dangers he might face, from wolves to finding food and shelter.*

** The harshest school of Sparta, a walled institution forbidden to adults apart from the gymnasiarchs (trainers) and the Paidonomos (boy-herder). The ephebes (youths) probably from 14 to 18 or 19 were sent to live and train at the ephebeion, where they would have been brutalized by the gymnasiarchs and by older boys. The brutality at the ephebeion is infamous in history, accidental deaths and serious injuries were without a doubt common.*

**Agent of the Krypteia, (hidden/secret) a sort of secret police of ephebes, (youths).*

TWO

'They're coming, Dioskouros. The fault is entirely mine,' Agesilaos said. 'It was all my idea. I wanted to follow you. Not them.'

Lysander turned back and watched the two boys wordlessly, both nimbler than Agesilaos.

Agapetos and Tisamenos stood beside Agesilaos, their hands clasped in front of themselves under their tunics.

Lysander considered the boys. They were persistent cubs; he'd give them that. 'Your efforts to follow me undetected failed. But an effort should at least be praised, so it is then, that I praise you for your efforts.'

The boys beamed.

'When did you know, Dioskouros?' asked Agapetos.

'He knew from Karystos,' said Agesilaos.

Tisamenos huffed. 'I told you he knew.'

'Are you going to beat us, Dioskouros?'

'Some other time perhaps,' he replied flippantly.

The boys smiled, as much with relief as with amusement.

'May we have the honour of walking with you, Dioskouros?' Agesilaos asked, grabbing at a second chance to draw Lysander's attention.

'If it please you, you may walk with me as far as the *Ephebeion*.'

Agesilaos stepped poignantly to Lysander's right, which is a place of honour. Tisamenos and Agapetos positioned themselves to Lysander's left side, as if making a subtle point to Lysander, so Agesilaos could let it be known that he wanted Lysander to be his Inspirer.

They started walking towards Sparta, still a few miles away.

Lysander was a hero to the boys of the Rearing. Lysander, Brasidas and Leonidas before them, were the ones all boys wanted to emulate.

'Tell us about Methone, *Hippeus* Lysander?' asked Tisamenos, his curiosity unfettering his tongue with, 'Is it true that you charged at the Athenian army on a horse?' There was a gleam of excitement in his eyes – in all their eyes; there's little a Spartan boy likes more than hearing a good war story, except a full belly, and at Sparta, both were rare.

'It's true.'

The boys' eyes lit up with the vision of it.

'Is it true you tamed a hundred Athenian hoplites?'

'I tamed hoplites that day, enemies all. But not a hundred, not even five, but a modest two or three. The day went to Brasidas, whose timely arrival saved us all from catastrophe.' He looked at Agesilaos limping beside him and gave him a wink.

Agesilaos blushed. It was a sign; he was sure of it. He had admired Lysander his entire life.

'You must have looked magnificent,' said Agapetos. 'Like Castor and Pollux.'

'Of course, he did,' Agesilaos snapped. 'He's a *Dioskouros*, you fool. Who else would a *Dioskouros* resemble, but the *Dioskouri*?'

Tisamenos gave Agapetos a friendly shove with his shoulder and Agapetos stumbled, but quickly recovered himself before making a complete ass of himself.

'You say some of the most ridiculous things at times.'

Agapetos's cheeks darkened with a flush of blood. 'Says you, who thinks there are horses with black and white stripes.'

'*There are*,' Tisamenos insisted. 'My father told me so. He saw them with his own eyes in Libya.'

There was obviously an old argument between the boys. Agesilaos seemed to rise above it, trying to give Lysander the right impression.

'Where? In the bottom of a wine jug?' mocked Agapetos.

Agesilaos shot his friends a scathing stare. They were embarrassing him in front of Lysander. 'Tell us about when you killed Amyklos the One Eye in single combat?' He had heard the story so many times, from his father, from *Geront** Tellis, from Brasidas, and Lysander's friends Kromios and even from Gylippos. But he had never heard the story from Lysander himself.

'Yes, tell us?' Agapetos said eagerly.

As they walked, Lysander told them the story without embellishments, and the boys listened with awe as he told them how he had to hack off Hoplite Kriton's dead hand to get his shield, miming the action as he spoke, enthralling the boys all the more with the gruesome details, feeding their blood-soaked imaginations with the images of it.

'Were you afraid?' asked Tisamenos.

'Of course, he wasn't,' said Agapetos. 'What sort of a question is that. Spartans fear nothing of mortal men.'

Lysander smiled. 'All men have fear in them, Agapetos,' he said. 'So, yes, I was afraid.'

The boys were shocked and they looked incredulously at him, shaken to their marrow to hear a Spartan say such a thing. Lysander of the Herakleidai, *hippeus* of the First Hundred – afraid? What nonsense.

'Let me tell you what my Inspirer Brasidas told me, when I was your age. He said to me: "*To be a good warrior, you must possess in good and equal measure these things: Strength, Speed, Agility, Cunning, Determination, Courage ... and Fear. If but one of these is missing, you will die before you find the glory for which you were born. Fear is in all men but the fool and the intoxicated. Fear feeds the instincts, instinct makes the mind swift of thought, a swift mind brings the body quickly to action, a strong quick body commanded by a swift thinking mind will fight and kill more efficiently than any other man on earth. Bravery will command the fear rather than the fear commanding all else. Fear is the instinct to survive*". That's what Brasidas told me, and I've never forgotten it. You must command your fear, boys, you must accept it, but you can never allow it to consume you.'

'Or you'll become a trembler,' said Agesilaos.

'Exactly so.'

'Like Timaios the Trembler,' said Agapetos.

Lysander nodded his head. Timaios had run away during the Battle of Hagios Floros in Messene during the Helot uprisings during the first war with Athens. He was often seen in the market, easily recognisable by the coloured patches sewn into his war cloak, and all the years since, he had been an internal outcast. He still served the morai, carrying out menial duties. He still attended his dining mess, but he sat alone and nobody ever spoke to him. He had to give way, and stand aside, even to the most junior of Spartans and their servants.

Brasidas once described the shunning of a trembler a living death, and Timaios was a broken man, a shadow in the world, without honour or respect. He was viewed with contempt, suspicion and served as a living reminder what cruel fate awaits the trembler in Lakedaimon. He not only damned himself, but his son too, who would never find a Spartan wife for fear of passing the trait of cowardice to their offspring. His wife killed herself, and his own family shunned him and cursed him to the gods for the shame he brought them.

'And what of you, boys,' Lysander asked, putting Timaios the Trembler out of his thoughts. 'Have you completed your *phauaxir*, your fox-time yet?'

'We have,' said Agesilaos, growing more hopeful that Lysander would choose him.

'And did you kill the child in yourselves and awaken the men you will become?'

'We did, Dioskouros.'

'And how many times have you been caught stealing?'

'Never, Dioskouros Lysander,' said Agesilaos.

'I've been caught once,' said Agapetos.'

'I've never been caught either,' said Tisamenos.

'Cunning Mister Foxes eh,' said Lysander.

Tisamenos blushed. 'Not cunning enough to fool you,' he said.

Lysander smiled. 'You're still young. You have much to learn. Your Inspirers will teach you these things. And who are your inspirers?' he probed. He looked at Tisamenos. 'I know who inspires you. My friend Gylippos.'

'He does,' Tisamenos responded. 'Since ten days ago.'

'What of you, Agapetos? Who inspires you?'

'Dithyrambos, Dioskouros.'

Lysander nodded his head. He looked at Agesilaos. 'And you, Agesilaos, who inspires you?'

'Nobody,' he said rather pathetically, looking down as if in shame. Who wants to inspire a boy with a lame foot? Even if that boy's the son of the King.

Lysander already knew that. He knew all there was to know about Agesilaos, but he didn't let on. He removed his folded blanket from his shoulder. 'Would you like to carry my blanket, Agesilaos?' He handed the blanket to the delighted prince. A Dioskouros has two emblems of his status, his blanket and his piloi cap, only the most honoured are privileged to carry either.

'I'm honoured to.' He proudly took the blanket and gave his envious friends a smug grin. It was a token of his affection and his intension to Inspire him. It had to be. Why else would he give him his blanket to carry? Agesilaos reasoned.

At the *Ephebeion*, Agesilaos returned Lysander's blanket to him and the boys ran up the hill to the *Ephebeion*, before they were spotted by the *gymnasiarchs*, *kryptes* or the dreaded *Paidonomos*, who would all beat them with birch, not for skiving, but for being captured skiving.

"Elder" Sparta was governed by Gerontes "elders" of the Gerousia, the Spartan senate/parliament. There were 28 gerontes aged from 60 up, elected for life by the citizen assembly called the Apella. As well as the gerontes, there were the two Spartan kings from the Agiad and Eurypontid houses, who ruled jointly, subject to the Gerousia's majority vote, but the kings could invoke their powers of veto, and when the Gerousia was split, the kings had the final say. When considering the Spartan political system, it's easier to think of them as a sort of constitutional monarchic, semi-democratic autocracy.

THREE

When the news arrived of Potidaea's demise, the Gerousia was called into session, a rare event, even in war.

King Archidamos sat in silence, his mouth closed, lips pressed tightly together, his bushy grey brows arching to an almost scowl as Tellis's voice filled the chamber, where the other gerontes sat in the same brooding silence as the King, listening to the important news that had come from Chalcidice that Potidaea had fallen to the Athenians after months of starvation.

So desperate was their situation, Tellis explained, '... There are stories of the besieged citizens turning to cannibalism,' he said.

For the first time, Archidamos's face expressed an emotion, albeit brief and barely noticeable.

There were other stories circulating of great atrocities committed by Delian irregulars and Thracians, who were loose in the countryside butchering every Potidaean they encountered, men, women – children, it mattered not to these godless men of opportunity, pillaging and looting for personal gain. Small change to rich Athens, big money for those non-land owning, poorly-educated privateers and marauders, for whom war offered opportunities they could not before have dreamed of. To such men, war was opportunity.

These honourless men were the unforeseen consequence of Athens' decision to fight a protracted and, as far as Sparta was concerned, an unmanly and dishonourable war, hiding their hoplites and nobility behind walls of stone. They had turned to low grade tactics instead of putting out those noble men of bronze, whose fathers had stood so bravely at Marathon against the Median invaders. Matters that could have been solved in a day's hoplite battle in the Plain of Eleusis in the traditional way, now dragged on and it would continue to drag on, year on year. The butchery and savagery would become increasingly more savage and bloodier on every side of the conflict. This war, Archidamos decided as he listened to Tellis's reports from Sparta's shadow men, was turning the good order of civilised Hellenes on its head, unleashing a storm of chaos and unspeakable atrocities upon each other. So, this then, was the great war upon which the fate of the Hellenic world would hang, and like the Lernean Hydra, this war was a beast with many heads in many lands, and it would not be easily tamed.

Archidamos neither sought nor wanted the war, but now it had come, and now, honour and gods commanded it continue, and Sparta must not waver.

Tellis had been speaking for almost an hour, when a *geront* interrupted, complaining about the cost of the war, and the setbacks Sparta had suffered. He thought Sparta had made its point, and now was a time to open the door for peace.

Archidamos rose to his feet and interjected firmly: '... Be in no doubt of it. This war, for all concerned, is now a matter that goes beyond setting examples. It strikes at the very heart of deepest honour. It goes to the very essence of the Hellenic states, be them Dorian or Ionian; Peloponnesian or Attican, we are Hellenes, and brother has taken up his spear against brother,' he said. 'So, hear me, Spartans; Ares is loose in the world of men and the fire of war now laps at every shore in Hellas and beyond. The survival of us all now depends on this gamble we have made and we must be resolved to pursue it with all the vigour and might for which we are best known, with an unbending will and an unbreakable resolve to victory or death. We must, where we can, inflict grievous wounds upon this hated enemy that is in our power to inflict. We must press the offensive in all places possible. In Hellas and beyond...' And then, as his hard eyes surveyed them, he warned: 'If we waver now, we forsake the strongest to the favour of the weakest, and so falls Sparta. So, I tell you now, Spartans...' His voice hardened with unyielding promise, 'we will not yield and Sparta will not bend while there is breath in my body. There will be no talk of peace in this land until this enemy is on his knees!'

The silence was ringing, the echo of his voice still booming in their minds; *There will be no talk of peace in this land until this enemy is on his knees...*

He looked at them, their grey and wrinkled faces like old leather, dried out in the sun. each had known war in their prime, each had delivered death to Sparta's enemies. When a man is young, he thinks himself immortal, when he is old, he knows he is nearer to his grave than to his cradle and clasps to every hour as if it were his last, and he knew most, if not all would be dead before this war was over. 'There will be no doors opened by us, lest to our own benefit,' he said, his voice quiet again. 'If Pericles wants peace, then he may come before us and we will hear what he has to say. Any man here now who desires peace with this enemy, let him depart from this kingdom now, for I will not suffer him in my presence any more than I would suffer a trembler.'

There was another stinging silence, the King's words swilling in their thoughts.

Ramphias rose to his feet and banged his staff down hard on the stone floor three times. '*Victory or Death*!' he cried.

The Spartans rose up, banged their staffs and all twenty-eight of them spoke enthusiastically with but one voice: '*VICTORY OR DEATH*!!!'

Archidamos resumed his throne and gestured to Tellis to continue.

'My Lord...' He moved into the centre of the chamber where the acoustics were better. 'Now Potidaea has fallen to the Athenians, Athens has sent orders to his generals to march on Spartolos in support of the pro-Athenian factions and democratisers, who want to overthrow our allies and friends at Spartolos and Olynthos. I've sent orders to our shadow men in the region to inform them of Xenophon's orders. I've also arranged for the delivery of weapons to our friends there. One thousand spears, four hundred swords, three hundred and fifty linothorax and two hundred shields and helmets–'

'And where do these weapons come from?' asked a geront.

'Captured from the Helots during the revolt,' said Tellis.

The old man nodded his head.

'What news of the plague, Tellis?' asked another.

'Athens is still under its curse and that city suffers the woes of Hades,' said Tellis. 'Pericles, now recovered from the plague, has been re-elected after his removal from office. He is inconsolable with grief for his sons who have perished in the plague. But he has still delivered a powerful speech to the Boule, that has, for now, settled the dissenters at Athens. The plague has also spread into their expeditionary forces and navy, with reports of it as far away as their Asian colonies. Before the Potidaeans surrendered, we were receiving reports that the plague was sweeping through the Athenian army besieging that city. Now they have surrendered, the plague has spread into Potidaea and among the colonisers who have taken the city over, and is ravaging the colonists they've installed there.'

'Now there's an irony for you,' Ramphias mumbled.

Tellis smiled to himself. Ramphias never did know when to keep his mouth shut.

'It's always a delight to hear the wisdom of Ramphias,' said Regent Pausanias with a half-smile. He liked Ramphias, who was old in his body, but young in his heart. He was plain speaking and a wise tactician. There was much to admire about him.

Archidamos spoke again. 'In light of this situation with the pestilence, we, with our allies have agreed that it would be the folly of fools to invade Attica this fighting season. We must instead turn our attention to taming the enemy in other places by other means. He will not ground his army to meet us in battle, where all can be resolved upon a single event. Instead, he trembles in fear of us behind his walls and uses his navy to good advantage against us...' He looked at Xenoklides of Corinth and Pagondas of Thebes standing side by side just behind Brasidas. 'The Ambraciots,' he continued, 'have petitioned us for help, and we are minded to render it, and at the same time, we must deny the enemy the roads and seaways into our territories, namely the Gulf of Corinth and the passes over the Cithaeron Mountains to cut the Athenians off from Boeotia. In order to achieve this, Plataea must either yield, accept a treaty and declare neutrality, or be destroyed...'

That will be music to Pagondas's ears, Tellis thought. Plataea had long been a festering wound to Thebes, and those fertile hills around Plataea would make a fine addition to Thebes' territory.

'It is equally as vital,' Archidamos continued, 'to drive the Athenians out of the Gulf of Corinth and seize their base at Naupaktos, and secure the narrows at Rhium, a task made difficult by the Akarnanians, Messenians, Zakynthians and Cephelanians and the fortifications at Stratos. For the possession of Naupaktos to be successful, we must tame these enemies to our will or destroy them completely. Navarch Knemos will be in overall command of land and sea forces, his objective is to take Stratos, and knock these enemies out of the war or bring them into alliance. He will be accompanied by Spartans and our immediate allies to launch an amphibious attack on Stratos. I will march to Plataea,' he added.

After the meeting, Tellis met privately with Archidamos and the five ephors.

'... Xenoklides of Corinth and I recently discussed sending emissaries to Persia to seek an alliance with King Artaxerxes, My Lord,' Tellis said in a quiet voice so as not to be overheard. 'We agreed that the Persians would have a great deal to gain in an alliance with us. The Athenian colonies of Asia and the Ionian islands, Samos and others that lie off the Asian coast. There are good sea ports, rich cities, fertile land–'

'*Earth and water*,' said one of the ephors, flippantly quoting one of the costliest misunderstandings in Hellenic history; that was what the Athenians promised the Persians for an alliance against Sparta, not understanding what the Persians meant by earth and water. That misunderstanding was the flame that ignited the Persian War.

Archidamos looked at the ephors.

'We agree with Geront Tellis, My Lord,' said one.

'It would force the Athenians to fight the war on two fronts,' Tellis said. 'That will weaken them even further. Once their Asian territories come under threat, they'll have to divert half their resources, ships, men and money to the defence of their Asian colonies.'

'They're vital to Athens,' said Ephor Isanor. 'Not only for their economy, but their food supplies also.'

'Who would we send?' asked Archidamos.

'I've a man in mind,' Tellis said. 'Stratodemos. He speaks the Median tongue and he's familiar with their customs. And our friend Pollis of Argos. He too is familiar with the Persians, and is acquainted with Artaxerxes.'

'Can he be trusted?' asked one of the ephors.

'Completely,' Tellis replied firmly.

Archidamos nodded his head thoughtfully.

'It may take some time to get everything in place,' Tellis said. 'Corinth will want to send their own man with them.'

Archidamos recognised the opportunity. If the Persians joined them in a formal alliance, Athens would be too overstretched. They would have no choice but to capitulate. 'We've nothing to lose,' he said. 'Begin your preparations and let all be done in the utmost secrecy.'

'As My Lord commands.'

FOUR

Lysander rode out into the chilly dawn, heading for Amyklai, towing a riderless horse he had borrowed from Brasidas's estate. He was going to the sanctuary of the Graces, Phaenna, the Shining and Kleta, the Glorious to meet Agesilaos.

The sanctuary nestles on the bank of the peaceful springs of Tiasa, meandering like a vein of silver blood across the valley, where it nourishes the fertile land and joins the sacred Eurotas. Nearby, Agesilaos could see the Amyklaian temple sanctuary of Apollo Hyakinthos, up on the Amyklaian Hill and the colossus of Warlike Apollo, his golden face shining in the cold morning sunshine. He had no idea why he was here. After the pre-dawn practices, beginning with line dancing, the gymnasiarch sent him here and told him to wait here. 'Why?' he asked. The gymnasiarch slapped him around the face. 'A spartan obeys orders without question,' he said, and then told him to go.

So here he was, the dawn had broken and he was here, waiting, but for what, he had no clue.

A low diaphanous mist hung over the nearby marshes, almost glowing in the heatless sun, the cold air sweet with the petrichor breath of the earth.

Someone was coming across the fields, a horseman. Agesilaos's heart jumped into his mouth with joy and nervousness when he saw Lysander riding towards him. He smiled – he tried not to, but he couldn't help it, such was the joy in him. He had been here about two hours already.

Lysander trotted passed him to a tree, where he dismounted and tethered the horses.

Agesilaos limped towards him. 'Good morning, *Dioskouros* Lysander.'

'Good morning, Agesilaos...' He removed something wrapped in cloth from the knapsack hanging from the riderless horse. 'A gift of honey for you.'

As gifts go, Agesilaos was unimpressed, but he hid it well. It was a token, and he knew boys who got even less from their inspirers. A loaf of bread and a cock up their arses. On the other hand, other boys were gifted knives and even bows for hunting, but Lysander was known for his modesty and his frugalness.

Lysander smiled to himself, he knew the prince was worthy of more than a pot of honey, he was the king's son after all. But it was a test of sorts, did he just want expensive gifts? If so, Lysander would reject him and Agesilaos knew that by taking the pot, he would be accepting Lysander as his Inspirer.

'May I ask. Does my father have a hand in this, or your friend Geront Tellis?'

Lysander did not answer, instead he took a deep breath and turned to the sanctuary, where he sat on the step, all the while, Agesilaos watched him carefully. 'Come here and sit by me, Agesilaos.'

There was an ominous tone in Lysander's voice that worried him. He went to the steps and sat down beside him.

'About five years ago, your father let it be known that he thought I'd be a good Inspirer for you when the time came. I'll not lie, since that time I've observed you in your training with your herd from time to time–'

'You have?'

'Yes. So, hear me now, Agesilaos, when I say, it's by your own merits that I'm here, not because it would please your father or Tellis, but because you're worthy to be inspired. But the choice is yours. You can accept my gift or you can reject it. Either way, the matter is resolved. Piety, obedience to the law and modesty are qualities that are as Spartan as black broth.'

'Even though I'm cursed by the gods to be lame?'

'Or perhaps you're blessed by the gods who made you lame. It's your lameness that has given you a courage and determination the Rearing could never teach you, Agesilaos. Your lame foot has served you better than you realise. It's given you a strong will to achieve, and a noble character...' He and put his hand on Agesilaos's chest and felt the strong beat of Agesilaos's heart in his palm...

Agesilaos's body tingled pleasantly at his touch, he could feel the warmth of it radiating through his chiton to the chilled skin beneath.

'You possess something others never shall, Agesilaos and that's the inner courage and strength in you to overcome this great difficulty. What you call a curse, I call a gift, and I admire you for it.'

Agesilaos was so moved by what Lysander said, he almost wept. Nobody had *ever* said anything like that to him before, except his beloved mother. In fact, he had never considered his lame foot anything but a burden and a curse. Sometimes he was overwhelmed by a crushing shame that sent him spiralling into an abyss of dark melancholy that could last for days on end; especially when the other boys taunted him and said that if he had been anyone else's son, he would have been cast into the *Apothetae* where the damaged and weakly are rejected and cast into the chasm of death. "*Toad Foot*" they called him, mercilessly mocking and imitating his limp.

But he was a fierce fighter, and any boy, older or younger, if they called him Toad Foot, he would turn on them like a mad jackal and tear into them, punching and kicking and biting, which was much encouraged by the gymnasiarchs. The Rearing was a school for wolves and jackals, not doves and rabbits.

He would make Lysander proud, he decided it there and then, and with that, he picked up the jar of honey Lysander had put on the step between them. 'It's the best honey in all the world...' His eyes glimmered with pure joy. 'I'll give you no cause to regret your decision, I swear it by the gods, and may they hurl me into the burning river of Lethe, forever cursed to forget everything, even my own name if I do.'

Lysander raised a brow and gave him a big smile. '*Pan's prick*...!' he said. 'That's quite an oath.'

'One I will keep.'

'I don't doubt it. It would be dangerous not to. The gods take such oaths seriously.'

Agesilaos shuffled up closer to Lysander. 'May I ask. What gift did Brasidas bring to you?'

Lysander smiled. 'The best gift of all ... *Himself*.' he said.

Agesilaos frowned. 'I don't understand?'

'That was his gift. He hunted me for three days in the mountains when I was on my fox time. *That* was his gift to me.'

Agesilaos frowned. 'That seems a strange gift, if I may say so?'

'That's Brasidas for you.'

Agesilaos chuckled. He pulled up a length of grass from a tuft that was growing through a crack in the step, a consequence of the great shaking of the earth years ago. Hundreds of Spartans and perioikoi and Helots of the Eurotas were killed. Houses and buildings collapsed on people and there were landslides that buried many people alive. Sixty boys of the Rearing were killed when a landslide crashed down on the boys' barracks.

The allies sent food and aid, even Athens, but Messenia to the west of the Taygetos Mountains was a different story altogether. The Helots there, seeing that Sparta was severely weakened by the crisis, mounted a massive revolt, which turned into a full-scale war, and then, Athens declared war on Sparta, accusing the Spartans of insulting them after they marched an army over the Isthmus of Corinth to offer assistance in Sparta's war with the Helots.

But the Spartans knew this was just a ruse by the imperialistic Athenians to occupy Messene and ferment more rebellion among the Helots in order to weaken Sparta further, so Agesilaos's father and King Pleistoanax thanked the Athenians, but told them they didn't need their help. This was the apparent insult that started the war with Athens that lasted fifteen long years, which were as many years as Agesilaos had been alive, thus to his mind, it seemed an eternity.

He fiddled with the blade of grass, twisting it around his finger, suddenly feeling anxious when he realised that neither of them had spoken for a long time. Feeling that he should say something, but he had no idea what. He thought Lysander would find him tedious and uninteresting, and the more he struggled to find words, the harder it became to speak.

Lysander suddenly stood up and walked to the horses. Agesilaos followed him, clasping his pot of honey.

'May I call you Lysander now I'm your Hearer?'

'Yes, if it please you.'

'Many things please me, Lysander,' came Agesilaos's ambiguous reply.

Lysander looked at him. 'Mysteries that will no doubt reveal themselves in the fullness of time,' he replied. 'Mount up,' he added as he mounted his horse.

Lysander was impressed by Agesilaos's riding skills as they headed east towards the Parnon Mountains, riding side by side.

'Do you like to ride, Agesilaos?'

'No,' he said. 'I love to ride. My father has many horses, and I ride them as often as I can. But I have my own horse, a gift from my mother.'

'Next time we go riding, you will bring your own horse.'

Agesilaos nodded his head. 'I will.'

They rode on for near three miles, coming to the dweller village of Selinus, where, just beyond the village is the ruin of an ancient shrine from the time before the Trojan war, dedicated to Zeus. It is said, that here is where Zeus transformed himself into a swan. There was little left of it now, just a few stone blocks that made up its walls.

'Why have we come here?' Agesilaos asked as they dismounted.

'Why not here?' he said. 'Besides, is there not something hidden behind that wall for you?'

Agesilaos frowned and looked at the remnant of the wall, growing out of the long grass. 'For me?'

'Yes. Go and find it.'

Lured by the mystery, Agesilaos went into the ruin, his keen eyes looking down, searching through the grass that was just as long inside the wall as it was outside. But what was he looking for? Was there anything here at all? He looked at Lysander, watching him.

'You're very close to it. Be careful where you step.'

Agesilaos looked down again, scanning the long grass intensely, and then he saw it. Something slender wrapped in linen. He stooped and picked it up – it was heavy but its shape gave it away. He unwrapped it eagerly, his eyes wide with excitement. And it was revealed, a most beautiful knife in a leathered scabbard with a long leather cord attached to it so it could be hung around the neck. The handle was ivory, shaped to make it a comfortable fit in the hand. It wasn't ostentatious, but it was plainly of the finest quality, and when he drew the leaf blade, instead of being iron, it was tempered bronze. It was beautiful, utterly magnificent – and a complete surprise.

'You didn't really think I'd show the measure of my affection with a pot of honey, did you?'

Agesilaos looked at him, he was speechless with happiness.

'My father gave me that knife. It goes back a very long way in my family. My father told me it belonged to Herakles himself, but I think that was just a story. But it is very old. Now I give it to you in token of my affection for you.'

'It's wonderful. Beautiful...' He sheathed it and hung it around his neck. 'I'll wear this always, Lysander, so I never forget the love with which it was given. And the love with which it is received.' He came over to Lysander and kissed him. 'For I do love you, Lysander.'

FIVE

It was hard country in the remote foothills of the Arkadian mountains. The hilltops were quilted with snow, vividly contrasting with the deep green of thick grass and heathers that swathed the lowlands, silvered with hoarfrost, incandescent under the midmorning sun sloping over the mountains, across the barren tundra.

Sometimes, on windy days, you can hear the mountains sing lamentingly as the wind cuts the peaks and howls through the ravines and crevices. Some say, these chilling songs are the Erinyes* portending bloody war and doom, others say they are the Moirai* singing as they weave the destinies of mortals. Mostly, the mountains do not sing, and the highlands of Skiritis lie still and quiet, but for the bleating of sheep and goats, and the occasional lonely tones of a shepherd's flute.

Of all the subject allies of the Eurotas Valley, Skiritis is the most powerful, and like their Spartan masters, they are fearsome and warlike, disciplined and most honoured by the Spartans to fight on the extreme left wing of the Spartan army, a place of honour.

A flock of shaggy-fleeced sheep and goats ranged under the watch of a shepherd boy, wrapped up as warm as possible in a fleece, his nervous eyes drawn to the two Spartan horsemen galloping their horses across the moorland.

They galloped full pelt along the valley, the icy wind blasting in their faces as they charged across the highland tundra. Ahead of them, the snowy peaks and slopes of the Arkadian mountains cut their jagged seams across the sky, skimmed by the rising winter sun.

The world was a blur of green, white and silver, the young prince was lagging far behind, and he could hear the distant shouts – 'C'mon, Agesilaos! C'mon!'

Try as he did, neither he, nor his horse were good enough or fast enough. 'Do it, boy. Do it for me,' he said to his horse as he flicked the reins and heeled the beast to go faster. The cold wind numbed his cheeks and his knuckles ached with the bight of winter's breath blasting him.

'C'mon!' Lysander yelled; he was a good two furlongs ahead of the prince, his crimson cloak billowing up behind him like a river of blood. Truly the best horseman in Lakedaimon, everybody said so. A Dioskouros worthy of his bones. He might lose the race, but nothing made him happier than to lose it to the best.

Finally, Lysander slowed his horse to a trot and Agesilaos quickly caught him up. Lysander gave him a big smile. 'What kept you?'

'My horse doesn't have wings,' he said sarcastically.

Lysander smiled amusedly. 'I think the fault lies more with the rider than his horse,' he said. 'You're too tense, and fearful you'll be thrown. Your horse senses it, and in his turn, he too becomes uncertain. You have to get to know your horse, Agesilaos. You have to become companions,' is that not so, Orion?' he said patting his horse's neck.

Sheep scattered in every direction as they trotted through the flock towards the river, where they slew their horses to a stop and dismounted.

Agesilaos could feel the weight of the knife Lysander gave him, hanging at is side. He touched it as if checking to make certain he hadn't lost it. He couldn't wait to show Tisamenos and Agapetos and the rest of his herd. The dagger of Herakles, the very dagger that had slain the Nemean Lion, he was sure of it and that's what he would tell his friends, and how they'll marvel at it...

Lysander stroked his horse's nose. 'You have your father Aiolos's spirit, Orion. He was just like you in his young days. Aye, he'd be proud to see you run so well...'

Agesilaos chuckled. 'It's true,' he said. 'You do talk to your horse?'

'Of course. Do you not talk to yours?'

Agesilaos shrugged his shoulders.

Lysander smiled. 'We'll rest here a while. There's some food in the knapsack.'

Agesilaos was hungry, but it wasn't for food. It was for knowledge and the arts of warcraft, and the good company of his Inspirer. He was so happy, he didn't want the day to end, but end it must, and after eating some bread and smoked fish, they set off back to Sparta at a steady pace.

'When will we meet next, Lysander?'

'I don't know. We'll be marching soon.'

Agesilaos nodded his head. 'Can we stay out late? I like being with you,' he said as he clasped his dagger by its scabbard and held it tight as if it were a talisman that would make Lysander agree to letting him stay out with him.

'You might not enjoy my company so much when we start training,' Lysander replied. 'I'll expect a lot from you and if you don't give me your best effort, I'll be disappointed.'

'I'll always give you my best effort...' His grip tightened around the scabbard. 'I'm a good fighter,' he said. 'Wrestling, boxing, pankration. The best in my herd, you can ask anyone.'

Lysander did not respond.

'I'm skilled at staff fighting too,' Agesilaos added. 'But I'm not very good at running of course.'

'One day, Agesilaos,' Lysander started up, 'by virtue of your birth and blood, you'll be an officer in command of men, possibly thousands of men, Spartiate and allies. Being an officer is about more than how well you can wrestle; it's about how quickly you can think and respond to unpredictable circumstances. An officer has to think quickly and respond decisively without hesitating. He has to make instant assessments of his situation and know how to meet them. Battles and wars are lost and won in a single moment; from a single thought or command. Make the wrong choices and you're food for the crows.

Agesilaos fell into Lysander's quiet and soothing voice, the motion of the horses made him feel as if he was floating on a calm sea, taking in every word Lysander said. 'How do you know if you've made the right decision or not?' he asked.

'If you're alive and your enemy's dead, you've made the right decision. It's important to understand your enemy. To learn how he thinks and what tactics he might use against you. Only by knowing him and his habits can you be conclusive about your decisions. Having good sources of information is vital. Knowing the enemy's strength and condition are just as essential.'

Agesilaos nodded his head. It worried him deeply that he might not possess these skills. It was such a responsibility. One mistake and so fall the Lame Prince, or even Lakedaimon itself. It was a frightening thought to a naïve fifteen-year-old boy trying desperately to be a man.

* ***The Furies.***

* ***The Fates***

SIX

Fortified city of Aphidnai, Attica

Eleusinios/February

It is said of Aphidnai, that after the Trojan War, Theseus brought the princess Helen of Sparta, who some call Helen of Troy here, where Theseus entrusted her into the care of his friend King Aphidnos, who took her into his palace and kept her there like a bird in a cage.

Upon hearing that their sister had been hidden somewhere in Attica, Helen's brothers, Castor and Pollox, the sons of Zeus, who the Spartans call Dioskouri, in their warlike state invaded Attica with the Spartan army to search for their beloved sister, for whom the Greeks had gone to war with Troy.

It was by means of treachery when the nobles of Decelea informed the Dioskouri of Helen's whereabouts in the palace of King Aphidnos, at the city of Aphidnai. Upon learning this, the Dioskouri mounted an attack on the town and took it complete and rescued their sister and sacked the city of its wealth. Thus is Aphidnai famed among the Hellenes.

*

It was a dreary morning, cold and damp. A thick mist hung over the fields and pastures below the hilltops rose like islands from a grey sea. Butting up against the stone walls of Aphidnai.

The six weary cavalrymen trotted through the gates between the towers, into the misty city, making for the garrison.

Citizens watched them clopping passed, their eyes fixed on the four riderless horses being towed by the two men riding at the rear. There were four bloody bodies draped over them,

Hipponikos came out from the administration and watched the hippeis trotting through diaphanous mist like ghosts into the garrison, their dirty and blood scabbed faces as grim as Thanatos after a mauling by the Peloponnesian invaders.

Their horses' hooves clip-clopped with a solemn loudness across the paving in the chilly dawn.

Hipponikos looked at the dead riders draped over the horses' backs like rugs, their arms and legs dangling either side, their bodies punctured and bloodied with javelin wounds, inflicted by fifty Corinthian peltasts* they had encountered on the road from Panakton.

They were led in by an elegant young officer with a magnificent black and white plumed Corinthian helmet on his head, tilted back, exposing his lean grimy face, a face Hipponikos knew – Alcibiades.

Alcibiades looked at the old general, his future father-in-law. In front of the administration, Alcibiades held his hand up to halt the men. 'Agrias,' he said as he dismounted his horse. 'Tend to the dead. Get the horses stabled and fed. Then get something to eat and some rest...'

A servant hurried across the concourse to take the reins of Alcibiades's horse.

'*Gods be praised*! *Alcibiades*!' Hipponikos exclaimed as he loped over. 'I did not expect to see you here, and glad I am that here you stand. But not in good condition.'

'We were ambushed by Corinthian peltasts. They came out of nowhere and took us completely by surprise,' he said. 'They killed four of my men and severely wounded three others. But fear not, we killed the bastards in the end.'

'Where are your wounded.'

'I sent them back to Panakton, it being nearer than here...' He raised a warm smile for his future father-in-law. 'It's good to see a friendly face...' He removed his heavy helmet.

'So, what brings you here, lad?'

'Orders, Strategos,' said Alcibiades formerly. He handed Hipponikos a rolled-up parchment. 'I'm here to take command of your hippeis.'

Hipponikos nodded his head. 'Then welcome. And I'm delighted to see you, lad...' They embraced warmly.

'As am I to see you...' They started walking towards the administration. 'How is Hipparete?' he asked.

'She's well, Alcibiades and she's going to be very happy to see you.'

'As will I to see her,' he replied as he followed Hipponikos into the administration.

It was busy with soldiers, officers and clerical slaves hurrying hither and thither, crossing the vast gallery, on their way to various offices.

'My commander told me that you have nobody in command of your hippeis?' Alcibiades said as they walked across the gallery to a door with two sentries posted either side. One of them opened the door as they approached and they went into a large room where there was a long table with scrolls and waxed tablets stored on it, and another table with a big chair behind it, a small burner was lit under a pot, keeping the sealing wax liquid. Another pot contained fine sand, and there were inks and writing pens...

'It's true. My hippagretas, Ganymedes died from the plague two months ago. Thanks to the gods, the plague is still more or less a stranger here. We've had very few occurrences.'

'My commander also said that there are also rumours that the Peloponnesians plan to attack Aphidnai?'

'Rumours circulated by the enemy to keep us scared, no more,' Hipponikos said gesturing with his hand to some seating. 'It's an old ploy. Besides, we're too far east of the Isthmus here. They won't come this far,' he added as they sat down. He gestured to a servant to bring some wine. 'Fear is a powerful weapon,' he said.

Alcibiades nodded his head.

'You will stay at my house as my guest-friend, Alcibiades. You're practically family now. Yes, I must insist on it,' he said before Alcibiades could draw breath. 'Hipparete would never forgive me were it otherwise,' he added.

'That's very kind of you and I except, Hipponikos. Military quarters are so uncomfortable...'

The servant brought wine for Alcibiades.

'It's unlikely any invasion will come this year. The Spartans have not mustered the armies of their allies; this can only mean they'll not invade. They fear the plague.'

Hipponikos nodded his head. 'We all fear the plague, my boy. *It is better at home, for it's dangerous outdoors*,' he said, quoting the old saying.

Not something the Spartans would agree with from what Alcibiades knew of them. And was that not behind Pericles's plan to wall everyone up in Athens? There was no honour in hiding, the Empire had to take the fight to the Peloponnesians. He loved Pericles, who had taken him into his home, along with his mad brother after his father was killed. But he just didn't agree with some of his policies. But then, the fools voted him back. 'Athens has become a necropolis, where the dead outnumber the living,' he said.

'It's a wonder Pericles survived,' said Hipponikos as he picked up his winecup, 'yet his sons did not.'

Alcibiades sipped his wine and savoured its sweet smooth taste.

'Some say the gods have a hand in it. They say that Athena herself cured him. At least, that's what his friends would have us believe.'

'Luck, is what I call it,' Alcibiades responded. 'Some die from it, others do not, even among slaves and fishermen and merchants, a number who fall sick survive and recover back to full health, others are left blind and lame, some are left insane; yet others are restored to perfect health. There is no order or reason to who lives or who dies. It's as random as where a raindrop falls. Luck, Hipponikos and nothing more.'

'Is that how Socrates has it?'

'Yes. Socrates doesn't believe in the divine, yet the gods love him, all the same...'

For the next hour or so, they sat supping wine as they discussed the war and politics, and over the course of their conversation, Hipponikos felt as though he were talking to somebody else. His young friend seemed to have grown up from the rowdy youth he had known at Athens before the war and it was a pleasure to be acquainted with this new Alcibiades.

The war certainly had matured him. He was no longer the drunken and carefree sybarite who courted scandal and was the cause of considerable embarrassment to Pericles, debauching with prostitutes and aristocratic youths. Now he was a soldier who had tasted war, even receiving an injury in battle at Potidaea. Hipponikos approved of this dashing new Alcibiades, the Alcibiades who was dutiful and courageous.

Just then, an officer came in and marched over to the old general. 'The magistrates are here, Strategos,' he said, casting a glance at Alcibiades.

Hipponikos nodded his head. 'They're early. Tell them I'll be there directly.'

The officer gave a curt nod of his head, about turned and marched out.

Hipponikos patted Alcibiades on the shoulder as he stood up. 'Get that down you, lad,' he said referring to the wine. 'Then go to my house, have a hot bath and a good sleep. We'll speak more later. For me, there are magistrates to appease,' he added as he moved towards the doors. 'They're unhappy that soldiers aren't out protecting their farms and estates. They think I should put the garrison out to protect their crops and houses.'

'How many men do you have?'

'Barely a thousand. Fifty hoplites, thirty horse and the rest are peltasts and light infantry. They believe the rumours and they're afraid of being ruined if their estates are devastated.'

Alcibiades nodded his head.

* ***A type of light infantry, named after the crescent shaped shiels (pelte) they carried. They were armed with several javelins.***

SEVEN
Island of Corcyra
Artemisios/April

It is said that before embarking on his ten labours, Herakles, seduced the naiad Melite, daughter of the river god Aegaeus the "goat-man". Melite bore Herakles a son, Hyllus, the leader of the Dorian Herakleidai who invaded the Peloponnese, and thus is Corcyra most famed.

*

'Forgive my rude dress, Iolaos, I came direct from my ship,' said Bulis, who was liveried in a leather skinned torso cuirass and armed with his sword riding high on his hip, his crested Corinthian helmet tucked under his arm.

Iolaos gave him a big smile. 'Nonsense, my boy, it's all the rage these days...' He looked at a servant. 'Bring our best wine to the sitting room and set an extra place for dinner. You will dine with us, won't you, Bulis? I won't take no for an answer.'

'In that case, I'd be delighted to...' He removed his sword and gave it to another servant along with his helmet and cloak and his cuirass. Much better he thought as he brushed his hand down his blue chiton.

'Everything went without incident I pray?'

'It did,' said Bulis as they walked out into the courtyard.

Upstairs, Iolanthe's heart skipped a beat with excitement when she spied Bulis in the courtyard, offering a prayer with father at the altar of Zeus-Herkeios. She beamed excitedly as she watched them through the upstairs window screen that overlooked the courtyard. He cut a fine figure, so handsome and a kinder, more generous man never walked the earth, in her eyes. Their marriage was arranged of course, but it was a very good match, because she loved Bulis and he loved her. 'He's here, mother. Bulis is here,' she said excitedly.

Her mother, Psamathe, who was sitting on a low wooden stool darning one of father's robes, looked up at her. Her daughter was happy and so she was happy and so was father.

Iolanthe had been so worried since Bulis went away, and when news came that he had been wounded in a sea battle near the island of Seriphos, she had been so worried she could barely sleep a wink for thinking the worse. She gave her mother an eager look. 'I must go to him, mother.'

'No, daughter. You must wait until father sends for you,' Psamathe insisted.

'Yes, Iolanthe, you must wait,' came a boy's haughty rasp.

Iolanthe looked round at her younger brother who was standing in the doorway grinning smugly at her. 'Did I hear a little squeak?' She pulled a face. 'No, it's the child who thinks himself a man, yet here he is, among women...' She chuckled, and watched that gloating grin wither on her little brother's face. His eyes narrowed with anger. Pallas, being just twelve years old wandered between the women's part of the house and the men's, like a phantom appearing at the most inopportune moments, usually to annoy her, and he liked nothing better than teasing his big sister. Such is the purview of little brothers who linger in that endless purgatory between boyhood and manhood.

'I wander here and there as I please,' he said. 'Unlike you.'

'Oh, go away, Pallas,' she said. 'Mother, tell him to go away.'

Pallas laughed. He took great pleasure in stirring his sister up.

'Be gone, child,' Iolanthe hissed, knowing how much Pallas hated being called a *child*.

But this time, he didn't scowl at her. 'Yes,' he said, the grin returning. 'I think I'll go and greet our guest,' he said and with that, he was gone.

Iolanthe was furious. 'Why can he go and greet Bulis, yet I cannot? This is unfair, mother.'

'This is how it is, Iolanthe. It's the way it's always been.'

It was a bitter truth, and Iolanthe hated it. She was an intelligent and free-spirited young woman, and she longed for the freedom to express her own will. It was her independents and her refusal to wear veils or be treated like a man's chattel that made her refuse every suiter father introduced her to. That was until she met Bulis, who was altogether different to any other man she had met before. They had intellectual debates and he respected what she had to say; he even asked her for her opinions. He would never cage a dove who needs to stretch its wings, he once told her, nor veil its beauty from the world. They were equals in his eyes, and he would never shut her away as father had shut her and mother away.

'I swear, I will be no man's Helen,' she said. 'I'm a Sappho and that's the truth of it.' Psamathe looked worriedly at her. This streak of rebelliousness was so ingrained in her, it would never be tamed. But as much as it worried her, she admired her for her convictions, even though she could be fined or even lashed for challenging the masculine order that denied women their voices.

To her delight, when Pallas went out to greet Bulis, father sent him away. What a joy it was to her, to see that look of disappointment of Pallas's face. She smiled.

Bulis and Iolaos went into the house.

Iolaos gestured to a seat. 'Be comfortable, my boy.'

The slave brought in two cups of wine and set them down onto a table as they sat down.

Iolaos gestured for the slave to leave them and without speaking, he left the room, closing the doors behind him.

'How did it go with our friends in Patrai?' Iolaos asked. 'You met with them, yes?'

Bulis nodded his head and cleared his throat. 'The Corinthians have agreed to the Navarch's plan. But it's going to take some time to bring it together.'

Iolaos picked up his winecup. 'How much time?' he asked anxiously. 'Our friends are growing impatient. They want us out of the alliance before we're dragged further into it.'

'That is what we all want, Iolaos. Once Koragos has convinced the prisoners, a way has to be worked out to get them back without raising suspicion. The Corinthians have separated the trierarchs from the crews, and they've been taken to the estates of the oligarchs, or into the custody of their families. The crews too are being treated well and aren't chackled, and are themselves boarded in the homes of Corinthians at the expense of the state, treating them more like guest-friends than prisoners of war.'

'The trierarchs will unite behind Koragos,' Iolaos said.

Koragos was a Corcyraean *navarch* who, had been captured last winter by the Corinthians, when his fleet of twenty ships, on their way home from Italy, were hit by a storm in the Adriatic, the fleet was scattered and two ships went down. Koragos's flagship became separated from the fleet, and to make matters worse, they had lost their mast which meant they had to row for hundreds of miles across winter seas back to Corcyra.

They ran into a squadron of Corinthian triremes, who took them captive. And Navarch Koragos was quite a prize, he was also one of the conspirators and as soon as they learned that the Corinthians had taken him prisoner, Bulis informed the Lady Hippodameia, who was Sparta's spy in Patrai. She passed the information onto the Corinthians.

'Peithias has informants everywhere,' Iolaos said. 'One cannot even trust one's own slaves these days,' he added.

Peithias was a powerful figure in the assembly, himself an oligarch swayed to democracy, he was one of the main architects of the hated alliance with Athens. He was Athens' man in Corcyra, charged with representing Athens' interests in the assembly, and curtailing the activities of the pro-Spartan and pro-Corinthian factions, who had been vocally opposed to the alliance from the very beginning. From their perspective, Peithias, a democratiser and his pro-Athenian friends had betrayed Corcyra and allowed Athens to enslave them into their inextricable tyranny, placing the oligarchic order in jeopardy with foolish ideas of democracy.

And what of democracy, Bulis thought as they sat supping wine and talking about the intolerable situation in Corcyra. Well, it might be such at Athens for the citizens of Attica, but it was anything but for their so-called allies, who were not free from the chackles of Athens, who behaved like tyrants with their allies, and if they did not fall into line with their Athenian masters, they would face Athenian wrath. This was the bondage into which Peithias and his friends had sold out their country.

Bulis, Iolaos and the other pro-Spartans who had not left the island, had gone underground, meeting in secret, engaged in a deadly conspiracy to overthrow the assembly, arrest Peithias and the democratisers on charges of treason, then to end the alliance with Athens and declare neutrality.

Bulis told Iolaos that he had met with Doreios of Sparta and Alexarchus of Corinth at the house of the Lady Hippodameia in Patrai; and they had assured him that both Sparta and Corinth would settle for Corcyraean neutrality. Having Corcyra's powerful navy and her hoplites out of the war would be, for both Sparta and Corinth an advantage neither could afford to reject.

In return, Alexarchus, on behalf of Corinth, gave Bulis his word that if Corcyra declared neutrality, Corinth would respect their independents and rescind their claims on Corcyra as their colony.

EIGHT

'... It's unlikely the Spartans will lead an invasion of Attica this year,' said Bulis as they went in to dinner.

It was an informal family meal, seated at a long table in the informal dining room adjacent to the kitchen, rather than reclined on couches in the formal dining room. 'They're fearful of the plague.'

Iolaos nodded his head. 'As are we all, my boy.'

'There's much to fear from it Iolaos.'

Iolaos leaned forwards and patted him on the knee. 'We're Peloponnesians, an oligarchy doing the bidding of Athens, a democracy fighting our brother Peloponnesians. The world's upside-down, Bulis. Upside down and mad.'

Bulis nodded his head. 'And Peithias with his democratisers are gaining support all the time to usurp power from us. He's a traitor to his blood, which is oligarchic to the marrow. His own father shuns him with shame.'

Psamathe and Iolanthe were already in the dining room with Pallas. They all three rose to their feet as Iolaos and Bulis came in.

Bulis smiled warmly at his betrothed. 'Good Lady Psamathe,' he said addressing Iolanthe's mother, a pleasure as always,' he said.

'Good day, Bulis. You are recovered from your wounds, I pray. We were very concerned when we heard of it.'

'Happily, I'm fully recovered, Good Lady.'

Iolanthe cleared her throat to remind him that she was there.

Bulis gave her the brightest of smiles. 'Sweet Aphrodite, you are the prettiest flower upon the Earth Iolanthe...' He put his hand over his heart. 'I thought of you every day, and when I was wounded, I thought only of you. And I swear by Apollo, your beauty glows brighter every time I see you anew.'

Iolanthe gave him a coy smile. 'Not too bright, I pray. I should not want to dazzle you.'

Her mother, standing beside Iolanthe, gave her a reprimanding look. Modesty is a virtue, whereas sarcasm is simply impolite.

Bulis's smile broadened. 'Any man would be dazzled to stand before such loveliness, Iolanthe. But it's a pleasing dazzle, I assure you, a balm to my eyes as you are to my heart.'

Pallas screwed up his face, it was so sickly to watch them. 'Did you kill many Spartans, Bulis?'

Bulis looked at the boy. 'Alas I did not. But we did sink a Theban trireme off the Euboean coast.'

'How?' Pallas asked excitedly, shifting in his seat, eager for a war story.

'We engaged four Theban ships, the Athenians pursued three of them, and we engaged the fourth,' he explained. 'First we ran along his side and broke his oars, then, as they flailed about trying to get control of their ship, we rowed off and then came about and rowed back at the Theban at ramming speed. They were easy prey as the Spartans say...'

Pallas's eyes were glazed over as he stared dreamily into space, envisioning the battle.

Iolanthe was listening too, but she cringed and pulled faces and shook her head. 'Oh, why must there be wars?' she gasped hopelessly, a despair lingering in her eyes.

'Alas,' said Bulis, who had barely taken his eyes off of her the entire evening, deliriously wanting to feel her breasts in his hands and to put his manhood inside her. 'War is in the nature of men.'

'Then the nature of men is cruel and bound by hatred and envy,' she responded.

'These are the weaknesses of men,' said Bulis.

'War is glorious,' said Pallas. 'History only remembers glorious war and heroic warriors, isn't that so, Bulis.'

'History remembers all those of note, Pallas,' said his father.

'History remembers poets, and great artists too,' Iolanthe put in.

'Yes. But mostly they remember great warriors,' Pallas responded. 'Homer is full of great warriors.'

'War is a teacher,' said Bulis. 'But its lessons a rarely anything but harsh. We all long for peace in our hearts,' he went on. 'But peace is not easily come by, but, as there was peace before the war, there will be peace again when it's over.'

'Until the next time,' said Iolanthe.

The head servant came into the dining room and whispered something into Iolaos's ear.

Bulis watched the old man's expression go from jovial to worried as the servant spoke.

Iolaos nodded his head. 'Show them into my study. I'll be there momentarily.'

The servant left.

'Is everything all right, husband?' his wife asked, seeing a tenseness in his eyes.

Iolaos smiled. 'Yes. Unexpected guests, that's all...' He looked at Bulis as he rose to his feet. 'Join me, Bulis.'

There were two men in Iolaos's study, Bulis knew one of them – Strophantes a blustery and effeminate aristocrat with a love for exotic robes and ostentatious jewellery. They said he spent more money on robes than he did his wife, who was just as gaudy. The man with him – the man Bulis did not know, was altogether different, he had presence about him, tall and lean with sharp features and sharper slate grey eyes, cold and pitiless. Sosthenes of Sparta, Bulis assumed correctly.

'My apologies for our unannounced arrival, but it couldn't wait,' said Strophantes. And to stress the secrecy in which they had arrived, both men were wearing dark homespun capes with hoods to hide their faces on the dark streets.

'The Athenians know that an oligarch met the Spartan Doreios and Alexarchus of Corinth,' said Sosthenes. 'Doreios is dead. He was knifed in the back shortly after you left Patrai,' said Sosthenes. 'Your mission was betrayed.'

Bulis could hardly believe what he was hearing and his blood chilled as a shudder of fear shimmied down his spine.

'*Betrayed*!' Iolaos gasped. 'Betrayed by who?'

'That we do not yet know,' said Sosthenes. He looked at Bulis. 'We don't think they know who you are either. The Lady Hippodameia of Sparta and Alexarchus were the only ones who knew your name. All the traitors knew was that you're a Corcyraean, nor do they know why you met with them. Athens has informed Peithias that there may be a plot underway to overthrow the assembly in order to end the alliance...'

'Gods preserve us,' said Strophantes, who, like Bulis and Iolaos, was hearing the news for the first time.

Iolaos lowered himself into a chair feeling suddenly vulnerable to the democratisers, his face became as pale at marble, realising the revolution might be over before it had even begun. 'They won't let it lie,' he said. 'Peithias will send men out to find us. They'll question all the oligarchs, and gods help us is any of them crack...'

His warning hung in the silence.

'We should find out exactly how much the Athenians know,' said Bulis. After all, it was his neck on the line.

'Could Doreios have talked?' asked Iolaos.

'No. He was killed in the agora,' Sosthenes explained. 'Someone in the crowd.'

'What're we going to do?' Strophantes said, in a thin shrill voice. 'We should leave the island while we still can...'

'No,' said Bulis. 'We should do nothing. Carry on as normal. If they don't know who we are, they can't find us if we give them no cause to suspect us. They think we're loyal to the alliance, they have no reason to suspect us.'

'*Bda*!' said Strophantes throwing out his hand. 'They suspect everyone...' He looked at them in turn.

Bulis gave him a severe look. 'If any of us leave, they'll know, and they'll suspect the rest of us through our association with each other. We must stay here and maintain the pretence until we're in a position to act. We must keep our nerve, Strophantes.'

'Bulis is right,' said Iolaos. 'As it stands, they believe us to be loyal to the alliance. Peithias and his men have no reason to suspect us...' He looked at Sosthenes. 'How long will you remain at Corcyra?'

'My orders are to stay for as long as it's safe to do so.'

Iolaos nodded his head. 'Where are you staying?'

'You need not concern yourself with that.'

'As you please.'

Strophantes was afraid, they all were, but only Strophantes wanted to run away and that instantly made Sosthenes wary of him. He had to ask himself, if Strophantes was questioned, could he be convincing enough? And if they put him to torture, Sosthenes had no doubt that Strophantes would not think twice about selling them out to the assembly or the Athenians to save his own skin.

NINE

Sparta

It was still three hours until dawn, and the might of Sparta was mustered in readiness on the road.

Archidamos, two ephors, the polemarchs of the morai, their subordinate officers, and twelve elites of the Dioskouri, all clad in their warlike state. They stood wordless in the gloomy sulphurous glow of the Amyklaian sanctuary temple of Apollo Hyakinthos, smoky from the lit bronze braziers and the fragrant smoke of frankincense and myrrh billowing from the impressive altar, from which the colossus of Warlike Apollo rises above the sepulchre in which lies God's beloved Prince Hyakinthos.

The only ones in the King's entourage who were not wearing armour, were the ephors and Tellis, draped in white and crimson, but on closer inspection, Lysander saw Father Tellis was wearing his armour underneath.

Archidamos's generals stood with their helmets under their arms, their dark faces cast in the hue of flames, anxiously watching the King and the haruspex, who was stooping over a shallow bronze dish, carrying out the hepatoscopy of the liver and entrails of the sacrifice for omens.

Archidamos, as high priest, poured libations of wine to Apollo into the eternally lit brazier stood before the altar, tipping it from a gold cup into the glowing coals, and they hissed and the flames turned blue and green, and smoke columned up for God to imbibe. As he poured, Archidamos spoke in the ancient Dorian tongue in a low incantatory cadence, his face limned in the flames and glowing smoke, his armour glinted as the light danced across the polished bronze.

He gave the cup to a novice and stretched his arms up at the colossus, and looked up rapturously and called upon Apollo: 'Mighty Lord of Ravens and time, you who gave us the Rhetra by which all Spartans live, stand in obedience to follow your command of us...' He looked at the haruspex.

The Haruspex gave the King a single nod. 'The liver and entrails are clear of blemish. The gods favour this time for war on Plataea.'

Lysander looked up at the colossus of Warlike Apollo, metamorphosed from a mighty bronze column that formed his body and rose from the altar above Hyakinthos's tomb, lambent in the glow of the low moon, casting a long black shadow across the temenos, dividing it into two almost perfect halves. Apollo's face of gold looked almost alive; his spear and bow growing from his arms.

Archidamos turned to the commanders. 'Tellis, what does Apollo say in the oracle?'

Tellis reached under his robes and pulled out a papyrus scroll, the oracle from Delphi, which nobody had yet read. He unfurled a papyrus and read it aloud: 'Thou arte mighty, you men of crimson and bronze, come thee as a storm to the place where the Mede stood defiant to fathers of all Hellas. But have a care, the gods will favour only him who is most pious in word and deed. Thus, will Potidaea be settled.' Tellis lowered the scroll. 'So speaks Apollo.'

What the oracle meant, nobody fully understood, but as usual with these things, Archidamos trusted it would become clear in the fullness of time. He turned to his commanders. 'We march at once to Potidaea where Thebes and the Boeotians await us. General Phoibos, send out your loyal scouts with ten horse.'

Phoibos of Tegea, gave the King a single nod. 'As My Lord commands.'

'Polemarchs of the morai. Command your men that no attack is to be made on Plataea, lest the command comes first from me. We must be mindful of the oaths our fathers swore when we drove the

Persians out of Hellas. This is the meaning of the oracle,' he said. 'Apollo bids us to give them an opportunity to come to reason.'

The generals affirmed the command.

*

Three morai of Spartan hoplites were on the road, mustered for the march, their bronze shields, helmets, cuirasses and grieves gleamed in the dawn sunshine, their backs draped by their crimson war cloaks. A fearsome monster of crimson and bronze with a spine of pointed spears behind a wall of bronze shields, as still as statues, as quiet as death, waiting for the order to march.

The wind blew down from the north and whistled thinly through the forest of spear tips, like the song of Nemesis, who stirs with glee upon the field of war, exacting merciless vengeance and carnage on all who stand before her.

The Three Hundred Dioskouri were in the forward position, closest to the King, who was mounted on his horse at the head of this mighty and most feared army upon the Earth.

Behind the Spartans, stood their servants in equal number and equal to their masters when it comes to warcraft. After the servants came the divisions of the subject allies of Skiritis, Tegea, Plataea, Gytheion Therapne, Geronthrai and all other Perioikoi towns of Lakedaimon; behind them, were the Helot divisions of light infantry, all perfectly disciplined to the Spartan standard. The line of warriors stretched back near a quarter of a mile, and beyond, were the supply wagons and a rear-guard of Skiritai hoplites.

TEN

Walled City of Plataea

Delphinios/May

Plataea had once been known as Gargaphia, named after the secret Caves of Artemis in the Gargaphia Valley in the Cithaeron Mountains, where a great misfortune befell Actaeon the Hunter, who was out with his pack of hunting dogs tracking a magnificent stag he had spotted in the forest, when he came ignorantly upon the sacred Caves of Artemis, where he was sure the stag had entered. He went inside, but instead of a stag, he saw the beautiful goddess bathing naked in the Parthenios Spring.

Artemis was enraged by this mortal's intrusion, putting his eyes upon her naked body. Her bow being out of reach, she splashed Actaeon with water and Actaeon metamorphosed into a stag. When the metamorphoses was complete, Artemis put the curse of fear into his heart and Actaeon, now a stag fled in terror, and his dogs gave chase and hunted him down and taw him to pieces. This is the story Spartans tell of Plataea, who to this day tremble before even mortal men, for they have the curse of Artemis in their hearts.

*

Plataea was a city of shadows, practically deserted since the outbreak of war, when, expectant of an attack from the Thebans and their Spartan allies, most of the citizens were sent to Athens for safety, leaving behind a few hundred men to defend the city, and a few old women to cook for them.

Daimachus stood on the rampart watching the clear dawn breaking along the rugged foothills of the Cithaeron Mountains.

Golden shards of light glimmered over the peaks and through the treetops in a glorious sunrise that belied the great danger they were in and a palpable tension hung oppressively over the city; disturbing news had arrived of a large Spartan army on the move. They had marched to the Isthmus, but instead of invading Attica, they turned left heading for Boeotia and they were coming this way. The dread day they had long expected had arrived. The Spartans were coming and Daimachus knew it – everybody knew it.

Plataean scouts had also reported a build-up of Boeotian forces at Thebes with the armies of the league encamped in the plains beyond their city walls and on the Kadmeia.

Daimachus dispatched a fast rider to Athens, to inform them of the situation and requested immediate relief be sent. The composition of the Spartan army being of such measure, Plataea could not resist by force without powerful help from their long-time ally, Athens.

To the northeast, a cloud of dust plumed in the distance from the road from Thebes. 'And so it begins,' Daimachus muttered quietly to himself. Then he shouted, 'BAR THE GATES! STAND TO! ARCHERS TO THE RAMPARTS!!!'

A lookout on a tower leaned over the parapet and called down: 'Lord, there...!'

Daimachus looked up at the lookout, who was pointing westward along the road to the Gulf of Corinth, in the shadow of the mountains, where he saw the glint of metal flaring in the dawn light and it was moving their way. He felt a tightness rising in his guts to his chest.

'*Gods of mercy, save us...*' murmured one of the other officers.

Daimachus watched in muted silence as the crimson and bronze dragon emerged from the dusty shadows. He knew at once what this monster was. '*Hades hath cleaved open the world and now cometh his engine of Death hot on his realm...*' Daimachus turned to the rush of activity as archers and warriors hurried up onto to the ramparts with their bows, their quivers loaded.

It was a pincer, with Thebes coming in from the East and Sparta from the west with their allies from the Eurotas and some Corinthians who had joined them at the Isthmus. There were thousands of them, including mounted hippeis of Theban and Boeotian knights approaching from the north with a division of hoplite infantry, moving through the fruit orchards and olive groves.

The advance guard of mounted Skiritai scouts and hoplites had reached the city approaches first, silent and highly disciplined; they immediately set to manning a perimeter and took up defensive positions on the road west of the city with the famed six hundred* elites of Skiritis, who had a place of honour in the Spartan army and acting as the advance guard for the kings.

Archers on the towers loaded their bows.

'Save your arrows, they're out of range!' their commander shouted gruffly.

'Skiritai,' said Daimachus. 'As fierce and as deadly as their Spartan masters.' He knew this creed of warriors and they were utterly ruthless in battle, known for giving no quarter to their enemies...

King Archidamos sat on his horse at the head of his army of near four thousand hoplites of the Spartiate order, including the Three Hundred, and there is no warrior upon the earth so feared as the Three Hundred horseless hippeis. There were three morai of elite Spartan hoplites, and behind them followed thousands more.

The Spartan divisions marched onto the western and northern plains in their formidable phalanxes of gleaming bronze and crimson, forming into their formidable phalanxes of eight ranks deep and sixteen files long, facing the walls of Plataea, and the three hundred deployed in front of the king with the phalanxes of the First Morai on the left and right flanks with the Tegean phalanxes on the extreme left. Meanwhile, west and south of the city, the Boeotians were moving in with light infantry, hoplites and mounted hippeis...

Up on the walls, Daimachus and the other stunned officers and several Athenian hoplites and aristocrats, gawped in horror at the Lakedaimonians martialling in battle order, their rigid lines silent and still, their faces hidden behind their crested Corinthian helmets, the horsehair crest swept by the morning breeze.

Archidamos, dismounted his horse, stepping onto a crouching servant's back.

Tellis, as ever, was at Archidamos's side and the two ephors just a stride behind them. They were quickly joined by the polemarchs and allied commanders.

Archidamos removed his helmet and looked at the Tegean commander. 'General Phoibos. Your Tegean hoplites and light infantry will secure the roads and the pass into Attica. Send out scouts, and bring me any reports of enemy activity on the Attican side of the pass.' he ordered.

'My Lord,' said Phoibos and marched away, beckoning to one of his subordinates.

The King looked round at the Three Hundred, boxed in three phalanxes. 'Hippeus Lysander, present yourself here to me!'

Lysander's heart jumped in his chest when he heard the King call his name.

Tellis, Brasidas and the other officers all looked at the First Hundred, from where Lysander liberated himself, fully liveried, he marched over to the King and his generals, all holding their helmets under their arms.

Lysander could feel his heart beating against his muscled bronze breastplate, his breath loud in his ears from inside his helmet. He came to attention.

Archidamos looked at him. 'You will take my message to the Plataeans and await their answer...'

Daimachus, still on the ramparts, flanked by Plataean aristocrats and their Athenian guests, watched the activity behind the Spartans; where their servants were busily building a town of tents, while engineers directed the digging and spiking of defensive trenches. His gaze shifted to King Archidamos and his officers.

The Spartan hippeus the King had been speaking to, marched fearlessly to the city walls, unarmed except for his sword, and without his spear and shield, his helmet was tilted back on his head. Once he was close enough to be heard, Lysander halted, removed his helmet and inclined his head slightly up, to see the faces of the city's nobility watching him from the ramparts. He looked directly, almost defiantly at an archer in the tower who was aiming his deadly arrow right at him. Looking back at the nobles, Lysander called up: 'Hear me, Plataeans! My king, Archidamos of Sparta bids you, open your gates and let us enter the city in peace as your friends? If you refuse, we will consider you our enemy and we will ravage and destroy your country, and put to death or into slavery, all that we meet. And yet, time still remains, Plataeans. Put out of your city the Athenians within, and our word is given, that no harm will befall them and they will be free to return to Athens without interference. The King further says: "Look you to the plains, where Sparta spilt her noble blood and mingled it with the earth not so long ago, when the might of the Mede was at your walls. Is the blood we gave then, worth less to you now? Barring your gates to us causes great offence!" So, prove you are Sparta's beloved brothers, and bid us enter your city and the King will sup wine with you as your friend!'

Daimachus leaned over the rampart. 'Will you wait for our answer, Hippeus?'

'I will.'

Daimachus looked at the others, many of them were visibly afraid and at a loss as to what they should do. The army in the plains surrounding the city was immense.

Lysander stood statue-like, waiting, facing the thick stone walls, behind him, he could hear the hammering and shovelling and shouts of the allied army digging in, preparing to put a siege on the city if forced to it.

Archidamos had honoured Lysander by choosing him to bring his ultimatum to the Plataeans, and Tellis for one was glad that his *trophimos** was getting noticed by the right people. His conduct at Methone when the Athenians attacked was exemplary, and he was Prince Agesilaos's Inspirer.

Up on one of the towers, a couple of lookouts were watching the Spartan; the archer had lowered his bow, but he was ready to kill the Spartan at a moment's notice. That would be quite a notch to his tally, killing one of the famed Three Hundred.

'It's not natural,' said one of the sentries.

'What's not natural?' asked the other

'That Spartan; look at him, stiffer than a barley in a fuckhouse. I could put an arrow right through the bastard's neck from, here.'

'Do that and the general will nail you to the walls by your chestnuts. Anyway, it ain't him you've got to worry about, Athanas. It's them...' He was looking at the Spartan army.

* ***Elite Skiritai hoplites.***

* ***At the Spartan Rearing, which in later years would be called the Agōgē, a trophimos was a boy from an impoverished family who was sponsored financially by a wealthier benefactor.***

ELEVEN

'If we surrender,' a voice echoed across the council chamber, where the commanders had gathered. 'The Athenians will kill our wives and children.'

He was right, the Plataean citizens they evacuated to Athens were virtual hostages. If they surrendered, Pericles will most likely order them to be killed. If they stand and resist, then *they* will die instead. Their mood hovered between anger and fear, and the dichotomy of surrendering and resisting left them with impossible choices.

'They'll occupy us and make slaves of us,' said another.

'They'll hand the city to the Thebans, who'll kill us all in vengeance for Eurymakhos.'

Brasidas's friend Eurymakhos had commanded the hundred and eighty Thebans who tried to capture the city. The spark that began the Delian war.

'We have to get word to Athens?'

'And risk a set battle with the Spartans?' said one of the aristocrats shaking his head. 'That's a risk Pericles will not take. He'll readily sacrifice us if it avoids a face-to-face confrontation with the Spartans. But we might be able to reason with them,' he said. 'Appeal to their sense of religion, honour and justice.'

'Do you really think so?' said Daimachus, who didn't believe it for a moment. He thought that the Athenians would come, and he thought there was no reasoning with the Spartans, especially as they had all the advantages over them.

'Can one reason with a harpy before it rips your guts open?' said another.

The officer who spoke first, looked at the man. 'What would you suggest, Demophon? That we march out and throw ourselves heroically onto their spears? What poetry they'd make of that slaughter, eh? It would exemplify the folly of fools.'

Demophon shifted his weight.

'We should at least hear what they have to say,' said Daimachus. 'It'll buy us time if nothing else.'

They were all agreed.

Daimachus returned to the rampart and looked down at the young Spartan. 'Hippeus! We ask your Lord, King Archidamos that truce be maintained, so we might send out a delegation to consult with him!?' he called down. 'But first we must consult our assembly to choose them.'

Lysander nodded his head. 'You have one hour, Plataeans. You will either send your delegation, open your gates, or upon the dawn you will see your territory wasted, and your estates destroyed...'

'We need longer, Hippeus. Three hours?'

'For what? One hour, is time enough.' Lysander turned about and marched back to the Spartan line to inform Archidamos, leaving the anxious Plataeans gazing woefully after him.

'Ignorant bastard,' said Demophon...

Archidamos was waiting with Tellis, the Ephors, Pagondas of Thebes and Brasidas at the perimeter of the camp beside the road spur to the gates of Plataea, along which Lysander approached.

'What did they say, Lysander?' asked Tellis.

'My Lord,' Lysander started up, addressing his reply directly to the King. 'They ask that a truce be agreed in order for them to send a delegation to speak with you.'

'*Bda*!' Pagondas barked impatiently, pulling a face and throwing out his hand. 'To what end? I say we attack without delay, My Lord. We can assault their walls and gates.'

Archidamos put up his hand. 'No. How long did they ask for, Dioskouros?'

'I gave them one hour, My Lord.'

Brasidas chuckled. 'That's put a fire up their arses I wager,' he muttered to Pagondas.

*

Within the hour, four wary Plataean emissaries led by Daimachus, entered the Spartan camp.

They were met by the same young Dioskouros who had delivered the message, who escorted them through the camp, where they saw the host of Archidamos's army, hardly any of the soldiers took any notice of the Plataean emissaries. They were dead men walking as far as the Spartans were concerned.

For some reason, Daimachus found that just as worrying as if they were aiming their spears at them. It was a collective contempt.

Ephor Isanor and another ephor were flanking Archidamos, and near them, were his officers, including Brasidas, two polemarchs from Skiritis, and Phoibos of Tegea, a Corinthian and two Thebans. Tellis was there too standing to the King's right half a step behind him.

The Plataeans felt intimidated as they surveyed the grim-faced warriors and magistrates, and the King at the centre of them, still clad in his armour and draped in his crimson war cloak, his long grey hair combed back over his shoulders.

Daimachus surveyed Archidamos's silent retinue, their hard dark faces staring at the emissaries as one might stare at scorpion that had the nerve to come too close, waiting for the right moment to step on it. 'My Lord,' he said keeping his composure. 'And Lakedaimonians ... Thebes,' he added, dropping his tone, his stare shifting sharply at Pagondas. 'Why have you invaded us? Wherein is there just cause to inflict this injury on us, and put to us such an army, when we have not aggrieved or slighted you...?'

'Not aggrieved us? The man's a fool,' said one of Pagondas's officers.

Archidamos raised his hand to silence the undisciplined officer. The Spartans remained silent and expressionless, like disinterred corpses, only their eyes showed signs of life.

'My Lord,' continued Daimachus, 'it honours neither yourselves nor your noble fathers who came here before you as our saviours from the Mede. And upon the great victory, they swore their oaths to the gods that we shall be free in our own land, without fear from any other Hellenic state forever? Yet here you stand, these fifty years later, ready to lay waste our country. Pausanias of Sparta, freed Hellas from the Mede with the help of those Hellenes ready to risk all in the great and bloody battle close to our beloved city. Our fathers who offered sacrifice to Zeus the Liberator in the agora of Plataea in celebration of your great triumph over the barbarian invaders, and Pausanias of Sparta and the Hellenic allies restored Plataea to its citizens, including our territory, and declared us liberated and independent and inviolate against aggressors or conquest. It was then agreed by Pausanias of Sparta and the allies, that if any enemy attack or conquer us, the allies of all Hellas would send immediate and powerful help. Pausanias of Sparta and the other Hellenes thus rewarded us for our courage and patriotism against the hated Mede, where others took a different road...' He looked pointedly at Pagondas of Thebes. 'But now you do just the opposite,' he went on, feeling his blood cooling under their icy stares. 'And you bring with you, our enemy Thebes, who would put us in chains and make slaves or corpses of us. We ask the gods to whom Pausanias of Sparta and the allies swore their oaths, and appeal to you, My Lord, that you too as the most pious man in all Hellas, think on these oaths sworn to by your fathers, and do not dishonour them by attacking our country and allow us to live free and independent, as Pausanias of Sparta decreed...'

Archidamos thought about the oracle from Delphi.

'You dare to stand before us and lecture *us* about the

Plataean oaths!' growled Ephor Isanor, who could hold his tongue no longer. 'You, who entreat and conspire with our enemy Athens against us–'

Archidamos raised his hand again and Isanor fell instantly silent. 'There is justice, Daimachus, in what you have said, and none are more obedient to oaths than are the Spartans. But I say this in response to what you say: If you obey your own words and oaths According to Pausanias, you would continue to be independent and free, by joining in freeing those Hellenes who, after sharing in the dangers of that war, joined in the oaths assuring your freedom. But you are cowed to the will of Athens and subject to their empire, therein, the oaths are void, for you are no longer independent...' His stare burned into the Plataeans like fiery arrows. 'It is to free those who wish freedom of the Athenian yolk, that this war has come, and all Hellas burns in the fever of war, and only Sparta came reluctant to it, and forces to break the fettering chains of Ares and set him loose upon the world, and come hot behind him, Nemesis. But what is done can no longer be undone. Sparta is sworn to war against Athens and her empire. So, I say to you now, Plataeans, you must either join us and abide by the oaths yourselves and declare yourselves free of Athens and join us in freeing those others under Athens' whip in this righteous war, and your city and lands will remain unscathed. If this is beyond your ability; then declare yourselves neutral and ground your arms with neither side, but instead, welcome Athens and Sparta equally as your friends but not invite them or us as your allies in this war. Do this, Plataeans, and we will be satisfied and be as friends, and your city will be unscathed. But if you stay with this foolhardy alliance with Athens, then Plataea and all your territory will be destroyed. I give you two days to save yourselves.'

Daimachus and his companions were taken aback by the king's generous terms. 'My Lord,' said one of them, a man who was old enough to remember the Persian army mustered to destroy them half a century ago. 'Our wives and children and womenfolk are in Athens and at their mercy; should we agree to these terms out of hand, they might bring harm to them. We must at least return and discuss the matter at the assembly and will return within three hours, if My Lord will permit?'

'I have no stomach to make war upon the innocent,' said Archidamos. 'I grant you these hours.'

After the Plataeans had left, one of the Theban generals commented: 'They're just trying to buy time, My Lord.'

'Let them play for time, Polymnis,' said Brasidas. 'In this, time's on our side. While they procrastinate, we'll be preparing to lay their country bare.'

Polymnis was about to respond when Archidamos rose from his chair, and everybody fell silent.

'One way or the other, Potidaea will be out of this war,' Archidamos said as he took a cup of wine from a servant. 'If they refuse to come to reason, we will destroy them, they know that as well as we do.'

'Thebes and the Boeotian allies will keep you supplied, My Lord,' said Pagondas.

The atmosphere relaxed and became less formal as servants brought some wine for them and the generals started talking among themselves.

Brasidas gravitated towards Lysander and stood just behind him.

Daimachus and his worried companions were back within the hour. Daimachus stood before Archidamos. 'My Lord,' he began. 'Your terms are most reasonable and most generous, and they give us hope. We seek no war with you, nor do we seek war with Athens. But our women and children, as I have told you, are at Athens as hostages. So, we must ask you, allow us the time to send our heralds to Athens and put before them what you have said, and ask them to grant us the neutrality you demand?'

Archidamos nodded his head. 'I'm in a mind to grant you this time. Go to Athens,' he said. 'And as you put before them your dire situation, you will plead with them to send out their army. And they will decline with some excuse or other. Then will Plataea see who their true friends are. In that time, we will make preparations to lay siege to your city. If you do not return within four days, then better you not return at all,' he warned ominously.

TWELVE

'Hippeus Lysander,' a young Theban said as he intercepted Lysander and Epiphanes walking through the camp.

Lysander stopped and looked at the young Theban, who was wearing civilian robes.

'May I speak with you on a personal matter? I am Coeratadas of Thebes, I was a friend of Leonidas's.'

Lysander looked at Epiphanes. 'I'll see you at the spring.'

Epiphanes walked away.

'Leonidas is dead,' said Coeratadas. 'He was killed at sea in battle with Corcyraean warships off the coast of Euboea last summer. His ship was rammed and he went down with it.'

Lysander lowered his eyes and took a deep breath. 'He was a true friend.'

'He spoke well of you, and when I saw you were here, I thought I should tell you.'

'And I thank you for it...' He wondered what Coeratadas's relationship was with Leonidas. Platonic friends? Lovers? He assumed the latter, Leonidas never struck Lysander as having platonic friends, just a procession of lovers. 'We should have a cup of wine to his memory.'

Coeratadas nodded his head. 'I'd like that...'

A snappy voice called, '*Coeratadas*!'

Coeratadas and Lysander both looked round. It was Polymnis who called him.

'My *Erastes*. I have to go.'

'Come to my tent tonight if you can.'

'I'll try.' Coeratadas hurried off to Polymnis who was waiting impatiently for him.

Lysander thought about Leonidas as he continued through the camp towards the forest along the lower foothills of the Cithaeron

Mountains. He felt a sadness that Leonidas had died so young, and that they'd never meet again, not in this world at least. He had enjoyed Leonidas's company during his time in Thebes with Brasidas just before the war. They had gone riding together, even wrestled together in the palaestra on the Kadmia.

He went into the woods where he fount Epiphanes waiting at the fresh water spring where it came out from the mountain and spilled down ten feet, where it spattered into the shallow pool that fed the spring's path down the mountain into the Oeroe River.

'Eurymakhos's brother Leonidas was killed at sea last year,' Lysander said as Epiphanes helped him out of his armour.

Epiphanes remembered Lysander telling him about Leonidas.

Once Lysander was stripped naked, he waded ankle deep into the pool and stood under the little waterfall, letting the freezing water cascade down his body. A short distance away from them they could hear the noises and activity from the camp.

Epiphanes sat at the water's edge, eating an apple he picked from an orchard. Lysander's shield was lent against a tree just behind him, the hideous face of screaming Medusa staring out at them, glowing in the evening twilight. 'He's very handsome,' he said and took another bite from his apple.

Lysander looked at him as he washed himself down. 'Who?' As if he didn't know.

'The Theban.'

'Was he? I didn't notice,' Lysander responded as he washed under his armpits.

Epiphanes knew Lysander as well as Lysander knew himself. Trying to play it down didn't convince him one little bit. Lysander was attracted to the Theban, and Epiphanes knew it.

Just then, a twig snapped in the woods. Lysander's lupine eyes were quickly on the figure coming towards them.

'There you are...'

'Good evening, Brasidas.' (Epiphanes jumped to his feet). 'Leonidas is dead.'

Brasidas nodded his head. 'As I've heard. But he died well, I was told.' He sat down under a tree near to where Epiphanes stood. 'We're going to lose many more friends before this war's done, Lysander,' he said as he picked up a smooth marbly white pebble and toyed with it. He looked carefully at Lysander. 'The Thebans think our terms are too generous.'

'The Thebans are personally invested in Plataea,' said Lysander as he got out of the water. 'They've a long festering hatred of the Plataeans. Anything short of Plataea's complete destruction will be too generous as far as They're concerned.'

Brasidas chuckled to himself. How well his Little Wolf understood the nature of men. This, he thought, would be one of Lysander's greatest advantages in life, he had always thought so. 'Told you that, did they?'

'They didn't have to. I saw it in their eyes when the King was putting his terms to the Plataeans...'

Epiphanes handed Lysander his cloak.

'They want to destroy the city,' Lysander continued as he wrapped the cloak around himself. 'They'll be satisfied by nothing less.'

Brasidas raised a brow and rubbed the pebble absentmindedly with his thumb. 'The Thebans have only ever had their own interests in mind,' he said. 'They've a tradition of letting their allies down,' he added, thinking of the Persian War. 'They want to control the Boeotian League.'

Lysander did not respond. He agreed with Brasidas, Thebes had ulterior motives, but they were committed now and he did not think that Thebes would desert the alliance for a minute. They were men of honour, like the Spartans. 'It wouldn't be in their strategic interests to pull out of the war,' he said.

Brasidas did not respond. They didn't often disagree on things, but when they did, Brasidas never tried to make him change his opinions. 'You spend too much time with my father. You're even beginning to talk like him.'

Lysander chuckled and gestured to Epiphanes that he was ready to get dressed. 'Father Tellis is a wise man, Brasidas. He says the Thebans would have too much to lose if they turned on us, not least because it would bring war between us, and leave them exposed to the Athenians, and Thebes would never make another alliance with Athens, not after the last time, when they all but succeeded in democratising the Boeotians.' He pulled his chiton on.

Brasidas smiled.

Epiphanes assisted Lysander in putting on his armour.

They were on their way back to camp, picking their way through the darkening forest as the sun slipped behind the horizon, when there was a distant shout from the Skiritai controlling the road to Leuctra, 'STAND TO!!! STRANGERS APPROACHING!!!'

THIRTEEN

Antigonos looked at the nebulous sprawl of Archidamos's camps as they came into view, the campfires glimmering in the plains between rows of tents and scores of silhouetted figures moving about, and idling in front of their tents. He could hear singing, Tyrtaios if he wasn't mistaken, a song to the glorious dead and battle. It is well known that the Spartans sing a great deal, and their voices, especially those from Amyklai, carry a tune beautifully, and the low lamenting chorus made the hairs on the back of Antigonos's neck stand on end. How is it possible, he thought, that these warlike men, knew such moving tunes as to stir the heckles of a powerful warlord like him?

Ahead of them, a squadron of Skiritai soldiers were blocking the road, spears sloped to the approaching party, who were heavily armed.

Antigonos and his party were in the company of the Spartan shadow men Salaithos and Brasidas's older brother Pheidon, with a Macedonian escort, a dozen servants, a supply wagon and twenty Phokians.

A long-haired Spartan and two young men, one a servant, came out from the woods to the side of the road.

'Brasidas,' said Salaithos quietly, leaning on his horse towards Antigonos's ear.

'My brother,' said Pheidon. 'The youngster to his left is Lysander of the Three Hundred.'

Pheidon was the first to dismount, he loped to Brasidas and the brothers embraced. 'Our father? Our Mother?' he asked.

'They prosper,' said Brasidas. 'Father's here, he'll be glad to see you.'

'Good evening, Brasidas,' said Salaithos as the brothers parted from their embrace and with a nod of his head, Salaithos added as he and Antigonos dismounted their horses. 'Allow me to introduce you to Emissary Antigonos of Macedon, come in goodwill and friendship from King Perdiccas.'

'Greetings, Antigonos,' said Brasidas, stepping forwards, a big smile on his face. 'I've heard stories of you, and your battles against the Thracians.'

'And I've heard much of you, Brasidas.'

'Have you heard that I like to drink my wine undiluted?'

Antigonos shook his head. 'This I did not know. I look forwards to sharing a jug with you.'

Brasidas smiled. 'We're brothers of the vine, my friend.' Brasidas clasped Antigonos's wrists in friendship, a friendship that would endure for years to come. 'This is Hippeus Lysander,' he said, introducing Lysander to the big ugly Macedonian.

'Greetings,' said Lysander.

'Greetings Dioskouros Lysander. Of all that is admirable of the Spartans, the Dioskouri are the most admired of all mortal men on earth,' he complemented. 'Handsome and deadly all at once.'

'You honour my creed, Lord.'

'... We were on our way to Sparta from Delphi, when we heard the King is here,' Salaithos explained as they walked through the vast camp.

At the King's command tent, Brasidas beckoned for Lysander to go in with them.

Tellis greeted Antigonos formally and brought him before Archidamos.

'My Lord, King Archidamos of the Spartans,' said the Macedonian, 'my King bids you good health, and extends his friendship as one king to another, and as cousins of the blood royal. I bring his gift...' He gestured to two slaves carrying a heavy chest between them. 'Three talents of silver and half a talent of gold from My Lord's personal treasury towards the war effort.'

'Our cousin and friend, King Perdiccas of the Macedons is most generous with his gift, and his good will and kinship towards us. His gift will go to our efforts in bringing this recreant enemy to our will. Join our camp, Antigonos, you're most welcome here as our guest-friend.'

'Gladly, My Lord. To observe the Spartan in his warlike state is indeed an honour I should not want to miss.'

*****

Later, in Brasidas's tent, Brasidas, Pheidon and Lysander were having a cup of wine.

Pheidon was talking about the Macedonians. Perdiccas's relationship with Athens had soured somewhat. The founding of their colony Amphipolis which threatened access to the gold and silver rich Pangaeon Hills, and the timber rich forests. But that was only the start. The Macedonian king had learned that Athens were also double-dealing with his troublesome brother Philip, who controlled Amphaxitis on the Axius river, with its port and easy access to the Aegean. The Athenians were also making deals with the Thracians, who were a grave threat to Macedon, and they made regular incursions into Philip's territory.

Pheidon told them that King Perdiccas also had trouble with other neighbours and warlords, King Derdas of Elimea for example, also being courted by Perdiccas's supposed ally Athens. Then there were the unruly, semi-loyal tribes in the north, up in the mountainous highlands, along the very frontiers of the civilised and barbarian world.

In consequence to Athens' lies and double-dealing, and the imperialist vision, Perdiccas was very quickly changing his allegiance to the Spartans, who he knew were not imperialistic, and were the only force on earth apart from Persia, who had the military might and skills needed to drive the Athenians out of his country, and at the same time, hold his local enemies in check.

Pheidon went on to say, that Perdiccas, who was a shrewd and fleet-footed politician, had sent agents in the Chalcidice to encourage those cities loyal to Athens into rebellion.

'Can he be trusted?' asked Lysander.

'To a point,' said Pheidon after taking a swallow of wine. 'But he's only truly interested in consolidating his kingdom. If he comes into full alliance, he has some very capable cavalry and infantry, many of a barbarian character, fierce as Hades. He also has gold and lots of it. Antigonos has implied that Perdiccas would contribute generously towards any costs of an expeditionary army.'

'The old bastards would never go for that,' said Brasidas. 'Macedon's a long way away.' All the same, it had planted a seed in Brasidas's mind.

Epiphanes lit the lamp when Lysander got back from Brasidas's tent, a little lightheaded from the strong wine.

Once he was out of his armour, he started to relax. 'Did anybody stop by?'

Epiphanes shook his head. 'Not that I saw.'

Lysander nodded his head and looked thoughtfully at the flame.

Epiphanes watched him, the light from the lamp flickered in his face, his eyes glazed in thought.

And then, just as Lysander came to his senses, Coeratadas arrived. Lysander greeted him and invited him into the tent and sent Epiphanes away with a look at the same time.

'I wasn't sure you'd come,' Lysander said as he poured wine, one into his *kothon*, * the other into Epiphanes's drinking cup.

'Neither was I,' Coeratadas responded.

Lysander smiled and handed him the cup. 'Then why did you?'

Coeratadas gave him an ambiguous look. 'Don't you know?'

'I'm a Spartan, stupid and slow. Is that not what they say?'

'Only your enemies,' Coeratadas replied, looking intently at Lysander.

Lysander met his stare and stepped closer to him. 'Is that so?' he said in almost a whisper.

'Yes...' He reached and pressed his hand to Lysander's crotch.

* ***Unique to Sparta. The kothon was a metal drinking cup with a turned in rim that formed a sort of cutter to collect grit and stones from river water. It was quite an art drinking from them.***

FOURTEEN

It was the final night of the armistice with the Plataeans, who had returned that day, and met once more with Archidamos, and it was clear that the foolish Plataeans were resolved through a misguided notion that a Delian army was going to come and save them.

Once again, Archidamos appealed to them. He offered to take their city and maintain it for the course of the war, even paying them rent for the land and crops and return the city after the war. The delegation returned to Plataea with the King's offer to discuss it with the council.

It was late in the evening, when a Tegean hoplite informed them that the Potidaeans were requesting to give their answer from the walls. It was at this moment that everybody realised that all of Archidamos's efforts had come to nothing. But he had proved himself to be the most pious of men. Now he would be the deadliest of generals.

For Thebes, the news could not have been better. Now they could raze Plataea to the ground and erase it from existence and occupy their territory.

Once again, Lysander made the long walk to the city walls, where Daimachus was waiting on the ramparts. Lysander removed his helmet and looked up at the Plataeans.

'Take this message to King Archidamos of Sparta. We have abided by the oaths sworn by our fathers. We do not seek war, nor will we cowl before it. But rather stay with the great oaths and protect ourselves from all invaders. This is our reply.'

Lysander pulled his helmet on and without speaking a word, he about turned and marched back to camp.

When Lysander delivered their reply, Archidamos rose from his chair, his stern eyes roving the generals of his allies. 'In war,' he said, 'the Spartan is before all things, mindful of the all-knowing gods. So, let it be known, that we, who seek no empires, nor do we contrive to seize or make war upon any place that does not first aggress against us, must now see Plataea as our enemy. And now come us to that burning nature that courses our blood and our very marrow, for those who make friends of our enemies, shall see us in our warlike nature and know for all time, that our resolve is final. So, I appeal to the gods and heroes of this land, be my witness, we have not shown ourselves to be the aggressors. It is because they broke their relations with us that brings us here to this place where our fathers swore the oaths unto you, and spilt their noble blood in defence of them. Plataea has chosen slavery and death over liberty and freedom. They, with hubris and arrogance in their hearts, have doomed themselves...'

Brasidas shuffled beside Lysander as Archidamos swore his oath and asked the local gods to be with them in their just cause to punish the aggressors of Plataea.

Archidamos looked sternly at the generals. 'We will begin the destruction of their estates, and let not one ear of wheat be spared our wrath. Send out your divisions and destroy everything you encounter in the land of the Plataeans, let not one stone stand upon the other, nor one field or one tree remain in this land. Meanwhile, begin the immediate construction of war engines and siege walls. Allow no Plataean to leave, lest he be dead on our spears first. Give them to Nemesis.'

FIFTEEN

Day after day, night after night, in the land of the Plataeans, a storm of carnage and death ravaged the countryside. The Peloponnesians and Boeotians swept through the country like the *Erinyes* burning crops and orchards, slaughtering livestock, slaves and citizens, robbing and plundering, they left ruin, destruction and death in their wake, the night sky was filled with smoke gloaming in a red hue.

A bitter stench of burning fields and scorched flesh hung oppressively in the air, so fowl Daimachus could taste it in his mouth, and ash rained down, coating every roof and street with a fine grey dust.

He stood uneasily on the rampart with his son and several of his commanders; his hands rested on the cold stone battlement as he and the others stared out wordlessly beyond the Spartans and their allies' camps, into the blood red glow as their fields, orchards and villas were put to the torch. The fires spread across the parched land spewing black smoke and glowing ash swirling up into the sky like a spreading mortcloth, and there was nothing he or anyone else could do but watch as their country was consumed in fire and violence.

There came from that glowing maelstrom the screams and cries of Plataeans, many of them farmers who had returned to their estates after the evacuation in a vainglorious and futile show of resistance, only to be cut down and killed without mercy.

And the old women who stayed behind to cook the bread for Plataea's brave defenders, wailed and wept momentously from the city walls, where they stood limned against the glow like ghosts, their heads covered in black shawls.

'How does it go?' Daimachus murmured in a low calm voice. 'Ah yes, "*A Dorian war will come and with it Death.*" The gods have forsaken us...'

An old woman climbed up onto the city wall and raised her hands to the smoky heavens palms up, fingers splayed out. She lifted her face and cried at the top of her voice: '*Oh mighty Zeus, God of the gods, why hast though forsaken Plataea*!?'

The men on the rampart and watchtowers at either end, looked worriedly at her.

'HEAR ME SPARTA!' she cried. 'I CURSE THEE! I CURSE THEE TO ETERNAL DARKNESS! ON MY OWN BLOOD I CURSE THEE!' She reached under her black robes and something glinted in her hand – a knife. Before anyone could react, she slit her own throat and the blood from her jugular gunned out from the gaping wound, and then she toppled over the rampart into the darkness.

Everyone stared in horror, if they did not express their fear in words, it was clear enough to see it in their dark faces.

'MAMMA!' a warrior shouted as he ran along the palisade and leaned over the rampart, staring down with wide eyed horror as his dead mother, lay buckled on the earth below. The warrior fell to his knees sobbing, crying inconsolably, '*Mamma-mamma-mamma...*'

What will come first, Apollodoros wondered, the vengeful Thebans? The merciless Spartans? The Plague? Hunger? By what terrible means was Plataea doomed? He looked across the camps where the campfires and tents were numerous.

'D'you think they heard her?' asked one of the officers.

'Oh, they heard her,' said another.

'And it'll not make the slightest difference,' said Daimachus. 'Archidamos is the high priest of Zeus, Apollo, Athena, Ares and Artemis. An old woman's blood curse cannot pierce that deified armour...'

Nobody responded.

How long could they endure without help? Some of the defenders, realising that the Athenians were not going to come to their rescue, pleaded with Daimachus to come to terms with the Spartans before it was too late. To declare Plataea neutral and open the city gates to both sides without favour to one or the other. The Athenians wouldn't murder their citizens, they said ... *would they*?

'*Cowards*!' the old women spat angrily at these spineless men, who were full of brave words and gestures when they volunteered to stay behind to defend the city, but now, in the face of the bronze clad killers of Sparta, they buckled and trembled in terror of them and the wrath they were capable of unleashing. It is not without reason they call them the Tamers of Mortals, the Gods of Men – the children of Ares...

'Where are they, Apollodoros...?' Daimachus looked him in the eyes. 'They said help would come. So, where are they?' He turned and looked at his Athenian friend. 'Athens told us to hold on and help would come.'

Apollodoros looked down in shame, lost for words. He knew that, if help didn't come, the city will be lost. It was clear that the Spartans were in this for the long-haul. There was no coming to terms now, the course was set, they would hold out until their final destruction. He was now resigned to their doom – deep down in his heart, Apollodoros knew his countrymen were not coming, and if they did, they would be annihilated, for what stood before them, were the two most powerful hoplite armies upon the earth: Sparta and Thebes.

'If they conquer our walls, they conquer *us*; and they'll likely kill us all and raze Plataea to the ground,' said Daimachus's son Eupompides, a fine-looking young hoplite with a short neatly trimmed beard. His dark eyes glinted in the coruscating hue.

'The Athenians will come; you'll see,' said one of the commanders, combing his hair back with his hand as a gust of wind swept along the palisade.

'Athens isn't coming,' Eupompides responded. 'They've deserted us to our fates. Athens' word isn't worth a dish of shit,' he said through clenched teeth. 'The time for clinging to hope's tit is done,' he added bitterly, casting a look at the commanders. 'We're on our own.'

He had said what the others had not dared to say in fear of the reality. Thinking that the Athenians might come had put false hope into their hearts, but now that hope was gone. Nemesis had but one name on her lips, and that was *Plataea*...

SIXTEEN

Spartans and Boeotians were everywhere, hurrying this way and that aglow in the firestorm around them, confused and terrified. Silhouettes moved in the dancing flames, shields gleamed in the fires; blood slicked Swords and spear tips bristling as the Peloponnesians chased down the fleeing Plataeans, stabbing and hacking them to death. Other warriors hurried off with booty.

All around the buildings and fields were ablaze. Only the Processional Way to the temple of Demeter was wide enough to pass along, choked with smoke, walls of fire either side of the road.

A young woman clasping a small boy by his wrist, ran out from the temple, their terror-filled faces aglow, every building in the village was ablaze, apart from the temple. Even these blood crazed Peloponnesians would not dare assault the house of an Olympian god.

The girl was practically dragging the little boy behind her down the temple steps.

There were Thebans nearby, and they could hear the cries and heinous screams of the villagers in the night, being chased down and killed without quarter or mercy.

Some Plataeans tried to fight, but to no point, outnumbered and outmanoeuvred, they were quickly killed.

The girl and boy ran for the Processional Way and vanished into the acrid smoke, covering their mouths and noses with rags as the smoke swirled around them. Huge tongues of fire lapped at the night hissing and spitting like the fiery tongues of dragons.

The heat was unbearable, pressing in on every side of them as they ran up the centre of the Processional Way, the boy stumbled and tripped, his shorter legs made it hard for him to keep up with his sister, but she held on firmly to his wrist, so tight, it hurt.

Black figures darted ahead of them in panic. 'We must hurry,' she said, her eyes watering and stinging from the smoke.

They stumbled on into the choking miasma, incandescent in the blood red glow.

'*Hurry, Dion, hurry...!*' She pulled the little boy along.

'I'm going as fast as I can,' Dion called back breathlessly, struggling to keep pace with his sister.

They were stopped in their tracks, as something ran out onto the road in front of them. It was a man! Burning on fire from foot to head, screaming in agony. He ran along the road towards them – a human torch, his screams so terrible, so horrendous and so animal-like, the terrified boy made water on the spot as he stared at the flames lapping around the man as he ran about demented for what seemed an eternity, when in reality it was but seconds. Finally, the burning man fell; his screams silenced by merciful death.

Dion started crying again.

'We must go, Dion. Hurry now...'

They continued on, both of them coughing on the smoke, slowing down, exhausted and blinded by the thickening smoke. Dion fell unconscious, overwhelmed.

'*Dion*!' she called in panic, turning back to him, but Dion didn't move. She crouched beside him and shook him. 'Dion. Get up, Dion...!'

Dion lay still and silent.

She coughed and gagged, becoming overwhelmed by the smoke. 'Dion!' she cried, her voice growing weak. 'Please wake up...'

Suddenly from out of the glowing smoke came a red cloaked Spartan. He had neither his spear or his shield with him. The flames coruscated across his shiny bronze armour, his face invisible behind his helmet.

The Spartan stooped over and scooped the boy up into his arms. 'Follow me...' He headed back along the Processional Way, Dion cradled in his arms, the girl staggering behind him.

When they cleared the fires at the junction of the trade road to Thebes, the prevailing wind blowing eastward, blew the smoke away from them.

The Spartan set Dion down on the grass on the opposite side of the trade road.

The boy moved and coughed – he was alive.

Epiphanes handed Lysander his shield and his spear back to his master as the girl knelt at her little brother's side. Dion was coming around, taking deep breaths of the clean air, coughing.

The girl looked at Lysander, luminous in the glow of the fires, his face still hidden behind his black crested helmet, his spear now clasped in his right hand, his shield cuffed over his left arm, painted with the face of screaming Medusa leering at them with her head of hissing snakes. 'Thank you, Lord. Thank you!'

Lysander stared wordless at the terrified girl for a long moment. He summoned the phylarch of a nearby unit of Tegean light infantry. 'See these children safe through the pass to Attica and make certain no harm befalls them...'

'As you command.'

Lysander turned to the boy and the girl. 'Go with them. When you reach Attica, you will be safe. Stay on the trade road, it'll take you directly to Athens.'

'Thank you, Lord. May I know your name, that I might honour you to our father?'

'Lysander of the Herakleidai.' Lysander turned about and he was gone, Epiphanes following behind him.

SEVENTEEN

For seventy days and nights, through the hot and airless summer, the methodical Spartans and their allies began constructing a mound up against the city wall, in order to scale it with infantry. First, they built two high walls either side from timber, driving huge posts into the ground and then latticed the wall with other long beams laid lengthwise between the vertical posts to contain and stop the fill from shifting and spreading. Day and night they worked, filling the earthworks with earth, boulders, wood and anything else that was at hand to fill the space. They had built a crude shelter covered with animal skins to protect them from boiling water and pitch and enemy missiles being dropped on them. The giant slope grew ever higher day on day.

The Plataeans quickly took countermeasures by building two massive inner walls from timber scavenged from around the city and its buildings and filled the cavity between the walls with rubble, city rubbish and masonry taken from the city's buildings, as well as that, and unbeknownst to the enemy, they secretly dug tunnels underneath the Spartan mound to dig out what the Spartans poured in to make the slope unstable, and they used what they dug out to fill the cavity of their counter-wall.

The Peloponnesians had built formidable siege engines, including a wooden wheeled scaling tower covered in animal skins to protect it against incendiaries, much as the Plataeans had done with the inner defence wall they had built. They built a battering ram too, to assault the city gates, but they too were strongly barricaded with thick wooden rafters.

In response, the Plataeans immediately installed countermeasures in the form of huge wooden beams that jutted out from the city walls from which hung long iron chains attached to thick heavy wooden beams that were drawn up and secured them with ropes, ready to swing down on the enemy's siege engines.

*

It was two hours before dawn and Lysander stood naked in the middle of his tent in the glow of a solitary candle. His arms were stretched out from his sides in a cruciform.

'Beloved Artemis, virgin goddess, bringer of light, mistress of the hunt, none more wondrous or divine, watch over my beloved Spartan, Lysander of the Herakleidai,' Epiphanes prayed as he tipped the sacred funereal oil from a small terracotta jar into the palm of his hand. As he anointed his master's body with sweetly fragranced oil, he said in a low incantatory voice, 'Greater, more noble, more terrible, Lysander, tamer of mortals, if you die this day, then die the beautiful death in glory and with honour...' He rubbed the oils into Lysander's chest, over his heart, feeling the hardness of his beloved Spartan's muscles and the power of his heartbeat at his fingertips. 'Greater, more noble, more terrible, Lysander, tamer of mortals, come to your warlike nature and meet the enemy with the courage of your creed...' He put oil onto Lysander's forehead. 'Greater, more noble, more terrible, Lysander, tamer of mortals, the power of Ares is upon you...' Epiphanes stoppered the jar and turned to Lysander and they looked wordless at one another; their eyes said it all, the flame of love still burned bright between them.

Outside, Lysander was now fully liveried in his armour, his helmet tilted up on his head. He looked out over the camp, quiet and dark, most of the fires had burned themselves out. A low mist mingled with smoke drifted through the camp with the petrichor smell of the dewy earth.

Epiphanes handed him his spear. 'May thine enemies tremble before thee...' He turned and lifted Lysander's heavy shield. 'With it living, or upon it dead.'

'Victory or death,' said Lysander and without any further words or ceremony, he turned about and marched away through the colourless pre-dawn gloom of the camp to join his brother hippeis in readiness for battle.

It was an impressive display of a highly disciplined force of some six thousand Peloponnesian and Boeotian warriors of the first order, the centrepiece being the presence of the bronze clad Spartans in their neat phalanxes, their faces hidden behind their bronze helmets, spears erect with broad iron spearheads and iron spike butt ends, the Spartans use to thrush down on the bodies of their enemies as they march over them.

They waited with limitless patience, not moving, not making a sound.

King Archidamos was with the commanders facing the great walls of Plataea. Their ramp had failed due to the enemy undermining it. Now they would try a direct assault on the walls and attempt to scale them and overwhelm the ramparts with light infantry under the command of General Gelon of Skiritis commanding his elite Skiritai, Tegeans, Theban and other Boeotian peltasts* who were assembled behind the scaling tower and battering ram.

The three Hundred formed three phalanxes of a hundred Dioskouri to the right centre and left of the King. The Theban, Spartan and Skiritai hoplites were assembled likewise in heavy armour in their phalanxes across the field behind the siege engines, spears erect. Shields cuffed to their left arms and resting on their shoulders by the dished-shaped taper around the rim to take the weight.

But these heavy soldiers would be redundant if they were unable to breech into the city, and nobody expected the Plataeans to turn out in battle order, they were vastly outnumbered.

Antigonos was impressed by the discipline and uniformity of the Spartans. Their Theban and other allied counterparts, although neat and disciplined, still seemed lacking in comparison. Yes, there was something very frightening about the Spartans. They were as calm as the mist at their feet, whereas the allies seemed antsy and unsettled.

Lysander looked at the scaling tower, pressed into the dawn like a wooden monster on wheels, dozens of men were around it, waiting for the order to advance it to the city walls with the battering rams. Futility, thought Lysander as his gaze shifted up to the Plataean countermeasures. If those chained beams swung and hit the tower, it would smash it to pieces. The battering rams too were within their reach.

* ***Light infantry.***

EIGHTEEN

The first attack began in the misty dawn, when Archidamos gave the signal, and a division of Tegean and Theban archers advanced and took up forward positions, well within killing range, their arrows trained on the city ramparts and watchtowers. The siege tower and battering rams started rolling towards the city, pushed, pulled and guided by the strongest of the mothones. Behind them, there were more archers and light infantry, keeping low as they advanced.

Almost immediately, Plataean archers in the towers and on the ramparts opened fire with a volley of arrows that whistled down on the scaling tower and battering rams advancing towards them.

The Theban and Tegean archers returned fire, letting loose two hundred arrows arcing up towards the ramparts with a thin whistle...

Some of the defenders were hit, their screams were clearly audible. Without pause, they reloaded and fired another two hundred arrows in an effort to keep the defenders pinned down as the siege engines advanced.

The Plataeans fired another round at the engines. Several men manoeuvring them fell dead and wounded and were speedily replaced man for man.

Archidamos, up on his horse, shifted his weight and watched the exchanges of arrow fire as the siege engines inched forwards, followed by the light infantry assigned to capturing the walls and opening the gates, whereby the Hoplites were to march in. Until then, all they could do was watch and wait.

Tellis, mounted beside Archidamos was completely expressionless and unmoved, watching the archers on the ground and on the ramparts firing relentlessly at one another.

Soon, both sides started firing flaming arrows at each other and the Tegean and Theban archers aimed high, their objective now was to try and set light to the city, and it worked in one or two places when they saw smoke and flames leaping up from some rooftops, which drew men away from the ramparts to deal with the fires.

Pagondas nudged Polymnis in the shoulder. Polymnis gave him a curious look. 'The old man's given Thebes the honour of going in first. I'll lead the men in personally.'

Polymnis nodded his head.

'Try and take as many as you can alive. I've a mind to nail them to the fucking walls as an example before we pull them down.'

Finally, the battering rams were at the city walls, each manned by a score of men who immediately struck the walls with their tree-trunk battering rams cradled in slings of rope. They struck with jarring booms.

The scaling tower inched steadily towards the city walls, the men manoeuvring it deploying all the strength they could muster to move the it.

One of the battering rams struck the wall with such force a large portion of the wall gave way and tumbled down.

It was looking promising and Archidamos exchanged an eager look with Tellis.

*

The scaling tower reached the wall, and as soon as it did, Daimachus shouted the order to release the countermeasures...

The huge heavy beams swung down on their chains with an air splitting WHOOSH and struck the battering rams and tower with such force, they practically destroyed them and killed at least a dozen men.

The scaling tower was made of sturdier stuff, and the first impact lifted the tower sideways up onto two wheels, almost topping it, but it fell back, still intact, or so it seemed...

Inside the tower, the thick beams and rafters vibrated and cracked loudly with a sound of splitting wood.

The infantrymen were ordered into the tower and started hurrying up the criss-cross of ladders each leading to a platform, and there were three platforms up to the enclosed top platform, from where they were to invade the ramparts.

The countermeasure beams were quickly pulled up by the Plataeans and released again and the huge beam swung down – VROOM and the tower juddered violently as the beam smashed into the side. This time it crashed through the wall, crushing several men within. A moment later and a second countermeasure beam swung in from the opposite side and the tower leaned to one side as the support beams snapped with a tremendous crunch of splitting wood. The tower gave out a loud whining groan as it buckled...

Archidamos and his army watched as the tower collapsed down and there was a raucous cheer of shouts from the Plataeans on the ramparts for their minor, but morale boosting victory.

Archidamos knew that there was no way they were going to get passed the Plataeans' countermeasures. He looked at Tellis. 'Fools' courage.'

The battle of the archers carried on a while longer as the men on the siege engines retreated back to the Spartan line.

A man tumbled from a watchtower with a scream of fear and pain, an arrow sticking out from his neck. He hit the ground with a heavy and fatal thud.

Another volley of burning arrows were fired by the Tegean and Theban archers and arced over ramparts, climbing into the sky before they plunged down into the city.

'The effectiveness of Plataean resistance has made our efforts fruitless, My Lord,' said Tellis. 'Those flying rams have us licked.'

Archidamos did not speak. His disappointment was clear in his face. He reined his horse around. 'Sobeit. We'll starve them out. Withdraw the offensive,' he said and cantered away.

Tellis and the Hippeis followed behind him, escorting him back to the camp.

*

There was a long silence in the tent, all of them were looking to Archidamos for the solution.

'The wind has been steady of late,' said Tellis, making no sense whatsoever.

Pagondas gave him an odd look.

'We should burn the city with everyone inside,' Tellis added. 'If we throw enough combustible material over the wall, which can be done from what remains of the scaling tower. All we have to do is move it back, where their flying rams cannot reach. From there, we can throw logs, brushwood and anything else that'll burn with sulphur and pitch and then light them up. raise a big enough fire, with the wind blowing into the city, the fire will quickly spread.'

Archidamos nodded his head, it was worth trying. The last thing he wanted was to lay in a long siege, taking away valuable manpower and money from the war.

'It could work,' Pagondas agreed.

Archidamos nodded his head. 'Do it. Meantime,' he added, 'begin preparations to circumventing the city with walls.

*****

They had thrown so much wood over the wall from the scaling tower, while crack archers once again kept the Plataean defenders pinned down from that part of the city. Tree-trunks and the broken battering rams, brushwood and pots of sulphur and pitch and lamp oil were thrown over the wall.

When it was lit, the fire that ensued was a monster of all fires, the flames reached higher than anybody had ever seen flames reach before, and the roar was so loud, men had to shout to be heard over it, and in the Peloponnesian camps, they could feel the heat of it radiating beyond the walls, and there was a glow in the night that outshone even the full moon.

Archidamos and his officers stood at the edge of the camp watching the fire, their faces lit in its bright orange hue.

'By the gods, did you ever see the like before?' said Polymnis.

'Not since the burning of Troy has there been such a fire as this,' added Phoibos of Tegea.

Archidamos put his hand to his head with the arrival of a headache. He had been suffering a good deal with headaches since they had arrived at Plataea, and on one occasion his head spun drunkenly and he almost fell over. Fortunately, only his servant saw.

Lysander looked worriedly at the sky over the mountains, where dark clouds were gathering, threatening a rainstorm, not only that, the wind had died down and changed direction.

Inside the city, Daimachus, Apollodoros of Athens along with every able-bodied man and woman were running around with pales and jugs and pans of water to fight the firestorm back, but it was hopeless, and an entire quarter of the city was burning and became inaccessible. As the fire swept through the streets, the screams of those trapped in the burning buildings fell gradually silent until the only sounds were the roar of the fire and the panicked shouts of the citizens rushing back and forth with water.

Daimachus had noticed those rainclouds too, now spreading across the sky over the plains. He prayed for it to rain, or the city and them with it, would be lost.

And then, the answer to his prayers, to all their prayers, there was a bright flash of lightning that streaked across the sky – moments later came the deep loud BOOM of thunder.

Raindrops, cold, glorious raindrops! Just a few at first, and then the heavens opened in a torrential rainstorm. Daimachus beamed and yelled out: 'The gods are with us! The gods are with us!'

Back at Archidamos's camp, the Spartans and their allies were thinking the same thing. The gods had sent a storm to put out the fire and save the city.

Tellis was the voice of reason once again, reminding them how prone the area was to sudden and ferocious storms. It was such a storm as this, that had hampered Thebes' attempt to take the city on the eve of the war. It had nothing to do with the gods but everything to do with the nature of this mountainous area.

Later, when Tellis and Archidamos were alone, sharing in a jug of wine before turning in for the night, Archidamos's winecup fell from his hand and he swooned and staggered–

Tellis was quick to his side, grabbing him before he fell, he helped the King to a chair. 'My king, you're ill.'

Archidamos shook his head. 'What happened, old friend? All about me spun and I felt I was about to die, I tell you...' He was trembling, but not from fear, but some inner malady, the colour drained from his face, which had pocked with beads of sweat.

'I'll send for the physician–'

'No, Tellis. No physicians.'

'You're unwell, Archidamos.'

'I'm tired, that's all,' he insisted. 'A few hours' sleep is all I need...' He rubbed the side of his head. 'And this headache isn't helping.'

Tellis acquiesced, but he knew it was more than that. The King was ill, he hid it well, but he couldn't fool Tellis. 'Then I'm staying here. In case you feel unwell again. This is my condition for not summoning the physician.'

Archidamos nodded his head. 'You've always been a good friend, Tellis.'

'As have you.'

NINETEEN

They had heard nothing from Knemos and his mission to capture Stratos and knock the Akarnanians out of the war before moving on the Athenian naval base at Naupaktos, where they had practically blockaded the Gulf of Corinth from the Gulf of Kalydon and the open sea beyond. What little they knew of the disaster unfurling for Knemos.

It was the middle of *Carneios,** when Archidamos and the bulk of the army mustered for the march back to Lakedaimonia, leaving a minimal force behind to maintain the siege with the Thebans and other Boeotian forces.

Antigonos of Macedon returned to his king with Archidamos's favourable messages and alliance and to expect his embassy, who would come to offer military expertise, and encourage Sparta's allies in the region to assist Perdiccas with any actions against the Athenians and Thracians they could.

How fine those Spartans looked, even among their allies, they above all others were the most noticeable and most enigmatic, swathed in crimson, marching in perfect step like a single entity, singing Tyrtaios to the glory of war:

Let a man learn how to fight by first daring to perform mighty deeds,
Not where the missiles won't reach, if he is armed with a shield,
But getting in close where fighting is hand to hand, inflicting a wound
With his long spear or his sword, taking the enemy's life,
With his foot planted alongside a foot and his shield pressed against shield,
And his crest up against crest and his helm up against helm
And breast against breast, embroiled in the action;
let him fight man to man,
Holding secure in his grasp the haft of his sword or his spear...!

The great crimson and bronze dragon marched passed the soot black fields, the air sang with the thump of five thousand warriors' marching feet upon the sun-baked road to the Isthmus, marching as a single entity, possessed of a single mind.

All before them lay wasted and burned, the trees in the orchards and olive groves stood as black as night, bare of fruit or leaf, but not dead, most would recover and in a few years they would once again bear fruit, as the fields would again be bountiful. But now, they lay wasted. They passed gutted villas and farms, their walls smashed, their innards burned beyond use by Spartan fire, so too the hamlets and villages of the plains. The Peloponnesians left not one stone upon another, nor one strand of wheat, or a or vine. War had swept this way with merciless abandon, and the air was fettered with carrion flesh and scorched fields still smouldering in places.

Amidst the blackness, they occasionally saw bodies, with what flesh the fires did not consume, black and crispy like the flesh of spit roasted boar. They were curled up in grotesque pugilistic poses, charred and grimacing faces with hideous grins accentuated by ivory white teeth.

This is how the banks of the Phlegethon look as it twists its fiery way through the Hades to the Pit of Tartaros, thought Lysander as he marched passed the macabre sites. The twisted remains of men, women and children. He thought about the girl and the little boy and hoped they made it safely to Athens.

'War is a merciless business, Little Wolf,' said Brasidas as he came up beside Lysander. 'From the meek to the mighty, none are spared its wrath.'

Lysander looked ahead, his helmet tipped back on his head, the dished rim of his hoplon rested on his shoulder, his spear vertical.

'I heard you let a couple of little rabbits go free?'

'There's no honour in killing children and women, Brasidas. That I leave to our allies, who seem lacking in such virtues.'

Brasidas chuckled. 'In war, one must be both merciful and ruthless,' he agreed. 'Not too merciful mind.'

Behind the army followed the baggage train, loaded with spoils, and supplies. In the front, on horses, were the King, Tellis, the ephors and some of the allied commanders.

Archidamos was talking to them in a clarion tone. '... The Athenians think we will tire of this war, Gentlemen. They think us feebleminded and too poor in our treasuries to maintain our armies and our navies. Well, I tell you, gentlemen, we will continue with this war until the Delians are defeated, or bring favourable terms for honourable peace upon which we are all agreed. The Lakedaimonians are committed to victory or death. We serve Ares in our warlike state and Ares commands us to press this war with all our vigour, and to his command, we will do just that, with all means available to us. Plataea will fall soon enough,' he went on. 'After a long winter without food or friendship. They will suffer as did the Potidaeans, and they will yield to us or they will die.'

Tellis looked at him.

'Once Plataea is tamed,' Archidamos continued, 'I want that city destroyed utterly. Leave it unfit even for rats to live in. We offered them honourable and generous terms, but they chose death instead, then let them have it.'

'It will be a pleasure to have it so, My Lord,' said Pagondas, who was looking contentedly at the King. It would be a pleasure to destroy that most hated city, which had for so long, been the bane of Thebes.

At the Isthmus of Corinth, they received some welcome news from the commander of a Corinthian patrol. He brought news that the Athenian Generals Xenophon, Hestiodoros and Phanomachus had met with defeat and death at Spartolos in the Chalcidis Peninsula. As well as the generals, more than four hundred elite Athenian hoplites had been killed and the remainder of their shattered army had retreated back to Potidaea. It was excellent news and welcomed with smiles and cheers.

*August.

TWENTY

Sparta

It was late afternoon and Agesilaos was in the river, having fun with his friends in the water after a gruelling and hot day of training. The entire afternoon had been spent in the valley plains phalanx training with staffs and training shields, divided into opposing phalanxes, "Spartans" and "Athenians".

It had been hard fighting, the boy phalanxes clashing like real hoplites, hard and brutal, lunging their staffs at each other over their shields, pushing against one another, two immovable forces. Agesilaos, who had been in the Athenian phalanx, in the middle of the front row, had a nasty cut over his eye from being jabbed in the face by another boy's jabbing staff. It had given him a splitting headache.

Most of the boys had cuts and bruises over their bodies from the violence of the battle.

Across their backs, they bore the recent wounds of the Artemisian whips, proving their worthiness through the ordeal of the ritual *Diamastigosis* of Artemis-Ortheia's long blood altar.

Agesilaos had endured fifteen strikes of the bullwhip before he fell. Nowhere near the legendary twenty lashes his Inspirer Lysander had endured, but worthy enough for it to be noted that the lame prince had endured the whip's keen kiss in silence as a Spartan must, a full fifteen hard licks. The average was ten, anything over seven was deemed good.

The boys were swimming in the deeper water under the shade of Old Herakles's sprawling branches. They pounced on one another, trying to duck each other under the water and wrestling playfully. Some boys climbed into Old Herakles and jumped into the water from the long thick boughs that stretched out over the river. The air was filled with their happy shouts and splashing.

The prince had a close circle of friends, Cinadon, Agapitos, Tisamenos and his lover-friend Tyndarios. The three boys were known for their mischief, and on food raids, where they always managed to get their thieving hands on a jug or two of wine for their mess contributions.

Agesilaos was recently caught on a food raid by two *krypteia* boys. For allowing himself to be captured, he got a skin splitting birching from the gymnasiarch, the wheels of the tendrils were still fresh on his backside.

Some boys further along the river shouted excitedly and ran towards the road.

'*Agesilaos, look*!' Tyndarios was pointing back along the road.

The King and his army were marching along the Hyakinthian Way, returning from Boeotia. All the boys without exception ran to the road and formed a long line at the side of the road, clasping their hands in front of themselves, those wearing chitons slipped their hands underneath out of sight as law requires. They watched in awe and complete silence as the army marched towards them.

First to arrive was the Tegean advance guard of mounted hippeis and light infantry, armed with shields, spears and swords, and they wore open faced helmets without crests.

It took several minutes for the main column to arrive, headed by Agesilaos's father; beside him rode Tellis, behind were Anakletos, Pagondas of Thebes, General Phoibos of Tegea and General Gelon of Skiritis.

Agesilaos looked proudly at his father and the Three Hundred Dioskouri. '*Lysander...*' he muttered, his heart quickening in his chest, his blood surging, eager to be reunited with his beloved Inspirer.

Lysander, who was marching with the First Hundred, looked at Agesilaos and the hairs on Agesilaos arms stood up on end with the power of Lysander's lupine eyes upon his, and Lysander gave him an imperceptible nod, which welled the prince with an immutable joy and pride.

The sounds of the flutes and drums and marching feet made a stirring song.

TWENTY-ONE

Argileonis was enjoying a stroll through the palace gardens with the Queen, admiring the flowers and making the most of the late summer. The air was sweet with the scents of flowers, and there were butterflies everywhere, and bees from the royal hives droned around the blooms gathering their nectar.

'... The King has a fondness for the sweet girl,' said Eupolia. 'And I so enjoy playing *Tavli** with her. She's very good and for one so young and delicate, she's really quite ruthless, *even* with me.'

'With her grandfather too,' said Argileonis. 'And we know how he hates to lose to a woman.'

Eupolia chuckled.

The Queen's favourite companions, Eudokia, Apollonia and the newest and youngest girl, (the very girl Argileonis and the Queen were discussing) Telephassa, daughter of Pheidon, were following several paces behind. They were all the daughters of high-ranking aristocrats who were close to the house of the Eurypontids.

Telephassa was arguably the most beautiful of the companions, one of the ephors compared her beauty to that of Aphrodite, to whom Spartan warriors pray as they prepare themselves for battle and the beauteous death. She was an intelligent girl, no doubt inherited from her paternal grandfather Tellis.

Eupolia was not yet forty-five and the King fell in love with her almost from the day he met her, when she was herself a royal companion of Archidamos's first wife Lampito, the mother of Crown Prince Agis, and she had tended her Queen night and day when she fell ill up until her death, something for which Archidamos was extremely grateful. "No gentler or kinder a lady ever graced these walls," he had told her. She was there in his grief, comforting and she became a mother to Prince Agis who was still a small child. Eupolia and Archidamos's love for one another was undeniable.

The ephors at the time, objected strongly to Archidamos's marriage to Eupolia, due to her small stature in comparison to most Spartan women, who are tall and robust, and therefore, the logic went, they would produce strong and robust warrior sons for Sparta. The ephors had used their considerable powers to forbid the marriage, one of them exclaimed in front of the King: "*She'll bear Sparta nought but kinglets instead of kings*!"

Archidamos flew into a rage an instant rage, drawing the sword from the scabbard of one of his guards, and was about to kill the startled ephor on the spot. Had it not been for the intervention of Tellis, he surely would have killed him.

Tellis told Archidamos to marry her and pay the ephors' fine. "*Once the deed is done, it cannot be undone, for when a king weds, it is with the blessings of Zeus himself*," he told Archidamos.

So it was, Archidamos married the woman he loved. He paid the fine the ephors levied, a talent of silver and a quarter talent of gold.

Rarely had Sparta had a finer or more loved queen than Eupolia. Small in stature she may have been; but she was strong in will and wise in thought like her husband. A king could never ask for a better consort. Archidamos never loved Lampito so well as he loved Eupolia, a kindly and most generous queen, beautiful and gentle with their children. She bore Archidamos two children, a son, the "lame" Prince Agesilaos, and their beautiful daughter, Kyniska who had a boy's heart and a passion for horses and sports that practically consumed her. She excelled at the Spartan Sisterhood, the fastest runner in her herd, and the finest horse rider in the entire sisterhood, and her skill with the bow would put any Delian needle-worker* to shame. All qualities that met with the ephors' approval.

Telephassa looked over to where several off-duty hippeis in the olive grove were relaxing, drinking wine, eating roasted chicken legs, crowded around something or someone she could not see.

Nearby, palace slave women, girls and boys were tending to the trees, checking the ripening fruits, picking off the bad olives and putting them into wicca baskets they carried over their arms.

'... I've never seen him so tired as he's been since they returned from Boeotia, and I fear another expedition might lay him low, or even kill him,' Eupolia confided to her trusted friend and confidante, stopping to admire the flowers. 'He's past seventy. Wars are for younger men,' she added as they continued walking. 'But it is these strange lapses in his memory and confusion that worry me most,' she said, the tone of her voice changed and she spoke in an almost whisper. 'Your husband says he is cursed by the *Maniai*.* Most of the time he's his normal self. But there are moments, Argileonis, when I fear he is losing himself.'

Her anxiety was clear to see from the well of tears in her eyes. She loved Archidamos completely. Argileonis cleared her throat. 'You must prepare yourself, Eupolia. Tellis's mother was also cursed by the Maniai.'

'As he has told me, and he told me that you were indispensable to her care.'

Argileonis nodded her head. 'By the end, there was nothing left but fear and confusion, she knew not even herself...'

The off-duty Dioskouri laughed again, and one of them declared: 'You've lost your army...'

'Besieged, surely,' said another.

'You have no moves left to make.'

'Gods save me. I've become Plataea,' said Agis.

They all laughed.

Argileonis and Eupolia looked over at the young men as their laughter carried across the gardens.

Where the path divided, they turned into the shady olive grove, towards the hippeis.

The young men were crowded around two other young men who were seated at a stone table playing *petteia* on a tactical wooden petteia board. Agis's pebble white soldiers had been decimated with just four pebbles left. Lysander's army was intact and had completely surrounded Agis's four remaining pebbles.

'He's got you, Highness,' said one of the young hippeis.

Agis shook his head. 'He's always got me...' He looked at Lysander. 'I swear you use magic.'

Lysander smiled.

Everyone fell quiet when the Queen and her entourage approached. Agis and Lysander rose to their feet.

Lysander recognised Telephassa, he had seen her several times at Tellis's estate, where she lived under Argileonis and Tellis's care on account that her mother died giving her life, and her father, Pheidon was hardly ever in Lakedaimon.

Eupolia looked at the board. 'Who is winning.'

'Hippeus Lysander, My Lady,' said a hippeus.

'I had the best teacher in Father Tellis, My Lady,' said Lysander.

'As Agesilaos says of you,' Eupolia complemented.

'He is gifted in many things, My Lady.'

'But not others,' she said, clearly referring to his foot.

'No man is a master of everything, My Lady,' Lysander responded quickly. 'But what he lacks on one place, he more than makes up on others.'

She smiled.

'Do you put the hardest lessons to him, as Brasidas did for you?' asked Argileonis.

'Always, Good Lady.'

Telephassa cleared her throat loudly.

Lysander looked at her and she met her stare. Was that contempt, or was it something else he saw in her eyes? Whatever it was, he responded with a half-smile and she looked irritated, clearly some sharp comment was burning on her tongue.

Eventually, the Queen and her party moved on and Lysander looked on after them.

The companions were whispering and giggling about something and Telephassa looked back at him and when she saw he was looking at her, she turned back smiling secretly to herself.

'By the gods, those girls are like the handmaidens of Athena,' said one of the off-duty hippeis.

'Especially the young one,' said another.

'You know her, do you not, Lysander?' said Agis.

Lysander blinked and looked at Agis. 'Not especially. I don't think she likes me.'

'Huh. Are you blind? She could barely take her eyes off of you,' Agis responded.

'Who is she?'

'Tellis's granddaughter.'

'Brasidas is unmarried,' said a hippeus stupidly.

'She's Pheidon's daughter, you idiot,' Agis snapped with a roll of his eyes. 'Set them up,' he said to a servant. 'Another game, Lysander?'

'Of course.'

An ancient Greek form of backgammon.

Spartan colloquialism for archers. The Spartans at this period considered archers to be cowards and the bow to be a coward's weapon as it could kill from a distance, leaving the archer relatively safe. The Spartans called arrows spindles or needles, in reference to women, who weave and sew.

Spirits of madness, manias and insanity. The root of the word mania.

TWENTY-TWO
Gytheion

It was the middle of the morning when Imbrasos arrived with two overseers. Quintius was leaning against the mast watching him walking up and down along the line of slaves, carefully examining them, nodding and shaking his head, mumbling inaudibly to himself, looking in their mouths, feeling their arms, and legs, and genitals. 'I ask you for decent brush, and pretty barley! That's all. It's not much to ask for, is it?' He looked at the Roman. 'Decent brush and pretty barley?' (Quintius rolled his eyes, he had heard it all before). 'And what do you bring me?' Imbrasos went on as he walked from one end of the shackled line of terrified captives to the other. Despite being washed and oiled, they still stank like farmyard animals. They usually smelled this way when they first arrive, sometimes worse. 'Sows and goats...' He shook his head despairingly. 'What have you been feeding them on?! ... Cabbage leaves? Look at 'em! They're half dead already, you ignorant Roman! It'll take months to feed them up, and what will that cost me, eh?!' He rubbed his smooth shaved chin, his eyes narrowly roaming the row of dejected humanity. 'All that red meat?' he went on. 'Eating my profits! What is it with you Romans, that you think we Hellenes would want to ravage girls who look like they were borne to a gorgon?' he ranted as he looked at the trembling young girls, examining their unfettered breasts. He reached to one of them and clasped his big fat hand under her chin and forced her mouth open and looked inside at her teeth, expressing his disappointment with a slow shaking of his head. 'Or boys as ugly as horses arseholes...'

Quintius was totally impervious. 'They've been in the hold for months,' he said. 'What do you expect? ... For them to be singing and dancing for you? ... Now take another look at them. I chose them for you ... no ... Aphrodite chose them ... she blessed them with rare beauty, I know you can see it. They'd do any whore-monger proud...' He added. 'Even a miserable old cunny like you,' he said, throwing in some good old fashioned Latin profanity for good measure.

They were everything Quintius said they were, and he had clearly chosen them with care, but letting the Roman know that, would put the price up. 'Barbarians you say?'

'From Gaul. They're as docile as kittens ... loyal as dogs. You won't get better, Imbrasos.'

Imbrasos sucked in his cheeks and puckered his lips.

'Slaves like these never come cheap ... cheap is what you get when half of them die on you a month after you bought them. These have got plenty of life in them; look at them, Imbrasos, Ganymedes and Helens of Troy...'

Imbrasos turned a sharp look on him. 'Helens of Sparta,' he corrected. 'We're touchy about that sort of thing around here.'

Quintius laughed. 'You Lakedaimonians are touchy about everything.'

'Lucky for you we're friends then. The usual price?'

Quintius flipped himself away from the mast and came over to Imbrasos. 'Plus, two hundred a head for the boys. You know they're worth it,' he added quickly, giving the captives a quick sweep of his eyes.

'Blood and dust! ... Are you trying to finish me off? I could buy half the boys and girls in Gytheion for less than that! ... Fifty extra, and not an obol more.'

'I'd like to see you try,' said Quintius lowly. 'One hundred and eighty, and your customers will think they died and went to Elysium...'

'You test our friendship, Roman. Sixty, and I'm risking the health of my children by not having money enough to feed them.'

'You better put them to whoring then, because I won't take an obol less than a hundred and fifty.'

Imbrasos threw his arms up in disgust. 'You wound me! Here was I thinking this Roman is like a brother to me, to bring me the flower of his crop, when all the time you just want to swindle me. Eighty drachmas.'

'I would plough a field with my prick before I took less than a hundred and twenty-five.'

Imbrasos turned to the slaves and considered them in turn, frightened and powerless, guarded by men with whips and clubs. 'Ninety.'

'One hundred, or I'll sell them in Lydia, where they like milky skin and appreciate beauty.'

'Ninety-five. Bare it in mind that I want all of them. The war is good for business. But not *that* good.'

Quintius made a gesture, and the deal was done.

An hour after Imbrasos left the ship with his purchases in chains, Quintius hurried to the usual meeting place at the acropolis, where he found Lysander waiting, 'Salve,' Quintius greeted with a smile.

'Greetings, Quintius. What do you bring us from your travels? Not the plague I pray?'

Spartan humour? He chuckled.

They started walking among the gravestones. 'With more than a little encouragement from Pericles,' Quintius began, coming directly to it, 'The Athenians are eager to bind their alliance with the Thracians, so they can install naval bases and colonies along the Thracian coast to make it easier to control what enters and leaves the Hellespont and Propontis. King Perdiccas of Macedon is unhappy with the arrangement as you might imagine. Relations between Macedon and Thrace are precarious at best and he fears the growing power of the Athenians in the region and the possibility of a joint Thracian-Athenian invasion of his country in order to seize the resources Pericles desperately needs; not least of them being the forests for the navy, and they're sure to support Perdiccas's brother Philip to usurp his throne, and Philip would become Athens's vassal. Now they have control of the Strymon through their colony at Amphipolis, the Athenians are denuding the forests and floating the timber downriver to the sea, where it's towed back to the Piraeus and the islands to be hewn into warships, and they've been fleecing the river for gold, and excavating the Pangaion Hills. The plague is slowing their efforts down and they've a drastic shortage of rowers and shipwrights. The plague has ravaged practically every quarter of the empire, high and low.'

Lysander nodded his head.

'The Athenians recently sent an engineer by the name of Diodotos to Amphipolis to improve the defences there and at the bridge over the Strymon.'

As they walked on, Quintius put his hand on Lysander's wrist and they stopped walking again. 'There's something else, Lysander,' he said in a quietly ominous tone. 'While at Odessos, I met an old acquaintance, Leocedes of Andros. He was a merchant when I knew him, now he's trierarch of an Athenian trireme...'

'Get to your point,' Lysander pressed.

Quintius took a deep breath. 'He told me that a Spartan embassy on its way to Persia on a secret mission (that is no longer such a secret), to seek an audience with the Great King of Kings, King Artaxerxes to offer the Persians an alliance...'

Lysander knew of this embassy. It consisted of three Corinthian autocrats, Aristeos, Aneristos and Nicolaus. As well as them, Archidamos sent Stratodemos of Sparta, Timagoras of Tegea, and a friend of Tellis's, Pollis of Argos.

'... They were betrayed to the Athenians, Lysander; by the Thracians...'

'*Thracians*!?'

For the first time in the five or so years since he first met Lysander, Quintius saw a look of surprise in Lysander's face. 'They interrupted their journey to appeal to King Sitalkes not to continue with his alliance with Athens. They also wanted Sitalkes's help to get them across the Hellespont into Asia, where they were supposed to meet Pharnaces, the satrap of Phrygia. He was to escort them on into the interior to Persepolis to meet with Artaxerxes...' He broke off and paused for a moment. 'But by a terrible happenstance, there was a party of Athenian ambassadors at Sitalkes's court, one is named Learchos, another is Ameiniades, both friends of the King's son, an ambitious worm named Sadocus, who I've had the misfortune of doing commerce with. The Athenians encouraged him to persuade Sitalkes into handing the emissaries over to Athens as a gesture of good faith and loyalty to Athens. Sadocus was recently made a citizen of Athens, which opens many opportunities for such a worm as him to better his position and grow his power. Now Athens owes him a service as well. It didn't take him long to overcome any reluctance and he agreed to betray the emissaries. Learchos and Ameiniades worked out a ruse, and your emissaries were tricked into thinking that the Thracians were providing safe passage through the country, to take a ship to Asia. Instead, they handed the emissaries over to the Athenians at the port, and it fell to my acquaintance Leocedes to sail them back to Athens.'

'Where are the emissaries now?'

'Dead,' Quintius said bluntly. 'Once they were handed over at Athens, they were denied any right to speak or trial, and were taken quickly and secretly out of the city, where their throats were cut and their bodies were thrown into a plague pit.'

Lysander made no comment, but Quintius could see the rage in his eyes.

Anything else?'

Quintius shook his head. 'No.'

Without uttering another word, Lysander leapt up onto his horse and galloped off, back to Sparta.

'You're welcome,' said Quintius sarcastically as he watched Lysander galloping away.

Lysander slowed to a canter as he passed a herd of youths carrying big boulders of rock along the road to Gytheion under the watch of their birch wielding *gymnasiarch*.

He looked at the youths' faces, twisted with the strain, anguish and pure misery as they clasped their heavy rocks, every muscle in their bodies as taught as iron, aching and strained. It was one of those hideous exercises the boys of the Rearing have to endure; to build stamina, strength and character. Lysander remembered these backbreaking, soul-destroying trials by ordeal well.

The boys gave him a curious and envious look as he cantered passed them.

'Dioskouros Lysander,' one youth said.

'SILENCE!' the gymnasiarch yelled raising his birch threateningly over his head.

When Lysander arrived at Archidamos's palace, he was ushered directly into a small chambre, where he was met by Tellis, who was alone.

The old man looked as though he had the weight of the world on his shoulders, his eyes heavy with some endless worry. Lysander almost asked him, but decided better of it.

Archidamos's health was failing fast, and with every passing day, the spirits of madness were stealing more and more of his mind, and it wasn't easy keeping the King's erratic and strange behaviour a secret either. Palace walls, like Persian kings, have a thousand eyes and ears. The whispers had already begun and the rumours were spreading that the King was ill. Some said dying, and others said that he had gone mad. In truth, it was something in between.

Even Lysander had heard the rumours, and noting the King's absence, he had to wonder if there was some truth to them...?

'What did you learn from our Roman friend, Lysander?' he asked quietly.

'It's not good news, Father Tellis. Stratodemos and the other emissaries are dead. Murdered by the Athenians...'

Tellis was visibly horrified as Lysander explained everything Quintius had told him about the intrigues with Athens and Perdiccas's brother Philip and the emissaries.

After Lysander had finished, Tellis stood silent for a long time, absorbing the information, and then he finally spoke. 'Athenian shadow men recently murdered one of my best men,' he said. 'Doreios. He was stabbed in the streets of Patrai, where Hippodameia has her house.'

'Hippodameia?'

'A very clever and resourceful woman, Lysander, who has lived in the shadows for many years. A whore-mistress like no other, with houses at Delphi, Phokis, Patrai and Thespiae. She has her whores well trained for gathering information. They're very loyal to her and that makes them loyal to Sparta. Officially, she's exiled from Sparta for sacrilege.'

'A deception?'

Tellis simply raised an ambiguous brow.

TWENTY-THREE

Once their meeting was over, Lysander left the palace and took the shortcut through the gardens and the olive grove, which ultimately led down to the heathland near the agora, from there, the hippeis' barracks were a short walk away.

That's where he saw her again, in the olive grove near the ruins of the old storehouse where nets and baskets used to be stored before the great shaking of the earth. Now all that remained were the tumbled walls and long grass and some sapling trees. Telephassa was alone, down on her hands and knees apparently looking for something in the long grass and the tumbled stones of the ruins, left where they had fallen.

Lysander moved in quietly towards her. He stopped and folded his arms and watched her, smiling amusedly to himself as she moved about on all fours, muttering indolently to herself as she brushed the long grass away with her hands.

She did not see or notice him at first, her head was down, searching frantically. 'Oh, where are you? I know you're here somewhere,' she muttered with growing irritation.

Lysander saw the glint of gold in the sunlight in front of two tumbled stone blocks, a sapling as tall as he was, grew between them. It was nowhere near where she was searching. He cleared his throat.

Telephassa looked round startled, the tiered gold disks of her earrings sparkled, her grey eyes wide with surprise to see him there. Of all the people ... why did it have to be *him* who happened by as she was groping around in the grass and blocks of half-buried stone on her hands and knees. It was so completely undignified and she felt such a fool.

'Good day,' he said, not moving, staring down at her, keeping his arms folded, seeming to be amused.

She stared back at him without speaking for a long moment; and then: 'Don't just stand there,' she snapped in a sharp tone. 'I've lost my charm.'

'Oh, I wouldn't say that,' came Lysander's mocking double entendre.

She scowled at him. 'If all you can do is mock me, then go away. Back to your wine sodden friends.'

'Mock you? I wouldn't dream of mocking you, Telephassa. Why, we're practically cousins, are we not?'

'Are you going to help me or not?'

Lysander puckered his lips as if considering the options. 'And what does it look like, your lucky charm?'

She scowled irritably at him. '*Tyche*!' she replied curtly. 'What does it matter? How many charms do you think are lost out here? Are you just going to stand there or are you going to help me find her?'

Lysander smiled and got down on his hands and knees. 'Are you certain you lost her here?'

'Of course I'm certain. What sort of question is that? Would I be humiliating myself if she were in some other place?'

'Hmm,' said Lysander. 'I suppose not. But there's just you and I here. No need to feel humiliated, Telephassa.'

'Blood and dust, you've a smooth tongue in your head, Dioskouros Lysander. They say as much of you.'

Lysander smiled. 'Do they? What more do they say?'

'It wasn't a compliment.'

'Was it not?'

They looked one another in the eyes, and for a long moment, it was impossible for Telephassa to look away. Snared like a rabbit in his predatory green eyes.

'So, what happened?'

His voice was as pleasing as his handsome features and his lean and powerfully strong body. She was falling into his power. '*Happened*?' She blinked and looked confusedly at him, a flush of blood darkened her neck and her cheeks.

'For you to lose Tyche?'

'Oh. The chain broke and she dropped. She must have landed around here somewhere.'

'How?'

'*How*?' she scowled again. 'How what?'

'How did the chain break?'

She took a deep breath. 'What does it matter how it broke?' She was thinking of him and that look they exchanged yesterday when he was playing petteia with Prince Agis; that's how it broke, he tugged too hard on it. He infuriated her and yet she wanted him to notice her. She had always wanted him to notice her, ever since she was a little girl and Lysander an adventurous youth of the Ephebeion. Popular and admired by both men and older girls of the sisterhood. Even the Queen liked him, and her son loved him, so did Grandfather Tellis and Brasidas. Even her own father thought he would one day make a fine officer.

'... It might,' said Lysander, moving on all fours closer to her, pretending to be looking for the charm. 'It might make all the difference in the world. Were you pulling on it? Could Tyche have flown off?'

'Don't be ridiculous,' she exclaimed. 'She fell...' Just as she had, when she met his striking green eyes, that's when she knew. 'If you're just going to mock me,' she said bluntly, 'you might as well go away, Dioskouros Lysander.'

Lysander raised a brow. 'Well, if Tyche dropped to the ground; where is she? The earth didn't swallow her up. But if you were pulling on it and it broke, it might have flown off. But then, why would you be pulling on it?'

She stared at him. 'I don't want to talk about it,' she said adamantly.

'Talk about what?'

'Blood and dust! Do you always ask so many questions?'

'Only if I'm interested in the answers,' he came back quickly.

Her cheeks flushed darker.

Lysander finally moved on all fours to the two blocks of stone and sapling. He reached and picked up the effigy of Tyche.

Her face lit up. '*Tyche*!' She rose to her feet and strode over to Lysander as he stood up. 'How did you get all the way over here?' She took the charm from Lysander a looked at him. 'You can go now.' She kissed Tyche and held her tight in her clenched fist.

'You should make an offering,' he said. 'Or Tyche may not give you her favour for losing her.'

Telephassa looked off behind Lysander. Her grandmother, who had been in private company of the Queen all morning, was coming spritely through the shady grove, elegantly draped in a pale blue peplos that hung with abundant folds down her tall slender frame.

Lysander turned to see who she was looking at.

'Good day, Lysander,' said Argileonis as she approached.

'Good day, Mother Argileonis.'

'You have come from my husband?'

'I have.'

She nodded her head. 'And now your business is concluded?'

'It is.'

Argileonis gave him a cool grin. 'Then do not let us keep you from your duties. Which I'm certain are of too urgent a nature than to wasting your time here.'

Lysander gave her a single nod of his head, and he gave Telephassa a purposeful look. 'Good day, Telephassa.' He turned away and walked off, the two women looking on after him.

'I've seen the way you look at him,' said Argileonis.

Telephassa looked at her hard-hearted grandmother, fully expecting her sharp tongue.

'Do you love him?' came Argileonis's unexpected question.

'I think I always have, Grandmother. I've tried not to.'

'Such things are beyond our control. Does he love you?'

The question shocked the teenager. 'He barely knows I exist.'

'Oh, he knows, Telephassa. He would make a good husband. He will give you strong sons and fertile daughters. But you must accept that he likes men too, and he takes Prince Agesilaos to his bed. But he's of marrying age and so are you. Yes, I think you will be a good match. I will speak to Brasidas and your father.'

TWENTY-FOUR

They moved into position, clasping their swords, teacher and student, learning the deadly arts of killing.

'*Make him dance*!' one of the boys called from the jostling line of excited spectators, as Agesilaos took up the fighting stance.

'*Pan's prick*!' exclaimed Lysander, feigning anger. 'What do you call that? *No, no...*' He shook his head disappointedly. 'That won't do. It won't do at all...'

Agesilaos looked startled at him.

'Left foot forwards. Bend your knees as I taught you! We're going to fight, not dance!'

The boys laughed and the lame prince spun on them, teeth gritted, lips snarling, his nose creased, rage burning in his eyes...

'Pay attention!' Lysander barked. 'Don't concern yourself with those fools. Hear only my voice. My command,' he said sharply.

Agesilaos turned back to him. 'Apologies.'

'Just get into the position! – That's it. Feel the bounce in your body ... good ... keep those knees bent. Now feel that blade in your hand, feel its girth and weight...'

'Grab it like your cock when you stroke!' a boy shouted.

Lysander saw which boy it was. He walked over, calm, silent, he swung his arm back and landed a hard open-handed slap across the youth's face. The boy staggered sideways and stumbled to the ground, a look of horror and shock on his face and a big red handprint covered his cheek.

The other boys looked down at him with big gloating grins on their faces as he sat in the dirt rubbing the side of his face, stinging from the slap.

Lysander turned about without uttering a word and returned to where Agesilaos was waiting for him.

Agesilaos was clad in a battered and scuffed linothorax and wearing an open-faced helmet, armed with a shield and a xiphos sword, and he looked and felt like a real warrior.

'Your weapons must be parts of you. Relax your arm a bit more, you're still too tense. Swing the blade a bit. Imagine you're fighting Athenians ... feel the power of your weapons, for they are Death. Now carve the air, and make your blade dance in your hand. On my command ... *Advance! ... Lunge! ... Defend! ... Behind you!*'

Agesilaos spun, lurched, weaved and gliding through the grass, whipping his unshod feet.

The faces of everyone becoming a blur as he spun passed them, the glinting blade slicing and lunging through the air at invisible foes.

'*Down! Defend! Up! Advance! Defend! Lunge! NEEDLES!*'

Agesilaos dropped to a knee and brought the shield up over his head to cover from the imaginary arrows.

'Up! Advance! Lunge! – ATTACK!'

Agesilaos ran at his servant, Harpalion, who froze in a moment of fear as Agesilaos launched himself towards him and plunged his sword just inches from stabbing him.

Harpalion took a deep breath, but he was unflinching. As with most *mothones* and their Spartan masters, Harpalion and Agesilaos were the same age and close in friendship, but Harpalion, knew his place. He had been Agesilaos's servant since they were six years old, and they were friends long before they fully understood their formal roles with one another...

'Behind you! Advance! ... NEEDLES!' Lysander shouted.

Agesilaos was swift and precise in his responses, reacting instantly to each command, despite his lame foot, his movements were smooth and agile and coordinated, his body flowing reasonably harmoniously.

'That's enough. You're supposed to be a warrior, not a *side-flasher*!'* Lysander assumed the fighting stance. 'Give me your very best, Agesilaos. To first blood...' With that, Lysander launched into fast, violent motion, thrashing hard at the air, leaping and thrusting with all the force of his body behind his blade a he swung at Agesilaos and in less than a heartbeat the point of Lysander's blade was at Agesilaos's throat.

Epiphanes shook his head. This was a bad idea, he thought. The boy wasn't ready for real weapons. Wooden swords and staffs were one thing, but bladed weapons were quite another. He could barely bring himself to watch.

'I wasn't ready,' Agesilaos said.

'Dead men don't speak. You must always be ready. Now. Let's try again, and don't disappoint me.'

They repositioned themselves, face to face, twenty strides apart.

The boys watching kept their silence, none of them wanting to feel Lysander's anger.

The contest began afresh. Lysander and the prince leaped and lurched at one another, blades crashing together and pounding on shields.

They attacked one another with frightening ferocity. Clashed – broke – hunkered down on bent knees, their eyes locked together. Agesilaos's eyes were glowing with determination.

Lysander suddenly charged, coming quickly at Agesilaos and swung his blade–

Agesilaos blocked with his shield as the blade whistled towards him and struck the shield hard with a bone jarring crash that sent Agesilaos staggering back several paces. But he was quick answering Lysander's opening offensive with a fast thrust, making Lysander have to defend and their blades smashed together, grinding as one pushed against the other, but Lysander had the advantage of strength and size on his side, and with a heaving shove, he pushed Agesilaos back – youth and man quickly regained their fighting stances, shields and swords at the ready.

Agesilaos ran at Lysander again in long leaping strides before he sprang into the death-leap, flying at Lysander, his blade honed on his body – Lysander countered with astounding speed and agility, smashing Agesilaos's sword away with his sword, leaping back, he swung his shield and slammed it into Agesilaos's back as he spun passed him; his shield hit him so hard, it sent Agesilaos stumbling forwards and put him on his knees gasping for breath as the impact took the air from his lungs...

'You're not ready for fancy moves like that yet,' said Lysander, watching Agesilaos pulling himself up onto his feet, staggering unsteadily and smarting with the pain.

The boys watched. Impressed by Agesilaos's audacity, even if he failed to achieve the objective.

Lysander and Agesilaos circled one another like scorpions, alert and expectant, their swords held high and inverted over their heads like scorpion stingers, shields at their sides leaving their midriffs exposed. They grew some distance between themselves, regrouping their tactics.

Agesilaos wanted to impress his friends and he wanted to prove himself to Lysander. He felt a surge of energy building up inside him and he took an unexpectedly bold offensive and ran at Lysander again, with long leaping strides as before, building up his speed–

'He's going to try another death leap,' Epiphanes murmured. 'The fool.'

He was wrong. Instead of leaping, Agesilaos swung his blade low at Lysander scything his sword through the air, and it smashed ferociously into Lysander's blade with a chilling crash of iron against iron, striking with such ferocity the blades spat sparks...

Lysander came back on the offensive, hammering Agesilaos's shield with an avalanche of hard fast blows that split the wood as he drove the hapless teenager back.

Agesilaos managed to escape the onslaught, and sped away behind Lysander, but not before Lysander sliced him across his arm, drawing first blood.

Shaken and somewhat battered, Agesilaos looked at his arm where Lysander sliced him and it was bleeding copiously, the wound was deep.

Undeterred, Agesilaos recomposed himself and sallied back at Lysander, more agile, thrusting with an upper-cut to Lysander's chest...

Again, Lysander blocked effortlessly with his sword, driving Agesilaos's blade down, he jerked his left arm round and smashed his shield into Agesilaos.

Agesilaos stumbled back.

'*Enough*!' Lysander sheathed his sword and handed his shield to Epiphanes before he unstrapped his cuirass and removed it.

Lysander sent the youths away, while Epiphanes and Harpalion tended to Agesilaos's arm.

'Will it scar?' Agesilaos asked as Epiphanes wrapped a bandage around the wound.

'Yes.'

Agesilaos smiled proudly. It was an accolade, a trophy he would wear with pride forever, as he wore the scars of the Artemisian whips with pride.

Harpalion helped Agesilaos out of the linothorax, and Epiphanes assisted Lysander.

'Tell me, Agesilaos; in battle, if you lose your spear and have to take to your sword, where are the best places to stab your enemy?' Lysander asked as Epiphanes walked away with his cuirass.

Agesilaos's response was instant. 'The neck, the groin, under the chin, in the mouth and in the side under the arms where the armour's weakest. The groin and neck are the easiest to get to.'

'In a phalanx, what is the first rule?'

'Never to break from the formation,' Agesilaos replied. 'The phalanx marches as one, and must be of one mind with every move precise to a man. He must advance in silence. Because this unsettles the enemy and shows us fearless in the face of our enemies.'

Lysander nodded his head.

Agesilaos gave Lysander a puppy-dog look. 'Can I come hunting with you tonight, Lysander?'

Lysander thought on it. 'If it please you. We'll sleep in the mountains and hunt boar for my mess contribution. If we catch one, you will come to *syssition* as my guest tomorrow.'

Agesilaos beamed with excitement. There was no greater honour or reward an Inspirer can give his Hearer than an invitation to dine.

*

They stalked slowly into the stygian darkness, Agesilaos clasping the hunting spear Lysander had given him.

They could hear the boar, rusting through the undergrowth, snorting into the grass, oblivious to the hunters as they moved in, creeping through the undergrowth.

There it was, the biggest boar Agesilaos had ever seen in his life before, tusks as long as swords.

Lysander gave Agesilaos a nod of his head, giving him honour of the hunt, and his prince proved himself worthy of his place at the dining table.

Once the boar was tied to the pole, Brasidas sent Epiphanes and Harpalion back to Sparta with orders to take it to the kitchens of his mess for tomorrow night's syssition.

Once they were alone, Lysander told Agesilaos to light a fire.

'My father will be proud to see what I've hunted,' said Agesilaos as he foraged for dry wood and kindling.

'Undoubtedly. It was a magnificent beast. You'll fill everyone's bellies with a fine feast that'll not soon be forgotten.'

Agesilaos beamed as he gathered up sticks and brought them to the where Lysander had made a circle of rocks.

Once the fire was set, Lysander opened the knapsack to see what food Epiphanes had left them. Bread, oats, a sealed jug of wine and some smoked meats. 'We'll not go hungry tonight either,' he said.

5th century BC contemporary colloquialism for girls of the Spartan Sisterhood. The female version of the Agógé/Rearing.

TWENTY-FIVE

After the usual rituals and religious ceremony, Archidamos welcomed Emissaries Androcles and Exikias of Leukas to the *syssition*. The King went on to give the usual thanks to the contributors to tonight's feast, namely Autokrates the Younger, who provided the wine from his vineyard and fish from the sea and rivers.

The diners called, '*Autokrates, hoi-hoi-hoi*!'

He then he thanked Lysander, and indeed his own son Agesilaos on behalf of the mess for the splendid contribution of the boar.

'*Lysander, hoi-hoi-hoi*!'

Unusually, Tellis was standing particularly close to the King, watchful and ready should Archidamos have one of his moments of confusion. Fortunately, this evening he seemed to be fully aware, his memory sharp, but a few days ago, he had several lapses of memory. Fortunately, Tellis was there to interject on the King's behalf.

The boar was being spit-roasted over big bronze braziers at the back of the mess behind the royal table. The mouth-watering aromas of cooking hog filled the mess, giving everyone a ravenous appetite. There was stuffed river and sea fish, squid, fresh oysters and lobsters, vegetables, olive oil, bread, honey and fruits – and yes, a cauldron of the infamous black broth, which every Spartan ate before starting on the good food.

The evening was going well, the voices and laughter of the diners disseminated around them with music and a boy reciting Homer, much to Archidamos's pleasure. He so enjoyed recitals of the Iliad and the Odyssey, which left Tellis to deal with the complicated matters of diplomacy with their guests from Leukas. They were in Sparta seeking more assistance against Athenian and Zakynthian attacks on their island and the harassment of their fishing fleet. Some of the fishermen had been murdered at sea by Zakynthians, their boats seized or sunk.

'It has been agreed,' Tellis told Androcles and Exikias, 'that a permanent naval base is to be established at Kyllene,' Tellis told them, and we're sending two hundred Lakedaimonian soldiers to Leukas,' he explained.

'Spartans?' asked Exikias.

'Skiritai and others,' said Tellis. 'Hoplites would be of no use to you...' He paused to take a swallow of wine, and to check on the King who was reclining on the dining couch on his left, having a conversation with Ramphias and seemed quite lucid. Tellis turned back to the two emissaries. 'Once the naval base at Kyllene is established, a squadron of Corinthian and Megarian warships will be in permanent occupation with a thousand soldiers garrisoned there. A Spartan harmost* will be in command of the base.'

Agesilaos was listening to Lysander and Glaukos having a conversation about their time in Messene and Methone. Agesilaos didn't know very much about Lysander's time in Messene, only the highlights of his legendary single combat with the treacherous rebel Amyklos the One Eye, and the Battle of Methone, when Brasidas, outnumbered eight to one, routed an Athenian army who had besieged the city.

Across the dining hall, Pagondas and Xenoklides were being entertained by Brasidas, who was telling them funny stories that had the two generals roaring with laughter.

They were about an hour into the mess, when doors suddenly flew open and an exhausted and unkempt hoplite marched in hurriedly and loped to the top table and stood before the king, bringing the mess to instant silence.

'My Lord,' said the hoplite, 'I am sent urgently by Navarch Knemos...'

'What news?'

'My Lord. We were unable to conclude the assault on Stratos after encountering an overwhelming force of Acarnanians...'

'Overwhelming force?' Archidamos shifted his weight on his dining couch.

Brasidas and Lysander exchanged looks.

'Yes, My Lord. Due to the allies being unable to put their men ashore to reinforce us. The allied fleet, led by Corinth,' the exhausted hoplite continued, 'itself has encountered disaster near Naupaktos against an Athenian squadron of war triremes numbering twenty, under the command of Navarch Phormio of Athens–'

'*Phormio!?*' Ramphias gasped. 'I thought that old bastard had retired.'

The hoplite glanced at the wily old geront, who had once been polemarch of the First Mora.

'How many allied ships were there?' asked Tellis.

'Forty-seven,' he replied. 'Most of them galleys which were carrying the soldiers to join the Navarch, My Lord. They were entirely unequipped for a naval engagement,' he added. 'They were transport ships, not warships, My Lord.'

That was of little comfort to the diners who exchanged looks with one another.

'... The Athenians have captured a number of their ships and taken prisoners, My Lord.'

'How many ships? How many prisoners?' Ramphias demanded.

The messenger looked only at the King. 'I do not know, My Lord. More than ten, along with their crews and other captives. Many soldiers and sailors have also drowned.'

Tellis took a deep breath as if a knife had been driven between his ribs.

'*This is a bloody disaster*!' Ramphias barked angrily. 'A Spartan army stopped by fucking pig herders and farmers!' he ranted. 'What, in the name of Zeus is Knemos doing!?'

The Hoplite glanced quickly at Ramphias. He could feel the anger simmering around him, he could see it in their grim faces.

From here in Sparta, many miles away from the gulf, this had a stink of cowardice about it – incompetence at best. Knemos's retreat in the face of the enemy, regardless that his reinforcements had not turned up due to the events in the gulf, implied weakness amongst the strongest. Simply put, this had the potential to be very embarrassing for Sparta.

'He was never the right man for the job,' Ramphias went on, casting a look to Brasidas. 'They should've sent you.' Ramphias stood up and looked across the smoky mess. '*How in the name of Steno's piglet* have we allowed these cock-shakers to better us…!?*' he billowed angrily. '*By the gods, I tell you, never have I felt such shame as now! And by the gods, I tell you this too; if we do not put all our might into this war, Sparta will fall…!*' Foamy flecks of spit flew from his mouth. '*A Spartan army forced to retreat by barbarians*! *A Corinthian fleet cast asunder in their own waters by an old man*!? *By Medusa's stinking breath, are we fighting a war or putting on a farce*!?'

This sort of thing was new to Agesilaos and he knew that he was in a unique position to be hearing it. News such as this, any news from the war was never relayed to the *ephebeion*. They were the children of ignorance, toiling obliviously at their exercises and training, preparing for when they came to the crimson and the bronze, to take their places in the morai to fulfil their destinies.

Ramphias suddenly pointed angrily at the ground, his eyes wide and burning like brimstone in the lamplight. 'Order him here! Let Knemos stand before us where he can explain this new tactic called retreat, for it is new to me!'

'No,' said Archidamos, maintaining his usual balanced calm, with no sign of the Lethean curse. 'And this is not the place for this debate…' He rose to his feet and all the diners rose with him in a sudden flurry of movement. The king had lost his appetite, but retrieved his mind. He swept out of the mess, followed by Tellis, Agis and several other high-ranking Spartans.

* *A harmost was a sort of provincial military governor of conquered or subject territories or cities. The position is unique to the Spartan system, and he had wide sweeping powers and authority of civil and military matters.*

* *Ancient Hellene slang for female genitalia, akin to modern "pussy".*

TWENTY-SIX

The cressets in the Gerousia were lit, the flames blowing this way and that in the numerous drafts that swept through the ancient building; the light from the flames coruscated in the tired and shocked old faces of the gerontes, seated along the benches, taking in the news of what had occurred in the Corinthian gulf.

Once he finished telling the elders what had happened, Archidamos sat back down in his throne next to Regent Pausanias who was sitting in his father Pleistoanax's throne.

'We're inferior in the sea,' said Tellis, rising to his feet. 'It's as simple as that, My Lords. The size of our fleet is irrelevant, the skills of our sailors, inferior. This is a weakness that must be rectified. Even with all the allied fleets combined,' he continued. 'We cannot match the enemy at sea, not in vessels or competent men to crew them. If the enemy possesses superior tactics over us, then we're always going to be disadvantaged and ravaged in the sea,' he added, his eyes carefully roving the assembly. 'Did Themistocles not prove this at Salamis? Because this is the nature of the enemy we fight, the enemy who produced Themistocles and Pericles. We will only beat the Athenians if we can master them in the sea–'

'This is an old argument, Tellis,' said Archias. 'We're hoplites. We fight on the land, not on the sea. It's for the allies to provide ships and men to row them.'

'If we don't do something, the Athenians will wear us down,' said Ramphias, who had always recognised Sparta's need for a larger navy and professional sailors to crew them, even before the war. He had recognised it as a weakness during the last war they had with Athens. But his arguments had made him unpopular, especially among the richest aristocrats who had coined and uncoined gold sorted away. They feared a financial burden falling on them to pay for it.

'The enemy ravages our shores at will,' said a geront. 'They're beyond the reach of honour,' he continued. 'They unleash marauders and men with dishonourable natures, lured by pillage, booty and the taking of slaves, the raping of women and the killing of the unarmed. We're practically defenceless against them. Without more ships, enemy confidence will grow and their raids will increase. There's also a risk of invasion in Messene, which might easily renew their rebellion against us, especially if the enemy give them the incentive by delivering weapons and money to them. They could ravage the crops and occupy key points along the coast. We leave our backs exposed at our peril. I agree with Tellis and Ramphias.'

The old man had hit a very raw nerve and there was a genuine feeling of unease among the opposing gerontes that they might be outvoted. Helot uprisings were always a worry, and in wars such as this, that worry was increased a hundred-fold.

'It'll take years to build, equip and man such a fleet as would be needed,' said another geront.

'Then better we start now then,' Ramphias responded.

'We have not the funds for such a vast and expensive undertaking,' said Archias, who was one of the richest men in Lakedaimon. 'It costs a talent a month to keep a single trireme at sea, then there's the cost of building them. Procuring the timber, finding the shipwrights to build them,' he went on. 'Put garrisons of dwellers into Messene at the vulnerable points, that'll keep the Athenians at bay.'

'You're talking about thousands of men to do that,' said another geront. 'Men who are needed elsewhere.'

'To defeat Athens, we must first obtain for ourselves parity in the sea,' Tellis insisted. 'It's as simple as that. On land, we're undefeatable, but as you now understand, in the sea, just twenty Athenian ships with good tactics and professional oarsmen and a good commander can defeat a superior force of more than double their strength if it's poorly manned and poorly led. Land tactics simply do not work at sea...'

'The cost is great, but if we fail to do it, the cost will be far greater than any amount of money,' said Ramphias. 'It would be a task easier done, and cheaper too, if we struck our own coin.'

There was an indolent murmur among the old men. Sparta had never minted money. To a Spartan, money was a vile thing to be shunned, despite those rich old Spartiates like Archias, Ramphias, Tellis and many others having personal fortunes of money. Such were the double standards at Sparta.

'Law forbids,' said a geront. 'Did Apollo not command so to Lykurgos. "*Love of money and nothing else will ruin Sparta.*" Let Sparta not be polluted buy a whore's reward, or you invoke the anger of the gods and invite calamity to Lakedaimon.'

'It's a step too far, Ramphias,' said another.

'We will never agree to it,' added a third, and it soon became clear that none but a few of them supported the notion of minting money, not even to lessen the cost of the war. Spits of iron had served well enough for hundreds of years.

'Is this navy truly a cost we cannot afford?' asked Regent Pausanias, who was finding his voice at these meetings more often. He was still young, but not too young not to understand and he was far from naïve. He was eager to go to the front too, but so far, the ephors had managed to stop him. Archidamos was the more experienced in both kingship and warcraft. Pausanias was too impetuous, too inexperienced and too young for the allies to loyally follow. Corinth and Thebes especially, required special handling and a confident commander and Archidamos was skilled in both areas, and above all, he never made rash decisions in the heat of a moment, but regarded them carefully first. But procrastination can be a costly habit in missed opportunities and tactical advantages.

'It is, My Lord,' said the geront who quoted from the Rhetra.

'Then you would sooner us defeated than meet these costs?' said Pausanias.

It was not a question, but a statement, and to make his point, he added. 'You would sooner defile our ancestors than bring glory, no matter what the cost? Have we already so in love with our private money, that we would sacrifice our children to Nemesis? We must send emissaries to the Persians and elicit from them an alliance.'

'My Lord. We've already tried that and our emissaries were murdered by the Athenians.'

Pausanias leered at the geront, who was taken aback by Pausanias's sudden display. Tellis was impressed, so apparently was Archidamos.

'Then we must try again. Tellis and Ramphias are right in what they say. It's simple tactics. We must match the enemy in every quarter, only then can we destroy him.'

'This doesn't solve the problem that we have now, My Lord,' said Geront Autokrates, formerly a very rare holder of the rank of *Strategos*, where the kings held the ranks of supreme commanders, or *strategoi*. 'We must vigorously oppose the Delians or they'll make slaves of us all. We can't suffer the Athenians to remain in the Gulfs of Kalydon and Corinth, hampering the ships of our allies and our war effort. If we can't afford to build ships, then we should seek an alliance with those who can, as Regent Pausanias has pointed out.'

It was still fresh in everybody's minds what had happened to the emissaries.

'I suggest we send the strongest encouragement to Navarch Knemos,' said another geront.

Archidamos nodded his head. 'We will send three officers to jointly enquire as to what went wrong, and to advise on our next move,' said Archidamos. 'Brasidas will be one of them, Timokrates and Lycophron will be the others. We will send with them four hippeis.'

TWENTY-SEVEN

Ionian Sea

Lysander, Gylippos, Aschines and Skiron made up the four Hippeis ordered to accompany the commission to Kyllene. Aschines, being twenty-nine years old, was in his last year as a hippeus, Skiron was twenty-six, the same age as Lysander and Gylippos.

Even though Aschines was the eldest and so the longest served of the Hippeis, it was Lysander who was chosen as their superior. Lysander had experience at command during his time at Methone, when he organised the Dweller militia into a fighting force and commanded the defence of that city when it was besieged, at least that was the reason that was given, but nobody was in any doubt that his close friendship with Brasidas and the king's cupbearer Geront Tellis were really behind it, that and the fact that Lysander was also Inspirer lover, to the Prince Agesilaos. That was how Aschines saw it at any rate, and the jealousy gnawed at him like a dog on a bone, and it filled him with seething hatred. He had never liked Lysander, mostly for the same reason he didn't care for Lysander's friend Gylippos. They were mothakes, bastards, come them one-part Spartiate and one part Helot. Born to inferior mothers. But it went even deeper with Lysander, who had once humiliated him when they were boys at the Rearing, when Lysander beat him up in front of the Paidonomos and Brasidas.

Aschines and Skiron were amidships. Aschines was moaning bitterly about his nemesis Lysander, who, so he said, strutted about the ship as though he were a warlord. Not only that, to his incredulity, the trierarch allowed Lysander to take command of the ship for an entire day. Whoever heard of such a thing? Just who did he think he was?

'...one day, that mothax piglet is going to get what's long overdue,' he said through his gritted teeth. 'He cheated his way here.'

Skiron felt the hatred and threat in Aschines's voice and it worried him.

The sail flapped above them in the fitful wind, the oars swished through the water below them.

'I don't know about that,' said Skiron. 'It was the ephors who decided the matter.'

'And who do you think influences the ephors, eh?' Aschines said.

He was bubbling on the inside, but he was in no position to do anything about it. 'Filthy half mothax piglet,' he hissed hatefully.

Skiron was of no opinion one way or the other. Orders were orders and there was an end to it as far as he was concerned. He was perfectly comfortable taking Lysander's orders, not that he really gave them orders. If he did, they were relayed down from the three commissioners. There was no point griping about it. But Aschines was consumed by resentment and envy for Lysander.

Only Lysander got to be present at the meetings between the commissioners and officers, and every other aspect of their enterprise, and he was as often in Brasidas's company as he was theirs.

Of course, to Skiron, that was perfectly natural, Brasidas had been his Inspirer, and they had a very close friendship. Lysander was completely loyal to Brasidas, and they were similar in many ways. Like Brasidas, Lysander could be gregarious and talkative, and he had strong opinions on tactics that differed from the traditional. His friend Gylippos too. They stood out and many people admired them, and many others did not.

What stung Aschines most of all, was being left out of the conversations and the decision making, the commissioners barely acknowledged him.

Lysander and Gylippos were on the starboard side of the ship, near the stern. Gylippos was sitting on the deck, Lysander was squatted down beside him, feeling the motion of the ship as they moved through the calm water.

'What d'you think of Skiron?' asked Gylippos.

Lysander gave him a vague shake of his head. 'I don't really know him well enough to have an opinion. But he seems to be a good man.'

'He told me that that cow-shit mouth Aschines has been insulting you to your back.'

Lysander nodded his head nonchalantly. 'Yes, I know. Aschines and I have history. He hates me and wants revenge for what I did to him?'

Gylippos frowned confusedly. 'What you did? What did you do?'

'I beat the shit out of him in front of the Cyclops and Brasidas when I was thirteen. Aschines was sixteen at the time, and the little boys saw it as well as the Cyclops and Brasidas. He's hated me from that day to this. It was the day I was sent out on my *phauaxir*, my fox-time. I broke his nose. He was then whipped by the gymnasiarch for letting a younger boy better him in a fight. He's never forgiven me for it.'

'That's a long time to hold onto a grudge, Lysander. And besides, everyone gets their faces punched in at the Rearing.'

'Try telling Aschines that. And now I'm in command over him, that must burn in his guts. It would mine.'

Gylippos chuckled. 'You just like being in charge, Lysander. Even when we were boys.' He looked at his friend. 'So, what're you going to do about Aschines? Skiron told me that he told him that you're a shit-sucking leach stuck to Tellis's arsehole. You can't let an insult like that pass, Lysander. You just can't.'

'What would you have me do about it? We're on a warship on active duty. Aschines can wait. I'll deal with him when I have the time.'

'Well, he would be well advised to keep his cow-shit mouth shut in my hearing. I'll not listen to my best friend being insulted.'

Lysander smiled. 'We're more than friends, Gylippos. We're brothers, you and I.'

Gylippos nodded his head, reminiscing on their long and close friendship. 'I still remember the first day we met,' he said with a growing feeling of nostalgia. 'Our first day at the Rearing. Do you remember?'

'Like it was yesterday,' said Lysander. 'We beat the shit out of each other.'

Gylippos smiled. 'We were evenly matched and the best of the herd.'

'Aye. From that day on.'

'Well, us bastard half-breeds have to stick together.'

Lysander smiled. 'Brothers unto death.'

'Brothers unto death,' Gylippos repeated. It was the oath they took when they were seven-year-olds, and it stood as strong now as it did then. 'You just make certain cow-shit mouth gets what's coming to him.'

Brasidas approached along the deck towards them and they both stood up.

'Go away, Gylippos,' Brasidas said, looking at Gylippos.

Gylippos walked away.

'Is something wrong, Brasidas?' Lysander asked, sensing a seriousness in his mood.

'My niece,' said Brasidas, feeling uncomfortable. He put his foot up on the table and leaned forwards.

'Telephassa?'

'Unless I have another niece, I know nothing about,' Brasidas replied flippantly. 'My mother is of a mind that you should marry her.'

Lysander gawped at him. '*Marry*!?' The idea horrified him. 'I like Telephassa, she amuses me and she's headstrong like your mother. But marry, Brasidas? I cannot imagine I would ever take a wife.'

'Would you sooner face the shunning? You will marry, Lysander. You will marry because it's what's expected of all Spartans. I too am to marry soon. Do your duty, give Sparta a son. Nothing more is required of you. Telephassa is fond of you. Perhaps she even loves you. But these things are irrelevant. She will make a good wife and bear strong children.'

It sounded more like Brasidas was ordering him to marry his niece. But there was merit in what he said. He did like her. 'What does your father say?'

'It would please him to bring you closer into the family. My father has always loved you as a son, Lysander. Marry Telephassa and a son you will truly be. But it's up to you. I only agreed to speak to you because my mother persisted and you know how she can be.'

Lysander nodded his head.

'Think about it at least.'

'I will. I'll be thinking about little else, Brasidas. This has taken me by surprise.'

*

A wind was getting up and the sea was getting choppy. Sea spray blown up by the wing speckled their faces as they looked eastward, where, in the distance, the sky was dark.

It was getting bumpy, the swells seemed to be getting bigger and the ships pitched and rocked as they splashed through them, Brasidas stepped to the safety rail, the wind was growing in strength, blowing through his long hair and platted braids. 'What're you think, Kossos? Should we find shelter?' he said to the trierarch.

Trierarch Kossos considered thoughtfully, looking at the darkening sky, the clouds looking angrier as they approached. The wind was getting stronger too. 'Yes. We can put in along the Kyparissian Gulf, but it's more than an hour from here, even at top speed under sail and oar, and that's going to hit us soon,' he said, looking ominously at the approaching storm.

They looked to the landward, where the rocky coast of Elis stretched for many barren miles, and there were deadly rocks just under the water, upon which many a ship had fallen fowl. The Kyparissian Gulf was the nearest safe water with a long sandy beach on which to ground the ships to protect them from being buffeted in the coming storm.

'Get us there as soon as you can,' Brasidas ordered.

Kossos nodded his head and turned about, beckoning to the boatswain...

TWENTY-EIGHT

It was mid-afternoon when the storm struck, like the vengeful Erinyes, commanding powerful winds that whipped and howled through the mast and rigging. Above, the dark fermenting storm clouds blotted out the sun and cast the world into a colourless grey twilight. The angry waters smashed against them and the ship pitched and shuddered as white spuming crests blasted over the starboard outrigger soaking the oarsmen.

Lysander and the others clung to whatever they could as the Stheno yawed and rose from the prow, lifting the bronze ramming horn clear out of the water and the apotropaic eyes leered defiantly into the storm and flared momentarily in the lightning and for a moment, they seemed alive.

The men at the rudders battled against the storm, wary of the rocky coast that might chew them up as the storm drove them towards the deadly shallows.

The three escorting triremes were having trouble maintaining their course and stability as they tossed and pitched in the rough water and the strong leeward winds cutting across them.

'GET THAT FUCKING SAIL UP!' the boatswain hollered.

'*Gods below!*' Timokrates gasped, clinging to a mast rope with both hands to steady himself as the deck suddenly pitched up from the prow again, like a rearing horse and rocked sideways to port at the same time.

The rowers struggled with all their might to keep them trim, keep them moving – keep them afloat.

Lysander and Gylippos were both clinging onto the securing ropes of the small forward mast, battered by the sea and wind, soaked through to the skin and holding on for their lives.

They were a mile from the coast and they started to turn landward, heading for shelter along the Kyparissian Gulf, where they could beach.

Lysander thought they weren't going to make it as the storm became a monster, spitting its wrath at them with a deafening roar of the sea, the rain and thunderclaps and flashes of lightning arcing through the dark heavenly firmament. The rowers on the outriggers ran out their oars in a futile effort to stabilise the ship as it was unrelentingly hit by huge waves. The lower deck had drawn in their oars and closed the hatches against the buffeting waves.

The Stheno rose and bucked in the mountainous swells and squalls, the air was filled with flying seawater and hard rain battering them relentlessly.

A mountainous wave smashed into the port beam, sending an avalanche of water and spume crashing over the outrigger and across the deck, where it became a waterfall into the lower rowing decks. The Stheno pitched further, the ship rolled and heaved as the sea reared up, swallowing men who fell into the fury.

The trierarch and deck officers yelled orders at the tops of their voices and still could not be heard as the wind stole their words.

Lysander stared into the salivating jaws of death snapping around them with terror fixed in his eyes. This was it; they were all going to die!

The prow rose again and crashed back down into the sea with a horrendous BOOM! Waves flew out either side of the keel like liquid wings glowing as another flash of lightning arced across the sky with white-hot fingers that plunged into the rising squalls.

The four Spartan warships made it to a sandy beach under the shadow of the forest swathed Mount Lapithas. The relief in the men was infectious, what a joy it was to feel the soft wet sand beneath their feet instead of the pitching decks of their ships. It was a miracle none of the ships had been lost and they all thanked their gods for it.

The boatswains wasted no time, ordering the men to pull the ships fully onto the beach.

The strong oarsmen and deck crews pulled and heaved the ships onto the beach. Once ashore, the boatswains issued orders to working parties to bale the hulls out; check for leaks; repair the damage.

Brasidas walked up the beach with the trierarchs and the four Dioskouri. 'Set camp for the night,' he said as the rain pelted them, the hard drops spattering off their armour and shields. They had to raise their voices to be heard over the noise of the downpour.

Twelve crew had been lost across the four ships and there was some damage to two of the escort ships, one had a cracked mast rendering it useless for a sail, another had sprung a leak that needed fixing and for that, they needed a shipwright.

'We can't be far from Samikon,' said Brasidas who knew the area. 'Send some men to bring supplies and whatever's needed to make repairs. Carpenters, shipwrights, and some decent food. We cannot dally here more than a day or so...' He looked along the line of five tents. '*Lysander*!' he yelled.

Lysander came out from a tent and ran over.

'You and your companions go with the shore party to Samikon in full livery, to make certain the locals know who they're dealing with. Eleans can be shy when it comes to helping their allies. They're miserly by habit, but timid by nature.'

'As you command...' He looked to their tent, where Skiron was starting a fire. 'Skiron, Aschines, Gylippos, be in your warlike nature immediately!' he barked officiously as he marched over to them.

'What's happening?' asked Skiron.

'We're going for a walk.'

'Where to?' Aschines asked as he came out from the tent.

'What does it matter? Just get your armour on.'

The four hippeis led the dozen sailors making up the shore party along a well-trodden track along the lower foothills, climbing above the beach.

'Why didn't he send the hoplites, eh?' Gylippos wondered aloud.

'He wants to make an impression,' said Aschines. 'And what better impression than Dioskouri? Is that not so, Lysander?'

Lysander felt a tightness in his throat and it was like speaking through fire, when he said, 'It is so.'

'Put the fear of Hades in them, I'd say,' said Gylippos.

'Try not to smile, we don't want to scare them too much,' came Lysander's quick retort.

The town was situated up on a rocky spur of Mount Lapithas overlooking the sea and a little harbour of fishing boats and some small houses. They had to ascend a steep path up to the main town, passing between some fruit orchards, where goats roamed, grazing on the rich grass and gleanings of fallen fruit.

Beyond was a sacred olive grove and the impressive temple of Samian Poseidon, perched high, where the god could overlook the sea, and the town.

Brasidas wasn't wrong; when the shore party escorted by the four Spartan hippeis showed up with a dozen sailors, they were a startling sight to the locals, many of them hurrying their children into their houses, others watched the Spartan warriors and sailors with nervous mistrust. Some of the menfolk and boys followed them to the agora, where the town elders had already gathered together in the square, no doubt wondering why were there Spartans in their town? Or perhaps the already knew their ships were caught in the storm?

'Greetings, Sparta,' said one of the grey-haired old men.

Lysander removed his helmet. 'Greetings, Samikon. Our ships were caught in the storm and we've had to put ashore and suffered damage to a couple of our vessels. We need food supplies, carpenters and a shipwright?'

The elders exchanged looks.

The second elder spoke in a low hoarse voice. 'We have a small fishing fleet, Spartan friends, but no shipwright as such. But we have a couple of men who may be able to assist in your repairs.'

'We have carpenters too,' said the third.

'And food we will gladly share with our friends and ally from Sparta,' said the first elder who spoke.

They were as good as their word, and they sent carpenters and three men who made fishing boats. Food would follow.

As well as the tradesmen, the boys of the town, possessed by their boyish curiosity and fascination with the legendary Spartans followed them back to the beached ships, where they hoped to see a trireme up close.

They hurried alongside the four dread Dioskouri, so mighty and powerful, legendary and enigmatic. Feared and revered by all Peloponnesians. Few people beyond the battlefield had ever seen Spartans liveried in their armour before, and this day would be a day to be remembered for the rest of their lives.

The boys kept their distance from them, wary of the murderous reputation the Spartans have, that when they march, they stop for nothing that stands in their way. That they possess dark powers given them by the gods of war, who love the Spartans beyond all mortal men.

TWENTY-NINE

Kyllene

The Spartan commissioners finally arrived at Kyllene, where Knemos's fleet was at anchor in the harbour along with the Corinthians and Megarians and other allied ships. Knemos's hoplites and sailors had more than doubled the town's population and temporary wooden palisades had been erected on the lower flank of the hill to garrison the soldiers and crewmen.

Up in the town, Knemos was in his headquarters with his senior officers and the Corinthian commanders; Machaon, Isokrates and Agatharchidas. They were discussing the reports brought back by Knemos's scouts and local spies who were keeping an eye on Phormio's squadron and the Akarnanians and Messenians who were encamped not far from Naupaktos, when Knemos's adjutant entered.

Knemos looked at him. 'What is it?'

'The Stheno has returned, Navarch...' He looked at the officers and seemed to hesitate. 'The spotter said there are at least two senior officers and four Dioskouri aboard. One of the officers was recognised as Brasidas.'

'*Brasidas*?' Knemos shifted his weight; he looked at the commanders. 'We will resume this later, gentlemen,' he said bringing the meeting to an end. He looked across the table at Melesippos, who was one of Brasidas's closest friends. 'Come to nail my balls to a tree, do you think?' he asked with a cool smile.

'That's not Brasidas's way, Navarch,' Messelinos replied.

Knemos knew the high command and Gerousia would not be pleased to have received his dispatch and he knew there would be some sort of repercussion from them retreating at Stratos and the Corinthian debacle in the gulf, which was entirely beyond his control, but that wouldn't be worth a dish of shit to those old snakes in the Gerousia. The question was, what that response might be? Relieve him of command? Execute him? that was the worse scenario after shaming of course. It was rare for Spartans to execute officers and hoplites. Unlike the Athenians, who were harsh with their generals who failed to deliver. 'Well, it'd be rude not to go a greet them.'

'Very rude, Navarch.'

Knemos rose to his feet...

Brasidas and Lysander looked simply magnificent stood at the prow of the Stheno in full armour, their crimson cloaks billowing in the wind, their crested helmets tilted back on their heads, the wind blowing in their stoic faces, both of them watchful as the Stheno manoeuvred into the harbour between the sea defences under slow oars, steering between Knemos's warships and gallies towards the quayside.

'BACK-STROKE!' the boatswain yelled, and the oars swept backwards to slow the ship with a SWOOSH of water.

The three escort ships followed in line behind them, their oars drawing steadily, their bronze tusks proud and deadly beneath the clear calm blue water.

Down in the port, the Stheno had docked, the gangplank was run out and Brasidas, Timokrates and Lycophron disembarked, closely followed by the four hippeis, their helmets tilted back on their heads, behind, followed by their servants.

Knemos glanced at the four Dioskouri behind them. 'Brasidas, Lycophron ... Timokrates. Welcome to our little shithole. And what brings you, Gentlemen?' As if he needed to ask.

'Orders brings us,' Timokrates responded in his usual, clipped and officious way.

Knemos narrowed on him. 'Indeed. And what orders are they?'

Brasidas smiled. 'We've had a terrible journey. So, first some decent wine and food, Knemos. There's nothing to worry about. You have powerful friends in Sparta.'

Knemos felt instantly more relaxed. 'My headquarters are this way, gentlemen,' he said and they started towards the town.

'Greetings, Lysander,' said Clearchus as they started walking up to the town.

'Greetings, Clearchus.'

'Greetings, Gylippos, you too Aschines and greeting to you as well, Skiron.'

'How goes it, Clearchus?' asked Aschines.

'It goes well enough...' He looked at Lysander. 'What news of Plataea?'

'Plataea's under siege,' Lysander replied. 'But they can't hold out much longer.'

Clearchus held Lysander back and they fell behind the others. 'Is my father ashamed of our show against Stratos, Lysander?'

Lysander shook his head. 'They've accepted that Knemos had no choice in his decision. A massacre would have been far worse for Sparta.'

'So why the commissioners?'

'Here to advise so far as I'm aware. They sent Aschines, Skiron, Gylippos and I to protect them and the navarch.'

Clearchus nodded his head. 'Knemos had no choice, Lysander. We were getting slaughtered in those hills. The Akarnanians were like harpies, coming at us from every quarter. They swept in in fast waves and swept out again. It was near impossible to tame the bastards. It was a wonder we got out of there alive. If the reinforcements had arrived, we'd have had them.'

It was hard to believe now, that Clearchus had been Lysander's nemesis at the Rearing, where they had been the bitterest of enemies, but from their many fights and struggles to outdo one another, there had grown a deep respect between them, and now, as men, that respect had blossomed into friendship. They were both tacticians, and the best of their herds and age groups at the Rearing. Now they were the best of friends.

Gylippos looked over his shoulder at them, lagging thirty paces behind, deep in conversation.

In the villa, when Knemos was alone with Brasidas, Timokrates and Lycophron, Knemos looked carefully at them and came directly to the point. 'Why are you here?' He gestured to a servant to bring wine. 'Is it because of what happened at Stratos? Are you here to accuse me of trembling or–'

'Whatever will be said of Knemos, being a trembler will not be among them,' Brasidas said reassuringly.

'Stratos and what happened in the Gulf between the Corinthians and Phormio,' said Timokrates as he gravitated to a chair and sat down. 'Was a great disappointment, it cannot be denied.'

'We were sent to hear your report on what happened, and to act thereafter as advisers to your command, Navarch,' said Lycophron.

Brasidas moved to the table and looked at the map. 'But you were impetuous, Knemos,' he said as he picked up a model trireme and looked at the craftsmanship of the carver who modelled it. 'You should have waited for the Corinthians before you mounted the attack. You took too much for granted in assuming they would arrive. But, likely, had you waited, you would have missed the opportunity, so you took it, and nobody can condemn you for that. There's no mark on your character that cannot be easily erased, Knemos...' He looked round at Knemos, 'I won't lie. Some of the old bastards in the Gerousia are so mad, they're farting lightning bolts out of their arseholes. And we have to be careful with the old bastards. Getting them too excited at their ages is dangerous...'

Timokrates smiled amusedly.

'But Ramphias, my father, Autokrates ... even Archias and the regent spoke in your favour. And there's an end to it. Of course, if you feel it should be otherwise, do say...'

'Is everything mirth to you, Brasidas?' said the joyless Lycophron.

'Mirth? I wouldn't dream of comedy at such a time, Lycophron.' His stare lingered judgingly on the smiling hero of Methone, who he felt was not taking the situation seriously.

Brasidas met his stare. 'Far from it.' He held the little ship in his hand and looked at the detail.

'Are you here to take me back?' Knemos asked.

'Of course not,' said Brasidas. 'We're here to help you.'

'To advise you,' said Lycophron.

Knemos looked squarely at him. 'Advise me? As a father advises his wayward son? Do you think me incompetent?' He was getting angry, the humiliation of it was hard to stomach, especially from Lycophron, a man for whom, it was well known, Knemos held in utter contempt. 'I will take no advice from you, Lycophron...' He looked at Timokrates. 'Who is senior man among you?'

'I am,' said Brasidas. 'Our orders are to listen to your explanation as to what exactly has happened? To make an assessment of your forces and fighting condition, and to assist you in your attack against this stubborn Athenian and seize Naupaktos before mounting an attack on the Akarnanians and Stratos. You're in command, as you must be as navarch. And we're here, not so much as to advise you, as we are to assist you,' he added diplomatically. Brasidas did have secret orders to relieve Knemos of his command, if he thought it necessary, but he knew Knemos and he knew him to be a competent commander and soldier. He had no intentions of removing him from command and shaming him.

Lycophron took a deep breath and he was about to say something, but Brasidas cut in over him:

'Once you've explained, and I'm certain your reasons are good and honourable, and militarily sound, we'll make an inspection of your ships and hoplites, then we'll make for the gulf, ready to attack Naupaktos and drive the enemy from Peloponnesian waters...' He took a cup of wine from the servant and placed the model ship back onto the map, poignantly onto its side. 'To the gravestones,' he said, raising his cup and taking a swallow.

'The gravestones!' they responded with a single voice.

THIRTY
Strait of Rhium

The Athenians at Naupaktos and their local Acarnanian barbarian allies had to be dealt with before their reinforcements arrived.

The morale of the Peloponnesian fleet was low, following their recent defeat and the capture of twelve ships along with their crews and a substantial number of allied hoplites.

Brasidas told Knemos to order as many of the men ashore as possible, he intended to address them, and they gathered on the beach in a half-moon, thronged together, shifting and having murmured conversations, curious as to why Brasidas had ordered the assembly, nervous as to what orders they might receive. They had tasted the bitterness of defeat against the stubborn Athenian and his landward Acarnanian allies and Messenian allies, not once, but twice. And Knemos's defeat at Stratos brought shame on Sparta, and that could not go unchecked. But in the ebbing and flowing tides of war, this would not be the last time Sparta would sup from Defeat's bitter fruit.

Knemos, Brasidas, Timokrates and Lycophron stood before the crews and soldiers.

'My Peloponnesian Brothers, hear me!' called Brasidas, holding out his arms to them. 'I understand your worries. That's why we're here after all, to bring you reassurance. So, hear me, boys! The last battle may have unsettled many of you as you contemplate the battle that's now before us. But I tell you this, and from my heart I say it. There's no just ground for your fear. In that battle you were simply unprepared. You didn't come here to fight a naval engagement. You came here to bring troops and supplies to enhance Knemos's forces against the troublesome tribes of our countryman who have put in with the Delians, not to fight on the sea. So, little wonder bad luck and catastrophe struck you when it did. But you were not lacking in courage that day...' he shook his head. 'By the gods that is not so, boys, I know this because I know your character, and if a Spartan points to a man and says that man has courage, then you know he is brave and true to his duty with an unbending will. You are courage incarnate. Added to this misfortune, it was your first naval engagement ... by the gods, do you see a new-born leap from the crib and sally forth like Ares into the storm of war? That'll be the day my prick falls off...' The men laughed amusedly. 'So then, our inexperience in the sea has set us back because we leapt from the crib, and went unprepared and unknowing into the firmament. Our defeat had nothing to do with cowardice...'

As Brasidas continued, Knemos surveyed the faces of the men. Brasidas's encouraging monologue seemed to be having an effect.

Timokrates leaned to Knemos's ear. 'When Brasidas speaks, all around him listen.'

'They love him,' said Knemos. 'That's why.'

Lycophron grunted indolently. 'He pampers them. The whip will sing a more encouraging song I'm sure...'

Knemos cast him a sideways look.

'... Fortune, in her whims sometimes brings disaster, but what is disaster but a setback for a brave man, who is unchanging in the fire of his warlike heart,' Brasidas continued. 'For him there's no room for doubts or wavering from his own inexperience, when set against that unyielding courage that I know burns in your hearts as it does in mine. Where we are inferior in experience, we're superior in courage. You fear the shadow of the enemy opposite us, for he is experienced in the sea sure enough, and I credit him for it, one warrior to another. But he does not have the same temperament as the Peloponnesian, who is tough and brave beyond all others in Hellas and the world...'

Later that night, the commanders; Machaon of Corinth and his colleagues Isokrates and Agatharchidas, met with the Spartan commanders aboard the Stheno to discuss the plan to draw Phormio into the Narrows and destroy him there.

'... Our spies tell us the garrison's unmanned, leaving Naupaktos unprotected. So, when we sail, they'll have no choice but to follow or pace us,' Knemos went on, placing the plan he and the commissioners had devised. 'We'll sail four ships abreast into the Gulf. Our right wing will lead with twenty of our fastest ships manned by our best rowers to break away from the formation and make towards Naupaktos under fast oars. This will force Phormio to speed in after them, and cut across our main wing. This is the moment we turn our ships and strike the enemy at our best speed...'

'As soon as they arrive,' said Brasidas, 'the twenty ships will turn about and block their way, and land their hoplites in the boatyards to secure the place from the Akarnanians and Messenian exiles.'

Lysander, who was standing near the Corinthians turned and looked across the Strait of Rhium to Phormio's twenty ships opposite, less than a mile away, he saw the lights from their lamps and ashore, he saw campfires from the Messenian camp...

Phormio's twenty ships were in position and at the ready half a mile away face to face with the Peloponnesian fleet of seventy-seven ships in a long line along the coast in the red dawn like a bask of crocodiles drifting in blood. The masts of both fleets had been removed with all other excess weight and put ashore to allow greater speed and manoeuvrability in the battle to come.

The timbers creaked and cracked in the silence with the pitching of the ships.

Phormio stood at the prow of his flagship, the Athena, with his officers, looking across the straits at the formation of enemy ships on the horizon. It was an impressive sight to behold, unsettling too, seventy-seven ships pitched against his twenty, and there was no sign of the reinforcements he had sent for. But unbeknown to him, the Athenian reinforcements had diverted to Crete to attack Kydonia after a neighbouring city and enemy Gortyna had denounced Kydonia as supporting Sparta in the war.

'Two days,' said Hippolytos. 'Two days and they just sit there. What are they waiting for? Are they so cowardly they will not fight us?'

'Have a care, these are Spartans,' said Phormio, 'for whom war is a brother. Don't mistake them for cowards, gentlemen...' He looked probingly at his officers. 'These men of bronze court battle with great care. Mark them well, they do not dally for fear of us, they dally to unsettle us.'

'Well it's working, Navarch, because the men are uneasy and afraid,' said Hippolytos.

Phormio nodded his head. Fear is like fire, once ignited it spreads quickly. 'Then I'll address the crews to reassure them. And the longer the Spartans take to make their move, the closer our reinforcements get.'

'*If they sent any*,' said another officer lowly.

'They know our situation,' said Phormio. 'The reinforcements will come.'

They looked back at the Peloponnesian fleet, where, aboard the Euryale, Phormio spotted several Spartan officers...

THIRTY-ONE

At dawn, on the seventh day, Knemos gave the signal and the Peloponnesian fleet finally put out, forming a long column four ships abreast, moving eastward towards the Gulf of Corinth – towards Naupaktos...

The Athenians were caught by surprise when the Spartan fleet started to sail, after sitting idle at anchor for so long.

'What are they up to?' Hippolytos adjusted his cloak against the chilly winter wind sweeping down the gulf from the open sea.

'They're going home,' said one of the others hopefully.

The Peloponnesian ships were beginning to move into the Gulf. Phormio ordered Hippolytos to signal the other ships to prepare to sail. 'We'll follow them in,' he said. 'Stay close to the coast, in a single line.'

Phormio's twenty ships sailed in single file along the northern shore under a steady oar into the dreaded narrows of the Gulf of Patras, which was the last place he wanted to be, knowing how vulnerable they were there. Exile Messenian hoplites were marching along the north shore, pacing the Peloponnesians who were moving steadily along the southern shore, rowing in their lines.

Phormio was cautious and unsure of what the enemy were up to. Were they really heading back to Corinth? Or was it a ruse to lure them into a trap?

The answer came, when, suddenly, the twenty leading Peloponnesian ships formed a single file, and steered northward away from the rest of the fleet, taking to fast oars, they swept diagonally across the gulf, making ten knots, their oars rising and thrusting forwards before dipping into the water a drawing back, completely unified, the sweat ran from their half-naked bodies as they repeated the process over and over like a machine with interconnected parts, raising – thrusting – dipping – pulling within three fast breaths and the twenty triremes speeded on determinedly like water-borne missiles gunning towards Naupaktos.

*

It was working, the Athenians increased their speed in pursuit of the twenty Peloponnesian ships in a race to reach Naupaktos.

Lysander, Gylippos, Skiron and Aschines, wearing their armour, stood amidships aboard the Stheno, poised and ready for whatever was coming.

The fire of Ares was burning in Lysander's blood, his heart pounded in his chest, the chilly morning wind blowing in his face as he watched the Athenian ships giving chase.

The trièraulès flutes sang loud and fast and the oars pulled back through the water SWISH – SWISH – SWISH to their rhythm.

Knemos, Brasidas and Clearchus were standing at the prow, watching the Athenians hugging close to coast, speeding towards Naupaktos, trying to get ahead of the twenty Peloponnesian ships.

'Now, Knemos,' said Brasidas. 'They're in the narrows. Give the order now...'

Knemos looked at him. 'Not yet. Let them get well inside. I know what I'm doing, Brasidas.'

Right now, Brasidas wasn't so sure. The enemy were well inside the narrows, much further and there would be a chance that some of Phormio's ships might slip through the snare.

'Do it now, Knemos,' Brasidas persisted insistently.

'Wait!' Knemos snapped back.

Brasidas shook his head and for the first time, he considered his secret orders to relieve Knemos of his command, but there was a deep reluctance in him. He knew if he invoked the orders, it would be the end of Knemos, he would be condemned as a trembler, and coloured patches would be sewn into his cloak to mark him out as a coward, and forever more, he would be spat upon, insulted, ridiculed and cast aside by all. It was a fate worse than death. Knemos was no coward, but he was no Themistocles either.

Clearchus and Lysander exchanged looks, Brasidas was far from happy and he tapped his foot anxiously on the deck, his hand clasping his spear so tight, his knuckled turned white.

Finally, Knemos turned to his second in command, Clearchus. 'Give the order.'

Clearchus hurried aft to relay the order to the boatswain and rowers, and signalled the fleet with coloured flags.

Brasidas turned away, fearing it was already too late.

Lysander saw the anxiety in his face, his mouth tightly closed, his eyes squinting. He put his hand to his chin and his fingertips sank into his beard.

Brasidas met his wolf's unblinking stare and gave a micro-shake of his head...

The coxswains heaved the rudder poles and the Stheno pitched as she came bout with a SWOOSH of water and bore down on the Athenians for battle.

'We'll run them aground,' said Knemos, giving Brasidas a determined look.

Naupaktos loomed into view, it was going to be a close thing, the Athenian ships rowed at full tilt, cleaving through the water, swift as the wind, making near fifteen knots, hurtling towards the twenty Peloponnesian triremes and closing fast on them.

As Brasidas had feared, Knemos's timing was disastrous, the Athenian ships were outrunning them as the Peloponnesian fleet hurried to engage them.

Eleven of Phormio's ship, including the Athena had slipped their snare and were speeding ahead of the twenty Peloponnesian ships in a life-or-death race to Naupaktos, and such an insignificant place it was too, full of old cargo boats and hulks, many hauled up on land resting crookedly on their keels, rotting away. It was the location that was important, tactically, as whoever held the place, controlled the traffic through the narrow strait between the Gulf of Corinth and the Gulf of Kalydon to the open sea, making it a vital possession for Athens, who could severely hamper the progress of the war and Corinth's naval power, forcing them to haul their ships overland across the Isthmus of Corinth into the Saronic Gulf.

Aboard the Spartan war trireme Artemis, leading the twenty Peloponnesian ships, the crew started singing the victory paean, encouraged by Timokrates who was aboard, standing on the aft quarter, shouting encouragement to the men.

Behind them, the fleet had engaged nine of Phormio's ships, in battle, and the Peloponnesians had the upper hand, but the eleven Athenian ships that had slipped through, were now passing the twenty Peloponnesians in their race to reach Naupaktos ahead of the Spartans.

'*Faster*! *Faster*!' Timokrates yelled at the trierarch as he watched the Athenians darting ahead of them. '*They're getting ahead of us...*'

Ten of the eleven Athenian ships made it safely to Naupaktos and swung their ships about, prows out in a defensive line in the harbour, facing the oncoming Peloponnesians.

The last Athenian ship was fleeing towards the harbour; behind it, the twenty Peloponnesian ships were closing fast.

'*More speed*!' shouted Timokrates. 'We've almost got him! More speed!'

Aboard the Athenian ship, the trierarch was standing on the deck with his officers. The crew were at their action stations working at double time in the race to stay ahead of the pursuing Spartans. He looked back along the ship, a Spartan ship was getting closer, its oars rising and falling like wings. 'They're gaining...'

'We're not going to make the harbour, sir,' said his boatswain.

Further back, the main force of the Peloponnesians had cut the last seven Athenian ships off, and were closing in like wolves for the kill, their beaming bronze ramming horns shimmered beneath the waterline with the promise of death.

The Athenian trierarch looked ahead to the harbour, where Phormio and his ten ships were holding their positions.

Aboard the eleventh ship, the trierarch, thinking quickly, spotted a Merchant grain ship anchored just beyond the mouth of the harbour, it was twice the size of his trireme. It was their only chance, he thought as he pointed to the ship. 'Make for that merchant and put it between us and the enemy so they can't see us. Maintain our speed and then bring us about and we'll ram the Spartan piglet before he realises what's happening!'

'As you command,' said the boatswain and relayed the orders.

The Athenian ship made for the huge grain ship, turning at its aft end, coming along side, he used the bigger merchant ship to cover their manoeuvre, and without slowing, he gave the order to come about at full speed, turning two-hundred and seventy degrees back out into the gulf. The ship pitched acutely in the turn, immediately putting its oars fast and hard to the water propelling it towards the Spartan ship, coming up on its rear, closing on it fast, too fast to give the Spartan time to turn about, the Athenian ship closed on the Spartan's amidships at ramming speed...

Down in the Spartan rowing decks, there was a tremendous CRASH and crack of splitting timbers just below the waterline, the ship shuddered with the impact as the Athenian's ramming horn punched through the hull. The oarsmen were thrown from their rowing benches, many were injured as the deck lifted beneath them, othered were trapped and some were dead, crushed and impaled on splinters of wood. Panic broke out immediately, the air was filled with the screams of men as the seat gushed in, rising into the rowing deck, dragging the ship down into the water.

The Athenian ship pulled back, revealing the extent of the damage. The Spartan ship was mortally wounded, a huge hole in its side, listing rapidly, she had but a minute to live...

Sailors leapt overboard into the cold water, those who could swim might have a chance, those who could not, were quickly drowned.

Timokrates went overboard, his armour dragged him under the water and he never resurfaced.

Phormio pointed to the Peloponnesians and shouted. 'Do we sit here like old women?! Or do we go out and show these arrogant Spartans what we can do?'

Buoyed by the lone ship's spectacular victory, the men aboard the ten ships cheered. Spurred on by the solitary Athenian ship, they now wanted to fight.

Confusion set in quickly among the Peloponnesians; some rowers in leading ships dropped their oars and seemed confused as to what their next move should be and they sat in the water, immobile and vulnerable to the Athenian assault...

Phormio, seeing the opportunity to gain the upper hand, or at least to inflict serious damage to the Peloponnesians, ordered his ships out at full speed.

The ten Athenian ships came out and engaged the numerically superior Peloponnesian fleet, throwing their enemy into even more disorder and confusion as they engaged in battle, sailing in among the Peloponnesians and made for the rest of his ships, captured by the Peloponnesians, attacking and capturing four Corinthian and two Spartan ships, and driving others onto the rocks.

It was a masterstroke and Phormio managed to liberate all but one of his ships and retreated to Naupaktos.

It was an unremitted disaster for the Peloponnese, outwitted for a second time by the elderly Athenian navarch. Brasidas was furious and he flew into such a rage, yelling at the top of his voice to re-engage the enemy; to attack Naupaktos directly, but his shouts went unheeded as Knemos and the Corinthian navarchs countered his orders, commanding the fleet to make for Corinth...

THIRTY-TWO
Corinth

Lysander had never seen Brasidas so angry, or his mood so dark. He could barely bring himself to look at Knemos, never mind speak to him, and Lysander knew Brasidas was giving serious consideration to killing Knemos where he stood for his poor judgement and his retreat, yet again in the face of the enemy.

'What happened at Naupaktos has exposed grave weaknesses in our abilities, Lysander,' he said as they followed the others into the city from the Corinthian homeport of Lechaion. Brasidas was still chewing on his anger and he and Lysander kept well back from the others. He didn't want to tarnish his reputation any further by being in their company any longer than he had to be, such was his disgust with them. 'As soon as Timokrates's ship was sunk, they hesitated when they should've continued to press the advantage, and close in on Naupaktos before Phormio had a chance to get out...' His voice was low and rasping with barely controllable anger. 'Their arrogance and their lack of discipline lost us an easy battle, and they strut like peacocks as if they had achieved some great victory. We achieved nothing, Lysander. Nothing but disgrace...'

A ragged torchbearer stepped out in front of them, his flaming torch held high, he offered them his services to light their way for an obol.

Brasidas threw out his hand as if shooing a bothersome fly. '*Be gone you cockless worm, or I'll have your head*!' he growled.

The ragged man scurried away fearfully without saying another word.

Brasidas and Lysander continued on, passing noisy taverns and brothels, and the air smelled of fish and cooking meat.

'Knemos made his move too late, Lysander. He gave the enemy too much time. Too much of a start on us. He should've gone as soon as I advised.'

'As soon as they were in the narrows,' said Lysander, who had already analysed the errors.

Brasidas nodded his head. 'And the Corinthians had the audacity to raise a trophy and call it a victory.'

'Old habits, Brasidas. They did the same thing at Sybota.'

As Brasidas remembered.

Knemos was with Melesippos, Clearchus, Lycophron, Machaon, Isokrates, and Agatharchidas outside the villa, talking – laughing, looking anything but defeated.

Timokrates was dead, the fleet was mauled and in disarray – he felt ashamed to be part of the debacle.

The commanders were gathered on the hillside with Lycophron, Machaon, Isokrates, Knemos and Agatharchidas.

They caught up with Knemos and the others.

'...It was still a victory...'

Brasidas glared at Agatharchidas. He could hardly believe his ears. 'Victory!' he barked angrily. 'You call that a victory!?'

They all looked warily at him. Brasidas rarely lost his temper, so his anger was somewhat surprising, especially to the Spartans who knew him.

'By the gods,' he spat, 'what manner of warcraft is this, to declare victory in defeat? To lift shame from the shit and polish it all up and call it Nike's diadem!? I'll have no part of it.'

The admirals were stunned.

'Did you not feel their cocks in your arses?'

'How dare you speak thus to us, Brasidas!'

'*How dare I*!? ... *How dare I*!?' he roared.

'Remember your place, Brasidas,' said Machaon.

'Remember my place?! Tell me, Navarch Machaon; what *is* my place here? I'm under the direct orders of the Gerousia and the King. There is no higher authority that I'm aware of that can issue a single order to me, save that of the King himself...'

Knemos put his hand on Brasidas's shoulder. 'Machaon meant nothing by it, Brasidas,' he said. 'The bulk of our fleet is still intact. We've lost but a few men, and we gave the enemy a bloody nose. In that, we have a victory.'

'And the Athenians still have Naupaktos,' Brasidas fired back. 'Our orders were to secure Naupaktos and tame the Akarnanians and Messenian exiles. These objectives have not been met. This is failure, no matter how much you gild it.'

'Battle at sea is very different to battle on land, Brasidas,' said Knemos. 'There are different rules. Different tactics, and the battlefield is more vast and more uncertain.'

'And that is precisely why Sparta will never master the sea as well as the Athenians,' said Agatharchidas.

Lysander shot him a look, and held his stare on him. 'There's nothing in war the Spartans cannot master!'

Lysander, Gylippos, Aschines and Skiron returned to Lakedaimon with a hundred hoplites and four wagons loaded with wounded men, wend their way through the rugged and mountainous country of the northern Peloponnese along dry dusty roads snaking into the shimmer.

It was a scorching hot day, the sun beating down through a cloudless sky, relentless and merciless.

The Spartans marched without the encumbrances of their armour; their crimson cloaks draped diagonally across their naked bodies. They were carrying their shields and spears and wearing their swords.

The thump of marching and the clattering of wagon wheels echoed from the near vertical walls of the pass. They were thankful of the cooling shade it provided, but it was short lived, on the other side of the pass, the heat hit them like the breath of a dragon.

'... Brasidas tells me that you're to be married,' said Menedaios as Lysander marched beside him.

Lysander shot him a quick look. 'Nothing is decided.'

Menedaios grinned. 'If that's what you think, then you're a gullible fool. And I know you to be neither gullible nor a fool, Lysander...' He chuckled to himself.

Lysander did not respond and fell into a moment of introspection as he gazed off into the hot shimmer that made everything beyond it invisible, and yet, like Menedaios's comment, he knew exactly what lay beyond it.

'Cheer up, Lysander. It could be worse. And look on the Brightside, once the deed is done, nobody can sing your shame through the streets as you pass by.'

He was referring to the public shaming of Spartiates who refuse to take a wife. They are publicly humiliated by the unyielding wrath of the women, who parade him naked through the streets of Sparta scorning him and singing of his disgrace. The women spit on him, beat him with sticks, and claw at his flesh, and pour scorn and curses unbound upon him, and his everlasting shame for not giving Sparta a son. You can love whoever you like, just give Sparta a son, beyond that, Sparta cares nothing of where you take your pleasures. As the saying goes, Sparta ends at the Spartan's door.

PART TWO
War in the Shadows

THIRTY-THREE
Athens

'Cleon has ambitions above himself,' said Diodotos as he reached for more of Nicias's delicious honey-cheese bread. 'Some say he still has the stink of the tanneries on him...' He took a bite and expressed pure joy. 'It's worth dining with you, just for this bread, Nicias. Your cook's a treasure.'

'He has an eye-watering fortune,' said Nicias. 'What Cleon lacks in breeding and morality, he more than makes up for in wealth, and he's used it to good purpose in all the right places to advantage himself with all the right people, and he's nowhere more influential than in the courts, where he sweettalks his way into the favour of the jurors as a whore into a drunk's purse, buying favour with many aristocrats who fall for all that shameless self-promotion and high opinion he has of himself.'

'Gullible fool's, Nicias.'

Nicias nodded his head. 'But I'll give him this, Diodotos, he has a way with words that can reach inside a man and raise him up to the point of feeling invincible. Not many men can do that.'

'He sniffs about in the gutters and sewers looking for rumours to use against those who oppose him. Bringing false charges and spewing outright lies about them for his own political ends. Of all the vile creatures I've ever encountered, Cleon's the vilest of them all.' He ate more honey-cheese bread and sipped his wine. 'And that's what makes him dangerous, Nicias...' Diodotos hated Cleon utterly, he thought he was uncouth and vulgar ... self-serving, making him unsuitable for high office of any title, making him General of Athens, supreme commander of the Delian alliance's land and naval forces was a huge mistake as far as he was concerned. A mistake that might cost Athens the war. Cleon was a reckless reactionary who lacked any sense of caution or tactical acumen. 'All the while he holds such sway, the idea of finding an honourable peace with the Spartans is impossible. He wants power, Nicias, endless power and I fear for our beloved democracy with him at its helm.'

'He's promised to raise the pay of the jurors,' said Nicias, 'and it's not unappreciated, they now firmly support him. Gods help any who Cleon thinks to prosecute now he has the juries eating out of his hand. You need to take care, my friend. We all do. Especially now that Pericles is dead, we're facing a crisis.'

'I agree. He's also become very...' He paused and looked at Nicias. 'Shall we say, generous with his coin. And those he once condemned when Pericles was alive, he now woos for support. The man has no scruples, Nicias.'

'He's cultivated all the graces of the aristocrat, while having all the vices of a rat...' Nicias inverted his winecup and the wine boy brought a jug of wine over and carefully refilled their cups before he retreated back to his place, like an object waiting to be used again.

'What more can one expect from a merchant?'

Nicias laughed lowly.

'That's something he'll never shake off, no matter how slippery and silky his words might be.'

Nicias was right, Cleon was loud, arrogant and clever like a ferret, and he hated the aristocracy to which he so desperately aspired to belong, needing their acceptance as one of them, and that was something he would never have. Diodotos hated him so much, he even thought about hiring a knifeman in the port to kill him.

'Tell me, Diodotos, what news did you bring back from Amphipolis? What's the situation there?'

'*Huh*. Now there's a story of woe, my friend. Perdiccas has proved yet again that he is the master of diplomacy, or trickery...' He pulled a face and shook his head. 'I know not which. But, when Sitalkes took his Thracian army into Macedon, sewing a harvest of destruction and death that would make even a Spartan blush, Perdiccas played a cool game, using his skills as a corruptor to outwit Thrace and indeed Athens. One has to admire him really. He did indeed resist the Thracians and managed to halt their advance. Sitalkes held his position with enemies all about him like wolves around a flock of sheep, as he awaited the hoplites Pericles had promised to send before he went to Judges of Hades. When they failed to show up, Perdiccas, who I tell you, is a man who could turn an Athenian priestess into a whore, went to Sitalkes's nephew in truce, and gave him his sister in marriage to bind the royal houses, and he gave the Thracians a chest of gold as a dowry that even King Midas would have envied. Consequently, Sitalkes has withdrawn his army back to Thrace, and Perdiccas once again escapes destruction through his cleverness.'

'The Macedonians are barbarians who want to be Hellenes,' said Nicias. 'The barbarian is always artful by nature.'

'I had little experience of them at Amphipolis. But I can tell you this much, Nicias; the entire region is vulnerable and as volatile as kindling to a flame, and that makes us vulnerable. If we lose control of our possessions there, we lose eight tenths of the timber needed to build our ships. I tell you, it's hard to know your friends from your enemies in that place, and I for one am glad to be back and I hope never to return there. I think I'd sooner face the Three Hundred Dioskouri, than go back there again.' He sipped his wine.

Nicias chuckled with amusement. 'Phormio did us proud in the Gulf of Corinth,' he said. 'Sent the Spartans home with their tails between their legs and all Athens has been celebrating as if it were the end of the war...' His face fell sallow as he stared into his cup and the wine within as if scrying for a prophetic vision, he could see the flicker of the oil lamp hanging from the standard behind his couch reflecting in it, but nothing more. 'Sparta is not defeated, and they'll not accept a peace in defeat,' he said, looking up. 'They would prefer death to such shame.' He looked at Diodotos, who had fallen into a thoughtful silence. 'They're not like other Hellenes. Nor Persians come to that. To defeat Sparta, you must kill her and all her sons. It'll be another year or two now before we can even consider proposing an honourable peace with them.'

'With Phormio's victory in the Gulf of Corinth, there's no appetite for peace, Nicias. Phormio's proved that they're vulnerable. At least at sea they are.'

Nicias nodded his head with disappointment in his eyes. He hated this war that had sucked all of Hellas into the maelstrom, Hellene killing Hellenes on a vast and unprecedented scale. War, he knew, was master of its own unpredictable nature, and the longer it continues, the more destructive it becomes, passing hatred and enmity from generation to generation, until war is waged for war's own sake, the reasons long forgotten. 'Then they should have a care, for they're fast learners, and the day might come, Diodotos, when they put an experienced navy to us that will not be cowed so easily...' He gave Diodotos a serious, almost prophetic look. 'On that day, they might destroy us utterly. Without the navy, Athens will lose.'

There followed a long and poignant silence as they imagined such a catastrophe.

Diodotos felt a cold shiver down his spine. It was unimaginable, even inconceivable to most Athenians.

THIRTY-FOUR

Sparta

Telephassa had quickly become the Queen's favourite. Her youth and her broad intellectual scope of interests made her pleasant company. And for a girl of barely eighteen, she was well versed in mathematics, poetry, philosophy and sciences and had an enquiring mind, which is to be encouraged among women of Sparta. All of Tellis's children and grandchildren were well educated by xeno sophists, and Tellis's trophimos Lysander was no exception, and the Queen and he confidante Argileonis, were both happy that she was marrying a man she knew, albeit from afar with very few actual encounters between them as children, she had always known who he was, and had secretly admired him for his brashness, prowess and his cleverness, and after Methone, he became something of a local hero too. He was also Inspirer to the Queen's beloved son Agesilaos.

Yes, Lysander was a rising light among the Spartans, but not even they could foretell the great destiny that awaited him, a destiny that would change the world forever.

'You're very quiet today, Telephassa?' the Queen commented as Telephassa combed the Queen's hair. Eupolia enjoyed it when Telephassa combed her hair. She was so gentle and tentative with the comb as to be pleasurable.

'Forgive me, My Lady.'

Eupolia's mouth curled into a gentle smile. 'Nonsense. There's nothing to forgive. He is probably just as nervous,' she said, knowing where her sweet companion's thoughts were.

'Do you think so, My Lady?' the idea that Lysander was nervous too made her feel a little easier in a strange way.

'Of course, he is. Young men are very clumsy and awkward at these things, just as are young women. You mustn't fret, Telephassa.'

'I fear I'll not please him. How will I know?'

'If he puts his phallus and his seed inside you, then you have pleased him,' intoned Argileonis candidly.

Telephassa reached up to her neck and took hold of Tyche in her hand, seeking her favour, on this day above all others. She looked at her grandmother who was sitting in a chair near the Queen's bed.

'Once he's finished, he will sneak away, and you will be his wife,' Argileonis continued. 'For you, and for him, tonight is not about pleasure. Pleasure comes later, sweet Telephassa. After you're married, when you share more than your bodies, but your minds as well, is the place from whence pleasure comes. Lysander knows this as much as you.'

'Does he, Grandmother.'

'Of course he does. Brasidas would have told him, as is his duty.'

Eupolia, who was of a gentler nature than Telephassa's grandmother, turned on her stool and took hold of Telephassa's hand in hers. 'What man could fail to be pleased by such a pretty bloom? The gods favour this marriage. You must not fret so, Telephassa.'

'My Lady is too kind.'

Eupolia took her earrings out. Polished lapis lazuli in solid gold mounts. 'In some places, it is customary to give the bride a gift, and I give you these, Telephassa.'

Telephassa took a step back and gasped in surprise. 'Oh, My Lady, I could not.'

'Yes you can. Here, take them, wear them, enjoy them as I have enjoyed them.'

Telephassa took the earrings. 'My Lady is kind and generous beyond my humble words.' She turned to Argileonis. 'Look, Grandmother.'

'They will suit you perfectly,' said Argileonis.

'Now, time slips away,' said Telephassa. You must go home.'

'But I've not finished your hair.'

'Andromeda will finish it. Go now.'

'I will come shortly, before the sun sets,' said Argileonis.

*

The hour had come and it was time for the wedding rituals to begin. Four hours before sunset, Telephassa was sent to her father's house and went to the bath, where she bathed in hot water. After her bath, her maid, Rhea, put scented lavender oil on her body, while in the nuptial bedchamber she could hear the loud incantatory chants of the priest of Protogonos, a most ancient and primordial god of fertility and procreation. He was just the latest of a procession of priests and priestesses, from Aphrodite to Priapos who had been coming and going since dawn. Fortunately, she had missed most of them, but the house reeked of myrrh, fremescence, dried hazel and sage, and all manner of perfumes to bring good spirits and good fortune to the womb of the bride.

Two hours before sunset, she left the house to go to the perimeter of her father's estate, and there to wait for the next part of her wedding.

At dusk, Telephassa was captured by three of her best friends; the friends she had grown up with at the Spartan Sisterhood. Of these three, Panora, daughter of Knemos was her closest friend and as such, she was her bridesmaid.

The other two girls seized her by the arms and led her back to the house, where they took her into an empty room, where like a prisoner to a dungeon, no words were exchanged, as law forbids it at this part of the ceremony.

The two friends left, leaving her alone with Panora and Telephassa's maid.

'Rhea, fetch me some water,' Telephassa said as she watched Panora pick up the shears. 'The Queen gave me a pair of her earrings as a wedding gift.'

'As I heard.'

'I tried to say no. But how does one say no to a Queen.'

'You do not. You accept and be pleased to accept. Only those she favours get such gifts. Are they the blue Egyptian ones?'

'Yes.'

'Her favourite earrings. You must make certain you wear them when you next go to the palace.'

'Oh, I will.' It was a refreshing diversion from what was going on.

'Are you ready?' Panora asked.

Telephassa nodded her head without speaking and Panora positioned herself behind her friend.

'Forgive me.'

'Of course. It has to be done.'

It brought tears to Panora's eyes as she started to cut Telephassa's beautiful hair.

Rhea returned with a cup of water, behind her was Argileonis. 'I feared you would not come, Grandmother.'

'He has beautiful eyes,' said Panora.

'He loves men,' Telephassa said candidly, being under no illusion as to Lysander's nature.

'Lots of men love other men. From what I've heard, they all do with one another. But I'm sure he'll love you too. If you want him to love you. It's not uncommon for husbands and wives not to be in love. It's perfectly normal.'

'Yes,' she sighed lowly. 'I suppose you're right.'

'He's very handsome,' Panora said as she continued cutting Telephassa's hair. 'I hope my husband will be so handsome,' she added with a dreamy smile.

Telephassa could feel every snip of the shears, cutting away the emblem of her girlhood, marking her transition to womanhood, which is the gift of marriage to a girl, liberating her from the constraints of her guardians. Still, seeing her hair lay in thick locks on the floor around her gave her a crushing feeling in her chest. But it would grow back, she knew.

'They say he is gentle in his nature,' Panora said.

*

It was noisy in the mess, the warriors were downing cups of wine, feasting on sea fish and venison. Lysander sat with a cup of water; wine being forbidden to pass the groom's lips on his wedding night, neither could he imbibe the cannabis vapours at the gas bath. He had to be in his perfect mind.

Brasidas was reclining beside him, trying to put his mind at ease. '... I was the same when I slept with a woman for the first time. Just be yourself, Lysander.'

'But your mother, Father Tellis, you and your brother ... I feel as if I'm being crushed, Brasidas. I fear I'm going to fail her and disappoint you.'

'And there's the problem. You think too much and you worry too much. Don't think about us. It's not us you're marrying, it's my niece. Think only of her. Now, it's time for you to take your leave of us.'

The tradition of marriage, is for the groom to sneak away unseen. Of course, the reality was different, but Lysander quietly left his place and made for the kitchen and the back way out of the mess, speaking to nobidy, and nobody looked at him, pretending not to notice.

Brasidas gave him a reassuring smile and nod of his head as Lysander rose to his feet, his heart filled with so many worries and uncertainties. He left the syssition and from this point on, he was forbidden to speak until his bride was lying upon the marital bed.

*

It was night, and after Telephassa's hair was cut as short to the scalp as it was possible to get, Rhea handed a boy's cloak to Panora and then stripped her mistress naked.

Panora put the cloak over her body – she took a leather cord belt from Rhea and tied it around Telephassa's waist. Rhea put a pair of boy's shoes onto her mistress's feet.

The final act, was to lay Telephassa onto a raised wooden pallet, and then the shutter of the window was closed.

'The gods are with you,' Panora whispered as she a Rhea left the room, closing the door behind them.

The silence was intense, she could hear herself breathing tremulously; her heart pounding hard in her chest as she lay there, not moving, staring into the perfect blackness – waiting with increasing uncertainty. Willing it to be done with one thought, praying it wouldn't happen yet with another. Or better yet, not at all.

She could hear the distant barking of foxes and a dog. She grew more anxious. Was he close? Was he outside, stalking around the house, searching for the best way in without being seen? Maybe he was already in the house? *Oh, sweet Athena…!*

*

The house was dark and still. Quiet all but that bloody dog yapping at the stars.

He felt more nervous than he ever did as a boy on a food raid, or at Methone when he saw all those Athenians at the walls. He couldn't compare it to anything, except possibly the first time he encountered Brasidas as a thirteen-year-old boy in the mountains, where Brasidas pursued him for three days and nights.

What if it all goes wrong? What if he was unable to perform as a man with her? What if she repulsed him? What if he repulsed her? The maelstrom of thoughts hit him like an enemy onslaught. Like a thief in the night, he approached the house, soundless as he went.

There was only one window that was shuttered, it had to be the window where Telephassa awaited him. His mouth became as dry as summer dust, his guts tightened with apprehension. He crept up to the shuttered window and pushed on them and they swung open–

Telephassa saw the shutters open, one of them creaked. She lay rigid with fear, her eyes wide open as the dark figure climbed through the window, not making a sound.

Lysander saw the silhouette of her lying on the pallet in the middle of the room. He was committed now, there was no going back, his very honour was at stake. He moved towards her, seeing the watery glint of her frightened eyes in the darkness as he leaned over her. Her hands were clenched into fists either side of her. He untied her belt and removed it, and then he scooped her up in his arms. He could feel her trembling. Or was it him...?

He carried her out of the room into the corridor, where every door but one was closed. Lysander carried her into this room, dominated by a bed. He laid her down on it. Only now could they speak.

'Do you fear me?' he asked her in a whisper as he stood beside the bed.

'Not you. But this.'

Lysander seemed to understand and nodded his head. 'We have until dawn.' He got onto the bed and laid beside her on his side facing her. 'We can take our time if you'd rather?'

She turned her head and looked at him. 'Perhaps we can touch one another, and embrace before...?'

Lysander nodded his head. 'I've never touched a woman before,' he said.

'And I've never touched a man.'

Lysander slid his hand under her tunic and rand it lightly over her smooth belly.

She liked the touch, he was gentle, just as her grandmother said he would be, and she turned to him, feeling something hard press against her...

THIRTY-FIVE

Neutral city of Patrai, Achaia

'You have very pleasing breasts, Hippodameia,' said Pheidon lying back on the bed giving her firm breasts close attention, his hunger satiated, his eyes dark and deep, like wells, the dark waters glimmering far below. She was still straddling him, sweating, breathing deeply, recovering from the immutable pleasure he had given her. He knew what he was doing with a woman, his fingers as lively as his phallus, making certain theirs was a shared pleasure.

Her body servant had been in the bedchamber the entire time, standing with her face to the wall as her mistress and her man enjoyed one another. She heard everything, the groans and pants, the movements of their bodies and the gasps as they fell into the climactic paroxysms of ecstasy. And then, her mistress said:

'Niobe, fetch us some wine.'

Niobe turned away from the wall and went to the little table on which stood a silver jug and two winecups. She filled them and took them to the bed.

Pheidon's eyes were on her. Pleasing to the eye. Small in stature, but buxom. 'Next time, Niobe should join us,' he said. 'Would you like that, Niobe?'

'Of course, she would,' answered Hippodameia, finally lifting herself off of him.

Niobe's face darkened with a flush of blood.

Pheidon smiled at the nervous slave girl. 'I'll fuck you both.' He took a swallow of wine and chuckled amusedly to himself as he looked at Niobe, who had a fearful look in her eyes. 'Yes. We'll do it tonight,' he said.

'Tonight!? Is there no end to your appetite?' Hippodameia exclaimed.

'Hardly. I want to do you both.'

Hippodameia looked thoughtfully at Niobe. 'As you like.' She got out of bed and took up her robes from a chair. 'I'll dress myself, Niobe,' she said. 'Fetch some fresh hot bathing water.'

'Yes, Kyria.' She left the room, closing the door behind her, horrified that she was going to be ravaged by her mistress's lover, who had only arrived here a couple of hours ago. No sooner had he arrived when he was tearing her mistress's robes off and throwing her unceremoniously onto the bed, ramming his phallus into her with what seemed to be a desperate need in him.

'I'll have rooms made ready for you, Pheidon,' she said as she tied her belt cord around her slender waist.

Pheidon watched Hippodameia. 'How was your trip to Attica?' he asked.

'Educational,' she replied.

'Did Epaphroditos speak of the traitor?'

'He did.'

Pheidon watched her as he sipped his drink. 'Did he name him?'

'He didn't know his name,' she said. 'He said only that the strategoi is receiving information from a Corinthian, but he didn't know who.'

'A Corinthian?' he repeated thoughtfully; that surprised him. He sipped his wine and let his eyes rove the bedchamber. Fit for a queen, a wide terrace beyond the columned portico and a splendid view of the gulf and the port. 'Did this Corinthian murder Doreios?' he pressed.

Hippodameia nodded her head. 'Epaphroditos says yes.'

Pheidon nodded his head slowly. Doreios was his friend and fellow warrior in in the shadow war. 'I want to know who this Corinthian cock-shaker is, so I can kill him myself. Were there any Corinthians in the city when Doreios was murdered?'

'There are always Corinthians in the city. Athenians too. Merchants and spies. Athenian spies spying on us, our spies spying on Athenians, Achaian spies spying on everyone. It's neutral. The ideal city for information to be passed from one side to the other. This Corinthian could be anyone, Pheidon.'

'He must be close. If he knew about Doreios, then he must know about you and what you do here, apart from renting whores out.'

Hippodameia did not respond.

'He probably comes here, Hippodameia? Possibly someone you trust?'

'There's but one Corinthian who comes here regularly. Lampon, who has a large estate in the valley of the Pirus River,' she explained. 'But mostly he lives here in Patrai, where he has a house near the Acropolis. He is also the nephew of Xiphilinus.'

Pheidon took a swallow of his wine without commenting. He knew who Xiphilinus was. Back in Corinth he was a powerful oligarch.

'He comes frequently to my house.'

'What else did Epaphroditos tell you?'

'He said Athenian resources are close to exhaustion. They're putting more and more burdens on their allies, forcing them to give more men, build more ships, more tribute to the Athenian treasury. They're even talking about taxing the merchants and aristocrats of Athens and Attica. They thought the war would be over by now. They thought Sparta and our allies would grow tired of it and run out of money. Potidaea has cost Athens a fortune, and the plague continues to take its levy. Epaphroditos says the Empire is struggling with internal strife. The proposals are being resisted strongly by their allies who say they're already struggling to meet the war's demands. Influential men like Nicias also oppose the measures. He thinks Athens should seek an honourable peace.'

Pheidon did not respond.

'How should I introduce you to Lampon? He'll know you're a Spartan.'

'Tell him I serve in the King's tent at Plataea. That should lure his curiosity. Tell him that I'm here on diplomatic business with Micythos.'

Micythos was the chief archon of the city and region around Patrai, he also happened to be a close friend of Pheidon's father Tellis from years past, when Tellis gave him vital information of a planned Acarnanian invasion. Due to that information, the invasion was thwarted and a peace treaty was made. Micythos had never forgotten this service Tellis and Sparta had done for his city and country. He was a young trierarch from the ruling house of Achaia. Now he was the most powerful man in Patrai – a very useful friend to have for a shadow man like Pheidon.

*

The House of the Hetaerae was really two, a brothel and tavern, which occupied the street and welcomed any with a few coins to spend. And then there was the grand villa, which sat in its own grounds behind the brothel and tavern. It had an imposing columned entranceway, that led into a palatial house with polished marble floors, and there were servants on hand to take the capes and robes of the "*guests*".

It was pure luxury, where only the best and richest guests were permitted. There was a large dining room, hot baths with massage alcoves and comfortable bedchambers.

The dining room was filled with music, panpipes, lyres, rattled and bells, played by youths wearing white chitons tied with red cord belts. They had little terracotta vials of olive oil hung from their necks on long leather cords.

'There,' Hippodameia whispered as they stood in the doorway, her eyes staring sharply at Lampon, who was reclining languidly on a dining couch, daintily eating honey glazed dates he skewered with a thin bladed dagger. He was watching the naked dancing girls, dancing erotically in the big square space in front of the tables, around which ten other aristocrats and wealthy merchants, chatting as they ate.

Pheidon knew one of them, his father's friend Micythos, who had presence about him, big in stature and his head was as bald as an egg, except for his grizzled beard.

'... So I had the bastard drowned in his own olive oil,' Micythos bellowed to the man next to him.

They laughed, so did everybody else.

'That's what happens when you think you can try smuggling your merchandise through my port without paying what's due.'

'What of his crew?' asked one of the diners.

'I confiscated their cargo and sent them on their way...' He reached for his wine cup, his gaze settling on one of the beautiful dancing girls.

'Still as bald as a baby's arse, I see, Micythos.'

Micythos looked round slowly at the speaker, wondering who had balls enough to speak so disrespectfully to the chief archon of Patrai, and then he saw it was Pheidon, and his angry face instantly softened and his lips curled into a happy smile and then he rose to his feet and gave out a loud belly laugh. 'Pheidon! My old friend!'

The two men embraced.

Lampon and the other guests all looked curiously about them. Who was this man? How did he know the Archon? Where was he from? Why was he there?

'Come, dine by me. Dine on me if you please...' He looked at the man he had been speaking to and bucked his head in a gesture to vacate his place for the stranger. 'How goes it, Pheidon?'

The aristocrat, knowing his place in the pecking order, quickly vacated his place and relocated next to Lampon.

'It goes well.'

They settled onto the couches.

'And your father? He prospers I pray?'

Pheidon smiled. 'He does.'

'Who is that man?' Lampon asked the aristocrat.

'I've no idea,' the aristocrat replied, looking resentfully at Pheidon. 'He's not from these parts, I can tell you that.'

Hippodameia came in a few minutes later, regal as a Persian queen, wearing exquisite robes. She worked her way around the room, greeting her important guests.

She greeted Lampon with a kiss on his cheek. 'I trust you're enjoying yourself, Lampon?'

'I always enjoy myself at the House of the Hetaerae. Tell me, Hippodameia, who is that man with Micythos?'

The question came sooner than she thought it would. She looked over at Pheidon and Micythos, who were deep in conversation, and unusually for Micythos, they were speaking quietly. 'Pheidon of Sparta,' she said. 'He's here as an emissary of King Agis,' she explained. 'That's all I know of him...' She looked at the aristocrat who had to move places. 'How are you this evening, Syloson?'

'As well as always I am when I come here.'

She smiled. 'I have some new boys,' she said. 'From Sicily. I'm sure you'll find one to enjoy.'

Lampon's attention was now fully engaged in Pheidon. He wanted to know why he was here?

THIRTY-SIX

Athens, Hecatombeus/July

Eponymous Year of Hagesistratos, 427 BC

Cleon had a lean cadaveric face with dark brown eyes that often looked as black as pitch when the light was right. He wore fine robes cut from the most expensive cloth, unlike the man. He had come into his own in the past few days, his skills as a litigant who believed in the persuasive power of fear, and nowhere did he demonstrate that more than yesterday, when he strongly advocated for the executions of every Mytilenean male from the age of thirteen upwards.

By whipping them up and instilling the Bouleuterion with fear and paranoia of secret plots as yet undiscovered, and yesterday, in the heat of his rhetoric, they had voted in favour of executing the men of Mytilene for making treaties with the Spartans and revolt against Athens. The vote was almost unanimous, to order the immediate executions of all the men and boys of Mytilene, and a death note was signed and dispatched the same day to Paches who was in command of the situation on Lesbos.

But no sooner had the ship departed, when many of the Boule, stabbed with conscience, had changed their minds and wanted to overturn the order for a more lenient compromise of executing only the ringleader and conspirators.

All those senators who had not died in the plague, or were recovered or unaffected, were in attendance, listening to Cleon as he reminded everybody of the events that had led to the crisis on Lesbos.

'... Last year,' he told them as he moved about the speaker's floor in that ungainly and ungraceful way he had, 'Mytilene revolted against us and their plan was to unite Lesbos and divorce herself from us, and they intrigued with our enemy Sparta and made alliance with them, and pledged their navy, which we have left independent for friendship's sake against us. Such is the loyalty of this friend, who plotted with other cities on Lesbos for the purpose of armed revolt...' He paused for a deliberately long moment, his eyes roving them carefully. 'At the same time, they secretively got their preparations underway to take advantage of our plight from the plague, which has killed three times the number of Athenians and our allies as have the Lakedaimonians. Further, they hoped to exploit our finances, knowing we're hard pressed in our treasuries...' He nodded his head broadly, giving them a severe and penetrating look. 'Oh yes, they were advanced in their plot against us, and they were fortifying the city and harbour and filling their grain silos and training their hoplites and navy in preparation of war against us. But they were betrayed by our loyal friends on that island. Once we realised it was true, we responded immediately, dispatching General Paches with a force of hoplites and ships to quell the rebellion and bring the Mytileneans to their right mind. But they chose to resist, and now they have surrendered and they come before us begging for mercy. Well, I say there can be no mercy for such cowardly treachery. If we are lenient with Lesbos, how can we be harsh with others of our allies who rebel against our authority? And you can be certain of it; if you are lenient with the Lesbians, it will encourage others to rebel.'

The senators shifted about on their seats, many were nodding their heads, murmuring agreement, while some were shaking their heads, uttering their disapproval of the mass executions of the Mytileneans, others sat without expression or comment.

'The Mytileneans deceived us by sending its embassy to the Spartans, who greeted them as kindred spirits and plotted treachery and war against us with them, and entered into a formal alliance with them, upon which oaths to the gods were sworn. And they now seek mercy.'

Nicias and Diodotos, seated beside one another, were also studying the mood of the assembly, so were Demosthenes, Alcibiades and Hipponikos, who had arrived at Athens from Aphidnai late last night – Socrates, who had been involved operationally in subduing Mytilene, sat between Alcibiades and Hipponikos.

'A vile man,' said Hipponikos.

'He has many ulcers on his soul,' said Socrates.

'... In times past,' Cleon continued, 'I've been convinced that democracy and empire cannot exist in the same space, and never has it been clearer than in your changing of your minds when it comes the problem of Mytilene. Safely here in Athens, where fear of plots are unknown to you...'

Alcibiades leaned to Socrates. 'He wants their blood, Socrates. He wants to kill all the men and enslave the women and children.'

Socrates nodded his head. 'And it'll serve Athens no advantage to do so in any place. More, it will advantage the enemy, who will say this is how Athens deals with those who wish to be free of the alliance. It'll serve to encourage hatred and fear among the allies and encourage them to revolt. And the Spartans will say, "This is how Athens treat their friends." But this is how it is with men like Cleon, Alcibiades. Strength through cruelty, which is really weakness of character.'

'... For myself,' Cleon continued, 'I'm of the same opinion now as I was before, that this most insidious treachery, can be met with only the severest of punishments. All men of Mytilene from thirteen upwards, should be put to death, and those women and children which remain, should be sent across the empire bound in slavery unto death. This you agreed by majority...' His stern eyes roved the senators. 'So I question the motives of those who now propose to reopen the case to seek leniency for the treacherous and rebellious Mytileneans...'

Nicias made eye contact with Hipponikos seated with Socrates and Alcibiades on the opposite side of the debating chamber. They nodded in greeting, both seeming to recognise what the other was thinking about this tanner's son playing high politics, litigating for the executions of thousands of men and boys.

Cleon's expressive, yet coarse voice disseminated across the chamber as he paced from one end to the other, speaking as much with his hands as with his voice, every gesture, like every word, was carefully calculated for maximum dramatic effect.

'... No other state has wounded us as deeply as Mytilene...'

Alcibiades yawned and made no attempt to hide it. He was tired of these debates about Mytilene. Yesterday, the Boule agreed to execute the Mytileneans and today, a good portion of them had changed their minds and called for the assembly to debate the matter again.

Socrates, who was elected to the Boule for this year, had predictably voted against the drastic measures. Mytilene was defeated, they had surrendered, and their delegation had put a strong case to the assembly. All this was done with honour, according to the ancient and noble traditions of war.

Yes, the campaign had been costly and bloody. It had stretched Athens to her very limits, and as their forces were fighting the rebels and besieging their city, a fleet of a hundred Athenian warships had ravaged the Peloponnesian coast, a deliberate show of force to demonstrate, or rather fool the Spartans into believing that despite the plague and expense, Athens could still radiate her power far and wide. But it had come at the greatest cost. The levies on the allies were practically doubled, and, for the first time in Athenian history, a levy of taxes was imposed upon the citizens, in order to maintain the cost of the war, which had endured beyond what Pericles had anticipated, and the enemy were showing no signs of giving up. To the contrary, they seemed just as determined to continue the war as they ever did.

'... Do not, therefore, betray yourselves,' Cleon went on, 'but remember the fearful urgency you demanded Mytilene be cowed. Stay to the course, honour your vote...' He shook his head, again his dark eyes perused them with the care of a cobra. 'Do not shake on fearful knees or forget the great danger the Mytileneans posed to us and the outcome of this war, coming close as we did to being attacked directly by the Spartan fleet by sea, while their armies mustered at our landward walls. Punish them as they deserve to be punished, and teach our other allies by cruel example, that the penalty of rebellion is exemplary death. Only then can we be saved from such rebellions in future times, as this will give them pause before they ground their arms against us...' With that, Cleon returned to his seat on the benches.

Nicias shuddered as memories of Samos surfaced, when, following their revolt some years ago, Pericles ordered all the trierarchs of the Samian navy to be crucified to the ground in the Samian agora. There had been a Spartan delegation there that day, and they made it clear how disgusted they were at the executions.

Suddenly, Diodoros rose to his feet. 'Oh, I neither blame nor condemn those citizens who have demanded that we reopen this matter concerning yesterday's vote,' he said, earning a surprised look from Cleon, 'which was made in the heat of anger instead of cool reason,' he said as he came out onto the speakers' floor. 'Yesterday, we spoke with hot blood and we voted in haste, without fully considering the matter. And that we can, in the space of but a few hours, decide upon the fates of so many. It would be immoral if we did not sit today to reconsider the matter of Mytilene and its fate...' He swept them with his eyes.

'Tell me, Socrates,' said Hipponikos, inclining to Socrates. 'You were there. Is such a punishment as Cleon advocates justified?'

'Such punishments are never justified, Hipponikos,' said Socrates soberly. 'To defeat an enemy in battle is one thing. To then put him and all his countrymen to death is unworthy of us, and will only serve to inspire anyone at war with us to fight to the bitter death, if they think they'll be murdered if they surrender. I fear that Cleon serves greater purpose to the enemy than to Athens in his policy.'

Hipponikos considered.

The debate went on with many adding their opinions, some in favour of executing the Mytileneans, but many more were now opposed, and when the vote was cast, they assembly voted to execute only the ringleaders. For Cleon it was a bitter political setback, for humanity, it was a saving grace.

THIRTY-SEVEN

Platanistas, Sparta

It was a warm afternoon with a pleasing breeze blowing along the valley from the coast. As usual, the old warriors gathered at the Platanistas to idle away the afternoon, admiring the youths from the ephebeion training on the race track, and to gossip about this and that, swapping old war stories for the thousandth time, and hearing the latest news from the front, and it wasn't good news for the most part. The humiliating naval defeats in the Gulf of Corinth and the debacle at Lesbos. Plataea was still besieged, the Athenians still refused to fight like honourable men in the field of battle, turning instead to butchery and unspeakable atrocities. Rhium and Naupaktos had badly knocked the confidence of the Peloponnesian navies, locked in a crisis of confidence and fearful of the Delian navy.

Archias couldn't remember a time when morale was ever so low as it was now.

Archias understood that some new tactical innovations were needed to balance the scale more in Sparta's favour, especially at sea. The Peloponnesian navies seemed to spend more time running away from the Delians than they did engaging them. It was shameful and degrading.

Sparta and her allies needed to put more effort in. As for the allies' obsessions with their farms, harvests, wives and children, their hardships, their losses and all the other gripes, well they were simply infuriating. They had come to Sparta demanding Sparta declare war on the Athenian Empire, and now they did nothing but complain about the hardships. Too bad, Archias thought. They wanted war, well now they had it, so now they had to endure and pay the costs. That was how Archias and many other Spartiates saw it. Total war demands total commitment.

Archidamos was right, this war would stretch into new generations. It might never end, with such atrocities thus far committed by all sides, hatred was now sewn deep into the souls of men, states and gods. The stain of Hellenic blood was a scar on the Hellenic heart, and there would be no rest until the bitter end, when one stands victorious over the other, or both will be destroyed.

This crisis in confidence had to be resolved as a matter of urgency, and when Archias brought his concerns to the King, ephors and commanders, they all agreed with him, which really took his breath away.

New ships were of no use without new tactics and skilled oarsmen to counter the Athenians.

To lose this war was simply unconscionable to the Spartan mind, Archias thought. If Sparta loses this war, she will never recover from it. Everything, the entire system and the Great Rhetra, their very way of life will fall apart and Sparta will fall into the abyss, never to rise again. The thought terrified him. Where was his bellicose advocacy for this war now? Drowning with his arrogance in an ocean of blood.

Brasidas had recently suggested the introduction of mounted cavalry and the emancipation of more Helot volunteers to create extra divisions of Spartan trained heavy hoplite infantry, even taking their sons into the Rearing!

Now that was a step too far.

These were radical ideas, and there was a growing feeling that it was an option worth considering. At the moment, Helot militias were light infantry, armed only with javelins and spears, sometimes with a xiphos or kopis sword as well, and they had proved themselves, as they always do, to be good soldiers. Brave too, running naked into the enemy, deploying their javelins into their phalanxes or at their charging cavalry. They were trained to the minimum standard, with good reason. Show a Helot how to fight and the next thing you know, he's fighting you. The losses of Helot peltasts were staggering in comparison to the losses of men of the Spartiate order, or the subject allies or any other belligerent in this war. They always had been, in every war Sparta had. But this war was different, it was a war like no other that had come before it. Not even the Median menace posed such a threat to Sparta as now confronted them.

Brasidas was in awe of those Helots who fought for Sparta, pressed men or volunteers, they were brave and heroic Peloponnesians, where most others simply saw them as slaves or fodder for Ares's insatiable hunger. They fought like soldiers, for their country against a foreign enemy, who was a common enemy, was Brasidas's response when Archias stressed his worries that arming and training more Helots in warcraft, would simply be creating a future enemy from within, who would murder the Spartans in their beds. But now he saw the true situation, Archias was wavering.

The Helots who went with Brasidas into the Gulf of Corinth and elsewhere, the rowers and light infantry followed him from loyalty to him personally. The respect and kindnesses he showed them, was returned in kind. The Tamer of Helots had become the unexpected friend of Helots.

Maybe he's right? Archias told himself. He and Sthenelaedas were seated in their usual spot at the far end of the running track on the long bench near to the bronze statue of Pollux mounted on his powerful warhorse, the bronze long since greened with age.

Sthenelaedas seated to his left was droning on about his pet hate – Athens; even now he was dead, Sthenelaedas was scathing and unrelenting in his hatred of Pericles, who he blamed entirely for the war and prayed he was now in the darkest and coldest spot of Tartaros, being tormented for eternity like Tantalos for the calamity he had visited upon Hellas and beyond.

Archias was too busy floundering in his melancholy to listen, besides, he had heard it all a thousand times before. He nodded and shook his head with an occasional grunt in the right places, while his eyes roved to see who else was enjoying an afternoon in the Platanistas, gossiping.

He spotted Geront Autokrates wandering around at the edge of the track, talking to acquaintances, his long suffering mothon servant stood a pace behind him. Over on the far side of the running track, he saw Kleisthenes the Cyclops, playing petteia with Tellis's beautiful wife Argileonis. Despite her age being past fifty, she was still a very good-looking woman of high birth and a close friend of the Queens, as her husband was the King's closest friend. She wore her hair up on her head with several tightly sprung locks that hung either side of her face. She came from a very wealthy family, her mother was the daughter of Eurycleia, sister of Eurybiades, Navarch during the war with Persia, her father was a Spartan general who was killed in battle at Plataea during the Persian War.

Kleisthenes's attention was divided between their game and the herd of youths from the *ephebeion* line-dancing to the song of a flute played by another youth, all under the watch of a gymnasiarch. Old habits die hard, and he may not have been *Paidonomos* anymore, but all the boys and *gymnasiarchs* still feared, respected and obeyed him.

Kleisthenes said something amusing to her and she gave out a hearty laugh. The cyclops was not a man known for his humour, but there it was, the beautiful Argileonis was amused by him. By the gods, it was a wonder she could understand him, so distorted was his voice. It was well known that Kleisthenes loved her, he had always loved her, but it was his friend Tellis who won her. They often came here to play petteia – the game of soldiers on pleasant afternoons, often drawing a crowd of spectators.

'Tellis is a lucky man,' said Archias.

'... He lied to Athens, he lied to his allies, and he lied to us,' Sthenelaedas went on.

'Who? Tellis?'

Sthenelaedas frowned at him. 'No. Pericles.'

'Such is the nature of Athenians, old friend. Have you not learned that yet?' He looked at young Libys, leaning on a wall with two other young men fresh out of the Rearing. Geront Dorian was with them, telling them about Methone, a proud day for Dorian who was there doing his bit along with Libys's brother Lysander.

The youngsters were listening enthralled to the old man, while Libys watched the people coming and going, in their little cliques gossiping.

Sthenelaedas's voice finally fell silent and for a moment, Archias listened to the flute, setting the pace of the line dancing. He admired the virile youths, full of hopes and aspirations, their blood hot for glory, impatient to come of age, when they too could join the war and slick their spears with Delian blood. These, he thought, are the generation to which the King alluded when he cautioned against the war.

Archias turned his attention to the five men standing away from everybody else, on the far side of the running track, shaded under one of the plane trees, from which the Platanistas takes its name, its branches stretched crooked and gnarled above them, heavy in new leaf and inhabited by chirping sparrows. Geront Khilon was one of them. He was the great-grandson of Khilon, the wisest of the Spartiates, famed for being one of the Seven Sages of Hellas. Khilon the younger walked with a staff he claimed to be the staff of the great man himself, but Archias didn't believe it for a moment. The men with him were Alkidas, another high-ranking commander Mindaros who was a friend of Brasidas, and two other *Gerontes*, Charon and Gorgythion

Autokrates was gradually working his way towards them, pausing to pass a few words with Dorian.

'Very fine buttocks,' said Sthenelaedas, looking at the dancing youths. 'Tell me, Archias, did we ever have such fine-looking arses?'

'I think we did.'

'The gods have a cruel humour, to make us wither away on our bones.'

'Says you who are fifteen years younger than I am. By the gods, you're melancholic today, Sthenelaedas–'

'Good day, gentlemen,' said Autokrates as he approached, aided by his staff and followed by his servant.

'Good day, Autokrates.'

'And what brings you here, Autokrates?' asked Archias. 'It's a rare thing to see you here.'

'I come to speak to you, gentlemen. To you and to others, but especially to you, Archias.'

Archias raised his brow. 'You have us intrigued, old friend...?' He gestured for Autokrates to sit with them.

Autokrates sat down beside Archias. 'Tell me, Archias, has Tellis said anything about King Archidamos's health?'

'No. Why?'

'There's a rumour that the King's gone mad, and that's why they sent Agis to command the army at Plataea with Ramphias.'

'The king is frail, it's true. *But mad...?*' Archias shook his head. 'Where did you hear this dangerous rumour, Autokrates?'

'Khilon told me. He said the King's been acting strangely. Shouting at the phantoms of his mind, roaming his palace late at night talking to people who aren't there; ranting about when the earth shook as if it were yesterday, and speaking to people long dead. Pausanias, his mother, his grandfather King Zeuxidamos. He even called Eupolia Lampito and forgot he had children...'

Archias looked over at Khilon, still deep in conversation with Alkidas and the others. 'And how did Khilon come by this?'

'From one of the palace guards.'

Archias and Sthenelaedas looked at one another.

'It's treason to say such things,' said Sthenelaedas. 'I saw the King just yesterday and I assure you, he was fully himself.'

THIRTY-EIGHT

Archidamos and Eupolia were out on the terrace, strolling towards the steps to the lower terrace, arm in arm as they often did, discussing their children. Agesilaos was proving himself a very capable boy at the Rearing, but he had not earned any great station there. He wasn't even a herd leader, which was somewhat disappointing to the King. Was it his lame foot? Or was he just not leadership material?

He rubbed the side of his head and pulled a face.

'Another headache?' asked Eupolia.

'It'll pass...' He glanced back at his retinue of courtiers who were following several strides behind them, being managed by Tellis, who seemed more determined than usual to keep everybody as far away from the King as possible; even the two ephors who were amongst the courtiers and the Queen's maids and companions kept far enough back so as not to hear the King and Eupolia.

Telephassa among them, was with child.

'The snakes look grimmer than usual,' said Archidamos as he turned back.

'Are they, Husband. I confess, to me they look as grim as ever they did, no more and no less.'

'Huh. They're waiting for me to die.'

'I think not, husband. The Lakedaimonians love you. And you're a long way from that day, and it upsets me to hear you say it.'

He took her hand in his and squeezed it gently. 'My dear sweet, Eupolia. You have been the brightest light of my life, and never have I loved so deeply as I love you. But you must know. You must prepare. The shadow of Thanatos is upon me and I feel him waiting. But know, when the hour comes, I die a happy man for the life the gods blessed me with to have you in it. And our children–'

'Stop it, Archidamos. I'll not hear it!' she said sharply. 'I cannot think of my life without you in it.'

He smiled and chuckled. 'Such a gentle thing you are...' They walked on. 'Now, what were we talking about? Ah, yes. Agesilaos. He fights his ambitions for fear of failure. But since he has come under the inspiration of Lysander, I have noticed much change in him.'

'Yes,' she agreed. 'Lysander was the right choice. Agesilaos is so much happier too. It's quite remarkable.'

'I will hear what Kleisthenes has to say at syssition...'

She stopped and turned a look on him. 'Husband, Knoethos is Paidonomos now, not Kleisthenes, lest you forget.'

He looked vague for a long moment, seeming to struggle with a difficult problem. *Knoethos*? He pondered. *Who by Zeus is Knoethos*? Then seeing a strange and unsettling look in Eupolia's eyes, he nodded his head. '*Yes* ... I meant to say Knoethos.'

She smiled gently at him, but there was a lingering worry in her eyes. Archidamos's behaviour had become stranger and even frightening, and his forgetfulness was getting worse.

Tellis feared the gods had sent phantoms to steal his mind. He had seen it before, with his own mother. She lost her mind little by little until she didn't even recognise her own children and saw murderers behind every door.

Ten nights ago, the King was found wandering about the palace naked, shouting at the shadows, hissing at the palace guards. The terrified commander of the watch, sent for Tellis and Tellis sent for the Queen and the physician.

The phantoms of madness had left their physical mark on Archidamos. He had developed a weakness in his left arm and his left eye was slightly closed, and he had a limp ever since that night.

Tellis ordered the guards to say nothing of what they had seen to anybody, warning them it would be treason to do so, and he would personally throw them into the *Apothetae** if he discovered anyone discussing what they had witnessed. The King was sleepwalking, he told them, the gods were speaking to him, as the gods often speak to their High Priests, Tellis told them.

That was when Eupolia and Tellis managed to persuade Archidamos to send Agis to conclude the siege at Plataea for his education in the arts of command, with Geront Ramphias, one of Sparta's most capable generals and two ephors to advise the prince.

'Kyniska,' Archidamos said from out of nowhere.

'What about her?'

'*What*?' He frowned at Eupolia.

'You said Kyniska, Husband.'

'Did I?' He thought for a moment. 'My little Kyniska...' He smiled. 'Rarely has there been such a headstrong girl as Kyniska,' he said.

Archidamos doted on her; he could not dote on his sons, who, in all aspects had to be princely warriors and leaders of men. Such sons are crafted not through the indulgences of a doting father, but through austerity, severity, discipline and the wisdom of the old ways. What Lykurgos called "*manly accord*". A king's son can be no less than any other Spartiate's sons, indeed, he has to be far more, even the younger brother, for a throne is never further than a brother or father away. But Archidamos loved Agis and Agesilaos no less than his overly indulged daughter and her headstrong ideas. And she sang such beautiful poetry to him, some of it her own compositions.

Eupolia had given Archidamos sharp words before about indulging their wilful and vivacious daughter, with her insatiable appetite for adventure. She was fourteen, and already noted for her skill as a rider and charioteer, indeed, at last year's Hyakinthia, Kyniska stood on the backs of two horses following behind the floral *kannathra** along the Hyakinthian Way, something only boys of the Rearing tend to do in order to impress their friends and families, leaping and somersaulting from horse to horse like monkeys. Eupolia did not go that far, but she certainly drew attention from horrified foreigners. A number of them expressed their disapproval to the magistrates of the *Biduoi*, for allowing girls to behave like boys and being permitted such liberty and freewill as to utterly horrify them.

They went down the steps to the lower terrace, passing between two bronze statues of the Dioskouri, Castor and Pollux mounted on magnificent horses that stood either side of the steps like sentinels.

Suddenly, halfway down the steps, Archidamos stopped dead in his tracks – he looked at Eupolia, the colour draining from his face. Something in his eyes frightened her–

'I feel unwell, Eupolia. A chill.'

'Let's go in.'

Tellis came to the top of the steps–

The left side of Archidamos's face dropped giving him a terrible grimace – Eupolia gasped in horror.

Tellis, looking alarmed and hurried down the steps.

'*Archidamos*!' Eupolia cried as her beloved husband collapsed to the ground in a heap–

'*My Lord*!' Tellis called.

'*Archidamos*!'

Eupolia and Tellis dropped to their knees beside him gasping and calling his name, but Archidamos was not responding – Archidamos, Eurypontid King of Sparta was dead...

Place of Rejection/execution. The lame Spartan babies rejected by the elders were thrown into this chasm (ambiguous) as well as criminals.

A wagon or cart decorated with flowers, often in the shapes of animals, and mythological creatures. The floral sculptures and displays were created by the women and pre-Rearing children of Sparta, for the three-day festival Hyakinthia (Lat. Hyacinthia) in homage of the lovers Apollo and Hyakinthos.

THIRTY-NINE

Archias, Sthenelaedas and Autokrates had been joined by Khilon, Alkidas and Mindaros. Khilon was habitually adjusting his himation, doing most of the talking, while the others listened, expressing their agreements to what he was saying with nods and murmurs as they discussed the King's health.

'... There's only one man who knows the truth of this,' said Khilon. 'And that's Tellis.'

Archias looked over at Argileonis. She knew, he thought, she was at the palace every day, but he knew she'd never speak of it to anyone, and she would report back to her husband if she had heard the rumour about Archidamos's health.

'Let's suppose you're right, Khilon and the King has gone mad, what do you propose we do about it? If the Delians hear of this, they'll take maximum advantage of it. They may even sway some of our allies into neutrality. After all, who would follow a mad king?' He shook his head. 'If it's true, and I do not think it is, there's nothing we can do about it, not without causing greater harm to ourselves from our allies and or enemies.'

'We should at least put questions to Tellis and the ephors,' said Sthenelaedas.

'I agree,' said Khilon. 'If it's true, Tellis now had more power. He could influence the king and the ephors for his own ends.'

'How many people have you talked to about this, Khilon?' asked Archias.

'Just Alkidas, Mindaros, Autokrates and you.'

'What about Eupolos and Teutamos who you were speaking to earlier?' asked Sthenelaedas. 'Did you not tell them?'

'We were talking about the siege at Plataea.'

'And Dorian?'

'Dorian knows nothing.'

Archias nodded his head. 'Then I suggest you speak to nobody else. I will call on Tellis this evening before syssition.'

Khilon and the others agreed. 'What about Argileonis?' said Sthenelaedas, looking over at her, still sitting with Kleisthenes. 'She's a friend of the Queen's, and Tellis is her husband. She must know something?'

'*Huh*. I think you'd sooner wrestle a bear than fall fowl of her quick tongue,' said Khilon. 'If she knows anything, she'll never say.'

Alkidas looked off to the track. The youths were now resting, sitting on the side of the running track, drinking water and chatting among themselves. Every now and then, they raised their rasping voices with cackling laughter as they teased one another. He looked at Argileonis and she was looking right back at him. Alkidas gave her a polite smile and a slight nod of his head...

Argileonis glared at him for an uncomfortably long time, then she looked back at Kleisthenes. 'Why would Alkidas and Mindaros be keeping company with such men? Archias I can understand, he's as much a worm as Khilon is a snake. But the others...?'

Kleisthenes glanced over at Khilon, Archias and the others deep in conversation, huddled close like conspirators weaving a plot, which, in a way, they were.

Geront Dorian approached with Libys and his two friends. 'Good day, Argileonis. Good day, Kleisthenes.'

'Good day, Dorian.'

Kleisthenes looked severely at the three young men. Libys, Pantares and to you Mnesos.

'So, young men,' Argileonis began, looking at three youngsters. 'Are you ready to meet our hated enemy?'

'We are, My Lady.'

'I only fear my sword will be too short in battle,' said Pantares.

'Step forwards, you'll find it long enough,' came Argileonis's sharp retort.

Pantares's cheeks flushed.

'And when do you come to your warlike state, gentlemen?' Argileonis asked.

'Pantares and I are marching to Plataea tomorrow, Good Lady,' said Mnesos, 'with Syntagmatarkhis Mindaros, to join Prince Agis's army.'

'And you, young, Libys?'

'I'm to join Syntagmatarkhis Brasidas. We sail in three days.'

Argileonis nodded her head, her thoughts momentarily turning to her famous son, of whom she was immensely proud, though she would never confess it. Argileonis was the very epitome of a Spartan woman, stoic, austere, frugal.

Suddenly, there was a commotion in the agora. Ephor Exarchos was shouting something as he hurried towards the Platanistas. '... HEAR ME! KING ARCHIDAMOS IS DEAD! THE KING IS DEAD!' Exarchos loped into the Platanistas. 'KING ARCHIDAMOS IS DEAD! THE KING IS DEAD!'

'Gods below...!' Dorian gasped.

Argileonis rose to her feet and clasped her chest, her heart was pounding with the shock of it, her first thought was to go at once to the palace – to the Queen, and then she saw Agesilaos on the running track, walking towards them with a dazed look on his face.

Everything stopped, everybody turned horrified and shocked.

'HEAR ME! KING ARCHIDAMOS IS DEAD! THE KING IS DEAD!'

Argileonis went to Agesilaos.

'... KING ARCHIDAMOS IS DEAD! THE KING IS DEAD!'

She loped to the stunned prince, who was clearly struggling not to cry, his eyes welled with tears. His friends followed close behind him, just as shocked as everybody else. Argileonis put her arm over his shoulder. 'Come, child. We must go at once to the palace.'

Kleisthenes signalled to the gymnasiarch that they were taking Agesilaos with them.

'My papa is dead...' Agesilaos's voice cracked under the strain of his emotions as he fought them with all his being, to maintain dignity and strength. But as soon as he spoke, the tears fell from his eyes.

Argileonis pulled her cape over him like a bird protecting her chick under its wing, so nobody could see his tears...

His father, Archidamos, Eurypontid King of the Lakedaimonians was dead and it broke his heart. '*Lysander*,' he muttered. He needed Lysander, his comfort, his strength, his wisdom.

Archidamos's death could not have happened at a worse time. Sparta was in crisis...

Heralds rode out across Lakedaimon, Kynouria and Messene, as well as to every ally, informing them that King Archidamos of the Eurypontids, hero of Sparta, the anointed High Priest of Zeus, was dead. A special envoy was dispatched to Delphi to inform the four Spartan pythioi, and to seek Apollo's wisdom.

Across the land, the women came out from their houses and pounded on bronze cauldrons, while their daughters whaled and wept in endless mourning from every village in the kingdom, from the tip of Lakedaimon at the sea's edge, to the Arkadian mountains, the air was filled with the sounds of crying and peeling bronze cauldrons.

'For forty-two years the great king had reigned,' said Tellis, addressing the Gerousia. 'A wise and noble king, even his worse enemies would say as much of him,' he added to their agreement. 'His death marks the end of an era...' Tellis turned to the young King Agis, seated on his father's throne, now claimed as his own. 'Rarely is a Spartan king so loved as was your father Archidamos the Second of that name, and rarely will a king be more remembered.'

Agis nodded his head. 'You were his true friend, Geront Tellis.'

Tellis was already thinking that Agis could not rule Lakedaimon alone, Pausanias could never be king while his father lived – Pleistoanax had to be recalled, but that would be no easy matter and it required some lateral thinking and he had already come up with the solution, the King not three days dead.

PART THREE

Sphacteria

FORTY

Archidamos's body was laid upon the long blood altar of Artemis-Ortheia, where processions of mourners could file by, weeping and praying, dressed in black funereal robes.

After three days and nights, the body guarded by Dioskouri from the First Hundred, Archidamos's body was laid upon a bier decorated with shields and pulled by two chestnut horses. Behind the carriage, up on his horse, the new king, Agis the Second, beside him rode two close companions, one was Lysander, the other was Clearchus, all three liveried in full armour, polished to the highest shine. Then followed the gerontes on foot, and then the hippeis, followed by the Spartan army, then then came the foreign dignitaries and the official mourners, all Lakedaimonians, who struck their foreheads and sobbed aloud and declared Archidamos the finest and best king Sparta ever had. The funeral procession made its way along every street in the city and every street was lined with thousands of mourners. It was a long and solemn ceremony, the boys of the Rearing and the girls of the Sisterhood danced to slow solemn music played on deep drums and flutes.

There was genuine mourning, for Archidamos was a much-loved king. To Sparta, he was a hero and a sage. Helots, dwellers, xenos, they were all there to watch Archidamos on his final journey.

Eupolia, Kyniska and Agesilaos walked on one side of the bier, Tellis and Ramphias the other, in places of honour, as Archidamos himself had requested.

Tellis had his hand up on one of the shields along the side of the bier, it was Archidamos's shield, and Tellis was having trouble keeping his composure, he hadn't just lost a king, he had lost his closest friend.

Eupolia had great inner strength, every bit a queen, draped him black, a dignified expression on her face as they slow-stepped beside the bier along the Hyakinthian Way with her children. Kyniska was holding her brother's hand, both of them had tears in their eyes.

Lysander was summoned to Tellis's house. Tellis was not alone, Ramphias was there, and so was Polemarch Iatragoras, who commanded the Second Mora, the three men were seated close together in the sitting room, speaking quietly, seemingly in agreement about something or other.

'Lysander, my boy. Come in,' Tellis greeted, rising to his feet, smiling happily, as if his visit was unexpected. 'Come, join us...' Tellis looked at the servant. 'Bing a cup of wine for Lysander,' he said and the servant went off to his command.

Lysander had an unsettled feeling in his guts as he greeted Ramphias and Iatragoras. Something was going on.

Tellis wasted no time getting to his point. 'We want you to go to Patrai,' he said. 'To Pheidon...' He picked up a ribbon strip of leather with letters written on it. 'Take this cypher to him. You will wear civilian robes and you can take only your sword with you for personal protection,' he added. 'You go now into the shadows, Lysander, as an agent of Sparta...'

The servant returned with a cup of wine and then Tellis dismissed him.

Lysander nodded his head. 'I understand,' he said, taking the cypher, furled into a coil.

'Pheidon will explain everything to you when you arrive,' Tellis explained. 'Our friend Quintius of Rome awaits you at Gytheion, to carry you to Patrai on his ship. When you arrive, seek out the House of the Lady Hippodameia, it's near the agora. Tell her I sent you and she'll take you to Pheidon.'

'As you command. When do I leave?'

'Immediately,' replied Tellis.

*****

Quintius almost didn't recognise Lysander when he came aboard the Minerva; it was the first time he had ever seen Lysander wearing civilian robes. They weren't just any robes; they were aristocratic robes no less. A fine white chiton, over which he wore a blue woollen cloak. Quality sandals on his feet. There was more a look of an uptight aristocrat than the deadly Spartan about him, he thought as he greeted Lysander warmly as an old friend. 'Dexius, cast off.'

Dexius relayed the order.

'I have something for you in my cabin,' said Quintius.

It was cramped in Quintius's cabin. It was also an example of just how much comfort can be squeezed into a relatively small space. Cushioned seats, a bunk and storage. The ceiling was low and they had to stoop their heads when standing up.

Quintius gestured to a comfortable seat. 'Wine? It's passum ... Brasidas's favourite...'

Lysander declined to sit and the wine. He heard Dexius shouting at the crew out on the deck; barking orders and insulting their mothers.

Quintius went to his bunk and pulled out a long wooden box from underneath and opened it. He reached in and took out a purse of money attached to a long leather thong, so it could be hung around the neck. 'You're a slaver from Argolis if anybody asks you. You get a lot of slavers at Patrai,' he added. 'They have the biggest slave auction this side of Delos there. I buy many of my slaves there, so if you have any problems, you tell them you're a friend of Quintius of Rome, most people know me.'

'I will.'

'You look after this,' he said as Lysander took the purse of money from him. 'They'll steal your balls for an obol in that city. They'd skin their own mothers for what's in that purse.'

'I'll bear it in mind,' said Lysander, feeling the weight of the purse. It was heavier than he expected it to be.

'You're to give it to Pheidon.'

Lysander nodded his head and hung the purse around his neck and concealed it under his chiton.

'It'll take us several days to get there, so make yourself comfortable...' He moved to the door and opened it. 'BOY!' he hollered. 'Boy will show you to where you sleep.'

A boy of about twelve came hurriedly from the deck.

'Show our guest to his cabin.'

'Yes, Dominus...'

Quintius went back out onto the deck.

FORTY-ONE

Patrai, Achaia

Within the city the streets seemed to glow in the lights of cressets set in walls and from the flaming torches of torchbearers escorting the good citizens and strangers safely about the city for an obol.

Lysander made his way along the dark smoky streets towards the agora. The taverns were all busy with evening revellers; beggars stood on corners, the blind, the lame and the destitute, begging for alms. Ragged street children darted about amongst the pedestrians, looking for opportunities to rob gullible strangers. Two such urchins were following Lysander, and Lysander, a wolf in civilian robes, knew it, and he didn't let them out of his sight, when they made their move, he would be ready.

The smells of cooking food reminded him how hungry he was. The last decent meal he had was before he left Lakedaimon, the food on Quintius's ship was the same fish soup day after day, with a loaf of unleavened bread, that got staler and staler as the days went on. He had been of the opinion that the ship's cook was incapable of cooking anything else.

Lysander stopped a man in the street. 'Excuse me, friend. I'm looking for the house of the Lady Hippodameia?'

'Lady, you say?' The man looked him up and down slowly with deliberation. 'Some might call her that. Others would not...' He chuckled amusedly to himself.

The two sharp-eyed boys loitered nearby, watching the stranger in his nice robes, and nice robes meant opportunity, and as he seemed to be alone, without even a servant, they thought he would be easy to rob.

'... Xeno, eh?' said the man. He had a short think and then he pointed to a street on the far side of the agora. 'Go to the end of that street, turn left. Then three streets further along, turn right. There you will find the House of the Lady Hippodameia,' he explained. 'You can't miss it, there are two wooden pricks five cubits tall* outside. 'If only, eh...?' he laughed again and hurried on, laughing as he went.

Lysander looked mystified. Was he mad?

The two grimy faced boys were getting ready to make their move, as Lysander walked on, they separated, one staying to Lysander's right, the other boy, who was younger and nimbler looking, crossed the street to pace Lysander's left, the boys never being out of eye contact with each other.

Lysander crossed the agora to the street the old man had directed him to.

The older boy came up to Lysander's side. 'I can show you to the house of Hippodameia, Lord,' he said in an effort to distract him, while the smaller boy moved in, ready to rob him.

'Be gone,' said Lysander.

'You can get lost easily in the city, Lord,' said the boy. 'The old man told you wrong. I can show you, Lord, for just an obol,' the boy went on.

Lysander ignored him, keeping half an eye on the little ferret to his left.

The older boy was annoyingly persistent. 'The streets are very dangerous in that neighbourhood, Lord. Make the wrong turn and you're like as not be murdered for your money and robes, Lord.'

'I can take good care of myself. Now go away, you bothersome fly, before we swat you.'

The younger boy took his opportunity and reached out and slip his hand under Lysander's cloak with a knife to cut his purse-strings–

Quick as a striking cobra, Lysander reached round and grabbed the artful boy by his bony wrist, to the boy's utter shock – his talkative friend leapt back, ready to run, but a mean faced man grabbed him by his throat. 'Where d'you think you're going, young'un?' Kromios growled. He looked at Lysander and grinned. 'What're you want me to do with this little shit?' he said. 'I can snap his neck if you like? It'll be easy, like snapping a twig – CRACK!' he barked, and both boys jerked with fright. 'And give him to the crows...'

Lysander took the knife from the young cutpurse's hand. 'And what was you going to do with that, eh?'

The citizens passed them by in both directions with indifference. The street children were a menace to society, like rats, they were everywhere.

The boy grabbed at Kromios's powerful hand, trying to pry it free from his throat, but the harder he tried, the tighter Kromios's grip became, cutting off his air, the boy was struggling to breathe, his face had turned mauve. He kicked and punched Kromios to no affect.

'Please don't kill my brother, Lord,' pleaded the younger boy whose wrist Lysander had hold of. Lysander released the boy. 'Let him go.'

Kromios gave out an ugly laugh in the boy's face. 'A god favours you today,' he said and released the boy.

The boy staggered back, gasping and choking, rubbing his neck, glaring at the big ugly man. His brother came to him and they hurried away.

'Local miscreants,' said Kromios. 'You have to have eyes up your arsehole here.'

'So, the Roman told me. Take me to Pheidon.'

'I spotted you in the port. We've been expecting you...' They started walking. 'One of our shadow men was murdered here not so long ago.'

'Doreios,' said Lysander. 'I heard. I confess, Kromios, you're the last person I expected to see here?'

'It's a long story, kid, and not that interesting. But it's good to see you.'

'Yes, for me also.'

Lively and noisy, the incomprehensible drivel of drunken voices roared from the open windows and doors of the taverns along with the songs of flutes and lyres.

Eventually, they came to the House of Hippodameia, which was the largest building in the neighbourhood, situated on a corner occupying two streets. It was three floors high, stone and wood and boasted a tavern, an inn, stables and brothel. Its portico was supported by two wooden columns fashioned into phalluses five cubits tall, just as the laughing man told him.

'That's some fuckhouse,' Lysander muttered.

Kromios nodded his head. 'Go on in. Just ask for the Lady Hippodameia,' he said.

Lysander frowned at him. 'Why, where are you going?'

'I have to be elsewhere; a scorpion needs treading on,' he said. 'Don't fret, Hippodameia will take care of you.'

Lysander crossed the street to the House of Hippodameia, and when the ganymedes and prostitutes saw him approaching, they mustered quickly like soldiers ready to do battle either side of the portico, girls on one side, ganymedes on the other, displaying themselves like meat.

|****7.5 feet 2.28 metres.***

FORTY-TWO

In the reception hall, there was a magnificent mosaic rendition of Priapos with an impressively large horn and a lustful grin on his face. The walls were frescoed with the seven winged Erotes: Anteros, who is requited love and was depicted with his brother Eros, who commands love, copulation and fertility. Then there was Hedylogos, the weaver of sweet words and flattery, who is the brother of another Erote, Pothos who fills the heart with yearning. Next was Hermaphroditos, who, as legend has it, encountered Salmakis, a nymph and temptress who was overcome by lust when she saw the beautiful youth Hermaphroditos by a river in the Forest of Caria. She tried to seduce him, but Hermaphroditos rejected her. Disappointed, she left the forest, or so Hermaphroditos thought, and thinking she had gone, he undressed and went into the river to bathe. But Salmakis was hiding in the forest, watching him, and when she saw him naked, her desired became an all-consuming fire, and no sooner was he in the water, when Salmakis appeared from the trees and she jumped into the water and wrapped herself around him, kissing and groping him. No matter how much he struggled, Salmakis would not let him go. She called upon the Olympian gods and asked that they should never be parted. The gods granted her wish and their bodies merged into one–

'Good day...'

Lysander looked across the entrance hall, where there sat a hard-faced old woman in a throne-like chair, flanked by two muscle bound bodyguards. She was adorned with gold and silver jewellery and wore gaudy green embroidered robes. Surely, this couldn't be the Lady Hippodameia? No, Lysander decided. No woman of Sparta would ever look so overdone as this woman did.

Before he had a chance to speak, the whore-mistress rose to her feet. 'Welcome to the House of Hippodameia...' She came towards him. 'I am Kythereia, mother of the house. Tell me your desires, and I will grant them ... for a small cost of two silver drachmas...' She looked him up and down, judging his wealth from his robes. 'Or perhaps you would prefer to dine with a hetaera, or a hetaeros, for thirty drachma you can be enchanted for the evening. A room for the night is thirty more...'

Lysander looked at naked youths and girls who were gathering either side of him like a guard of honour, youths to his left, girls to his right.

Lysander stared squarely at the woman, his expression as blank as a wall.

'... I have boys and girls who will make you sing with undreamed of joys,' she went on. 'Perhaps you'd like to have a closer look? Don't be shy. Have a little feel around if you like...' She stepped closer to him, the air around her was sickly with the smell of Egyptian perfume. 'Demigods, are they not?' she said softly looking at the youths.

'I'm here to see your mistress, the Lady Hippodameia,' said Lysander officiously.

The smile withered from the whore-mistress' face and she glanced at her bodyguards, who shifted menacingly towards them.

'What is your business with her?' said she.

'My business with her is not your business. Now take me to her.'

'I don't like your tone.'

One of the bodyguards shuffled closer, flexing his muscles.

Lysander flapped his cape back over his shoulder, revealing his sword. 'Have a care, slave. Come any closer and I'll tame you where you stand...'

The bodyguard stopped dead in his tracks, the whore-mistress' eyes glimmered with nervousness.

Hippodameia came out from a doorway. She gestured for the bodyguards and whore-mistress to step back. She knew he was.

Lysander looked coolly at her. 'You are the lady Hippodameia of Sparta?'

'Is that you, Lysander?' rasped a familiar voice and then Pheidon appeared. He gave Lysander a big happy smile and loped to him and embraced him. 'Welcome to Patrai. How is my beautiful Telephassa?'

'With child,' said Lysander. 'We pray for a son, but it'll be as the gods will it.'

Pheidon was delighted to hear it. 'Come. We'll drink to the child and the gravestones.'

The house was inhabited by a host of exquisitely beautiful hetaerae and hetaeroi and rich merchants and aristocrats, dispersed in various comfortably furnished rooms. There was music, and chatter and laughter, and youths wearing short white chitons hurried here and there with jugs of wine and trays of food.

The music was coming from one of the rooms, where several men were reclining on couches, imbibing cannabis fumes, watching and listening to a female voice singing verses of love:

Pheidon and Hippodameia led him through a back door to a flight of stairs and they ascended.

'These are the private quarters,' said Pheidon. 'We can talk up here.'

'I've had quarters made ready for you,' said Hippodameia.

'That's very kind of you, good lady,' said Lysander. 'I ran into Kromios outside. I was surprised to see him here, working in the shadows.'

'He was speared in the shoulder last year. He no longer has the strength in his left arm to carry his shield. A hoplite without a shield is of no use to a phalanx. He volunteered for the shadows and he's been with me since.'

They came into a large sitting room, lit by oil lamps. Pheidon's mothon servant came into the room.

'Kirphis, fetch some wine,' Pheidon ordered.

Kirphis went off to fetch the wine.

Lysander pulled the thong holding the purse of money from around his neck and handed them to Pheidon.

Pheidon threw the purse down onto a marble table. 'My orders?' he asked.

Lysander removed his sword...

Hippodameia and Pheidon watched him, as he peeled the thick leather strap of his baldrick apart, revealing they were two strips, carefully glued together with pitch Lysander had found aboard the Minerva. Sandwiched between the leather straps was the leather ribbon of letters making up the cypher. He removed it and handed the cypher to Pheidon.

'Clever boy,' said Pheidon as he took the cypher to a table and wrapped it around his scytale, so the letters were beside one another all the way along the scytale. Back in Sparta, there was another scytale in the ephorate that was exactly the same size and dimensions the leather ribbon was once coiled around, and then the message was written.

Hippodameia gestured to the seating. 'Be at home, Dioskouros Lysander.'

Lysander sat down and Kirphis returned with a jug of wine and three cups on a tray. He set them down and poured the wine...

'There's a Corinthian traitor in this city who's been selling us out to the Athenians. He also murdered Deion,' Hippodameia explained, while Pheidon read the message. 'Your friend Kromios has gone to kill him...'

The scorpion Kromios had gone to step on, thought Lysander.

Pheidon smiled. 'We're going to Delphi,' he said. Pheidon unwrapped the cypher from the scytale and gave the cypher to Kirphis. 'Burn it. Then get everything ready. We leave tomorrow.'

Kirphis, a man of few words, took the cypher and left the room.

The next morning, Kromios, Pheidon, Lysander and Kirphis took the flat deck ferry across the gulf to Khalkis with their horses, all dressed like civilians. Pheidon beckoned Lysander away from the others.

'Why are we going to Delphi, Pheidon?'

'Our mission is to corrupt the temple priests into delivering an oracle that favours Pleistoanax's return...' (Lysander balked at him). 'Agis is too young to command this war, Lysander. He lacks the experience and wisdom needed. Regent Pausanias is a cat without claws, the ephors command him in Pleistoanax's absence and they're opposed to Pleistoanax's return.'

'You do know that as a hippeus, I'm answerable to the ephors, Pheidon?'

'I also know you can see the reasoning in what I'm telling you. And I know you're loyal to my father and to Agis, that's why my father sent you here. The balance must be restored; Pleistoanax has to be recalled.'

'Then why hasn't he simply been recalled?'

'It's not as simple as that,' Pheidon replied. 'The Apella and the Gerousia are divided on the matter, so divided, a vote could go either way. So, our mission is to make certain the oracle favours Pleistoanax's return.'

FORTY-THREE
Delphi

Delphi is the city of God, not of mortals. Mortals merely inhabit it to the pleasure of the gods, keeping the holy city prosperous, maintaining the great temple and ornaments that adorn the steep slopes into the mountainside; and none may enter the sacred precincts unless they first purify themselves in the sacred waters of the Castalian Spring. The temples themselves are washed in the water of the spring to purify them.

The pythian season had begun and there were thousands of pilgrims in the city from every corner of the world, from princes to slave, all were welcome to Apollo's beautiful city, a gleaming jewel of marble, bronze and gold, unrivalled in all the world.

It was a hot and humid evening, and the lower city was busy with evening revellers, almost all of them pilgrims who had come from far and wide, seeking an oracle, or simply to pay homage to Apollo with small votives and their prayers.

Even at night, the sybils sat under stoas in lamplight, selling fortunes next to the money changers and street vendors selling small votive statuettes and talismans, and the ubiquitous beggars calling for alms, and the artful children from nearby villages taking full advantage of the rich pickings to be had, so it is in every city, even in God's sacred city, greed, vice, thievery and piety merge together in the visceral mass of people in ceaseless motion, pushing and shoving, moving in different directions, speaking in a myriad of languages; Persian, Hellenic, Etruscan, Latin, Phoenician, Aramaic and many more besides, disseminating incomprehensively around them as they pushed their way through the noisy crush of pilgrims, jostling about aimlessly.

'Wait here,' said Pheidon as he went into a seedy tavern.

Lysander and Kromios looked through the open door into a tavern where the noise of loud coarse voices and ugly laughter spilled out onto the street. Every wine-slopped table was crowded with rowdy revellers and the shrieking laughter of lowborn prostitutes. They watched Pheidon, who was speaking to the innkeeper, offering him money. The innkeeper took the money and nodded his head.

Pheidon beckoned to Lysander, Kromios and Kirphis to come in.

'Well, I've stayed in worse shitholes,' Kromios said lowly. 'Not many I grant you. But one or two.'

The stink of wine, bad breath and rancid sweat was almost overpowering as they entered the tavern. Lysander looked up into the smoke from the candles, floated like a sea mist across the ceiling and vented out onto the airless street like exhaled breath.

'There's a room upstairs we can have for a few days,' said Pheidon, and they followed a grubby girl through a doorway and up a flight of stairs.

It was basic, there was just one bed with a semen stained mattress and no other furnishings.

'A fuck room; how nice,' said Pheidon, making for the window overlooking the crowded street, the din of pilgrims was as constant as the din of drunks downstairs in the tavern and sex noises coming muffled from the rooms on either side. 'Kromios, go and find Phrynon and get the name of the priest from him.'

Kromios nodded his head and about turned and left.

'Phrynon's our shadow man here at Delphi,' Pheidon explained, looking at Lysander.

Lysander nodded his head. He had heard Tellis speak of him.

'Kirphis, go and organise some food and wine. Tell them to bring it up to us.'

Kirphis left to go to his master's command.

Pheidon moved away from the window and sat on the bed. ‘Once we know the name of the priest, we’ll set up a meeting.’

Lysander squatted on the window ledge. ‘Are you certain this is going to work? What if there is no corrupt priest?’

Pheidon chuckled. ‘You’ve got a lot to learn, Lysander. There are always corrupt priests; especially here, where their influence is greatest. Oracles have a lot of political power, Lysander, none more so than the Delphic oracle. So, relax, it’ll work,’ he said with utter conviction.

Lysander folded his arms and glanced out the window, down onto the street, watching the bobbing heads and shuffling bodies. He had never seen such crowds before.

Kirphis returned. ‘They’re bringing the food up,’ he said.

‘Good.’

‘Did the innkeeper ask you any questions?’ Lysander asked.

Kirphis shook his head. ‘He’s too busy to be curious.’

Lysander and Kirphis sat on the floor, there being nothing to sit on, and when Lysander saw the stained mattress, he resolved there and then not to sit or lay on it.

The food was as basic as the accommodation, tasteless and bland, like the food on the first day of the Hyakinthia, but they ate it without complaint. The wine was like watered down vinegar, but again, they drank it without complaint.

Kromios had been gone for over two hours before he returned.

‘Did you find Phrynon?’ Pheidon asked from the bed, where he was sitting back with his feet up on the bed with his feet crossed at the ancles.

Kromios nodded his head. ‘At the palaestra.’

‘Did he give you the priest’s name?’

‘The high priest himself,’ said Kromios. ‘Megadates…’ His eyes roved the room for a moment before they settled back on Pheidon. ‘But we might have a problem,’ he added.

Lysander, sitting on the floor with his back resting against the wall, raised a brow.

'What do you mean we might have a problem? What sort of problem?'

'It seems we're not the only Spartans seeking an audience with Megadates,' he said. 'Aristocles is here–'

'Aristocles?' Lysander echoed, frowning with surprise. 'As in King Pleistoanax's brother?'

Kromios nodded his head. 'The very same. He arrived here yesterday with four of Pleistoanax's men...'

'*What's he doing here*?' Pheidon mused aloud.

Lysander had never met Pleistoanax's brother Aristocles; he had been sent away to the Spartan colony Taranto in Italy after his brother's exile. The ephors at the time feared that Pleistoanax's allies might rally around Aristocles and use him as a figurehead to cause dissent and internal unrest, or even attempt to put him on the throne and declare him king. That sort of thing had happened before and it almost caused a civil war. The ephors were determined it wouldn't happen again.

'Phrynon says that the prince sent a messenger to Megadates at the temple this morning.'

For a long moment, nobody spoke and the noises from the street, tavern and sex noises from the rooms next door filled the void.

'He must be here for the same reason we are,' said Lysander, breaking the silence.

'It must be. There can be no other explanation for it,' Pheidon agreed. 'Pleistoanax knew he couldn't come back to Lakedaimon while Archidamos was alive,' he speculated reasonably. 'And his supporters and friends in Lakedaimon keep him well informed of everything that happens at Sparta, including what people think about his return...'

'Then, he'll know there's a lot of opposition to recalling him,' said Lysander.

Pheidon nodded his head. He laughed. 'The irony,' he said.

'What should we do? Do we still bribe the priest? Or let Aristocles do it for us?' asked Kromios.

'I say we let the prince do it,' suggested Lysander as he stood up. 'That way,' he added with cool calculation, 'if it goes wrong ... if the corruption is ever discovered, Aristocles can be blamed for it.'

Pheidon considered Lysander carefully for a long moment. 'I like the way you think...' He looked at Kromios. 'Where's Aristocles staying?'

'At the house of Melesippidas, near the palaestra.'

'I know the house.'

'Who's Melesippidas?' asked Lysander.

'He was a Phokian strategos during the last war, and a friend of Pleistoanax's.'

'Phrynon says to meet him in the Sacred Grove in two hours. He says he'll have more information by then.'

FORTY-FOUR

Pheidon and Lysander went alone to the sacred grove, dark and silent, except for the wind whispering to the olive trees as it swept along the mountainside. There was no sign of Phrynon, or anybody else for that matter, but it didn't mean he wasn't there; there were a hundred places for a man to hide; behind the trees, the rocks, in the long grass, a hill, a bush. Phrynon could be anywhere, but Pheidon was confident Phrynon already knew they were there, watching them, making certain nobody was following them.

'The bastard's hiding from us.'

Lysander thought he was there too, and his eyes slowly scanned left and right. There was a certain spot on the high ground, where mountain rock jutted from the hillside. It was a perfect vantage point, above the grove with clear views in every direction. If he was hiding, that's where he would be. 'He's up there,' he said confidently.

Pheidon followed his stare. He couldn't see anything but grey rock and a sheer cliff rising a hundred feet, but he didn't doubt Lysander. 'Stop playing games,' he called up.

For a long moment, nothing happened, but then someone appeared behind the screen of rocks and scrambled over them, a tall lean figure, he moved quickly down the hill and through the grove towards them. Phrynon gave them a thin mouthed grin as he approached. 'It's been a while, Pheidon...' He looked at the young man with him. 'And you must be Lysander?'

Lysander didn't answer him.

'This is an odd place to meet, Phrynon?'

'One learns to be cautious in Delphi. The place is crawling with shadow men.'

'Kromios said you'll have more information about Aristocles?'

Phrynon started walking deeper into the grove; Lysander and Pheidon went with him.

If shadow men came in types, then Phrynon was the reptilian type, sneaky by look as well as by nature; the sort of man you would, by your very instincts, never put your back to. He was a lithe figure with a long narrow face and pointed features, like the snake he was, but he was, so Pheidon had insisted, a loyal Spartan snake.

He was an aristocrat from an old Amyklaian family, his uncle Xiphilinus was a respected geront, highly respected for his integrity and honesty, unlike his lubricious nephew, who had a taste for intrigues and plots, especially against the Athenians, with whom he had been engaged in his own personal war since his father was killed in battle during the previous war with Athens twenty years ago, when his father was speared in the back by an Athenian hoplite.

When war broke out, it was the happiest day of Phrynon's life, and he was completely dedicated to the shadow war, where he could cause mischief, and corrupt Delians for useful information to pass back to Sparta.

'There's a certain hetaera I'm fond of,' Phrynon started up as the walked slowly through the darkness. 'It happens that this hetaera, is also Melesippidas's hetaera, and she happened to be staying at Melesippidas's house when Prince Aristocles arrived–'

'Does this story have an end?' Pheidon interrupted impatiently.

'I'm coming to it. It was she who informed me about the prince and the message he sent to Megadates. She was at Melesippos's house again this evening, and she learned that the prince is to beet Megadates tomorrow night two hours after midnight, at the temple.'

'Does she know why Aristocles his meeting the high priest?' asked Lysander.

Phrynon looked at him. 'No; but we can guess why.'

'Hmm. I have no faith in guesses,' said Lysander.

Phrynon raised a brow. He looked back at Pheidon. 'Once you're done here, you're to make your way to Plataea, where the King awaits you...' He opened a small leather pouch he wore under his cape and pulled out a leather cipher strip. 'It's a dispatch from the commanders of our new colony, Herakleia,' he explained.

Pheidon took it. 'Then our business is concluded.'

*

The holy city was as quiet and as still as a necropolis, uninhabited except for the bones thin foxes and wild dogs and cats scurrying about in the dark, scavenging for discarded food and hunting for mice and rats.

It was two hours after midnight and there wasn't so much as a slick of moonlight to guide the prince's way up the steep hill into the stygian darkness, draped in a dark hooded cape, rendering him invisible to all but the keenest eyes.

The prince hurried towards God's holy house; as furtive as a fox, his watchful eyes constantly surveying the night. But he saw nothing but the dark outlines of the statues, treasuries and sanctuaries pressed into the dark, and yet, he had the strangest feeling that he was being observed by unseen eyes.

He had come alone, as Megadates instructed. Megadates also told him to bring the money with him.

Aristocles spotted the priest, silhouetted on the temple steps, the temple looming above him.

Megadates started down the steps to intercept the dark clad prince on the concourse. 'Not here,' he said, fearing Apollo might witness his corruption and curse him for it.

Aristocles followed him under the shadow of the Polygonal Wall below the temple, under the columned marble porch of the Athenian Stoa. 'Do you have the money?' asked the priest.

Aristocles patted his robes, looked out over the sleeping city. 'I have it here. Is it arranged as we agreed?'

'Everything is arranged. I have only to give a nod of my head, and all will be done.'

Aristocles scanned the night again, shifting his weight. He looked at the high priest again. 'Apollo will tell the Spartans to return my brother to his rightful throne?'

The priest gave him a look. 'It's arranged,' Megadates repeated. 'Beyond that, it is for the Spartans to decide.' Megadates put out his greedy hand.

Aristocles, satisfied, nodded his head and reached under his robes and pulled out a heavy leather purse of coins.

Megadates took the money and felt its weight in his hand, a very satisfactory weight indeed, he thought as he sorted it away under his priestly white robes.

'When?' asked Aristocles.

'Soon. The oracle will be delivered the usual way to the Spartan envoy,' Megadates said and then he walked away briskly under Aristocles's watchful stare.

The Agiad prince hurried back down the Sacred Way without looking back, there was nothing more to be done now, but wait. He would return to Arkadia, where Pleistoanax was in exile, and inform him that the deed was done.

Had Aristocles looked back, he might have seen Pheidon stepping out onto the road from behind the ornate treasury of the Corinthians, from where he watched Aristocles vanish into the night.

Lysander came out from his hiding place on the other side of the Sacred Way, where he had been hiding behind the statue of his muscle-bound ancestor Herakles doing battle with the Nemean Lion. He joined Pheidon on the Sacred Way.

'Shall I follow the prince?' asked Kromios as he stepped out from the shadows.

'No. Wait here,' said Pheidon. 'Lysander, come with me.'

Megadates was glad to be home. After his servant lit a couple of lamps with a taper Megadates told him to go to bed.

Once the servant had gone, Megadates opened the purse Aristocles had given him and looked inside and the vision of the gold coins within brought a beaming smile to his face.

He took the coins into his bedchamber, where the lamps were already lit and retrieved a dagger from under the pillow of his bed, and then he got down on his hands and knees and slipped the blade of the knife between two flagstones on the floor and prized one of them up.

It made a grating noise as he pulled the flagstone away, and revealed a cavity in the ground beneath, in which there was a large oak strongbox with a mesh of iron reinforcing bands around it.

Megadates heaved the box out of the cavity and opened the lid, revealing a small fortune in bronze, silver and gold coins within. The accumulation of years of bribes. His greedy eyes glimmered in the twinkling reflection of gold. He placed the purse in the box and closed the lid and lifted the box back into its hiding place before he slid the flagstone back into place.

Corruption paid very good rewards, but the best rewards were the political bribes, which paid the most and this bribe from the exiled Spartan king was exceptional. He named his price to the prince and it was agreed without quibble. Yes, today was a very profitable day indeed, he thought as he rose up to his feet–

'They take a very stern view of those who corrupt the temple priests...'

Megadates spun round on his heels, a look of utter horror on his face as he looked at the grinning man standing in the doorway. His dagger fell from his shaking hand and it clattered to the floor. '*Who are you*!? *How did you get in here*!?' He took a couple of steps back towards his bed...

Pheidon stepped towards him and Lysander followed him in, his green eyes fixed on the High Priest, who sensed something scarily preternatural in the wordless younger man.

'A hefty fine,' Pheidon continued. 'Of course,' he went on calmly, 'for the corrupt priest it's much worse; death by stoning...' Pheidon's smile broadened, his dark eyes fixed on the terrified priest. 'What did he ask of you?'

The priest shook his head, fear burned in his eyes, which flitted between Pheidon and Lysander. 'You must go, you're defiling Apollo by being here...'

Pheidon laughed. 'Call for the temple guards then. And while they're here, I'll point out your chest of bribe money under the floor. Or you can tell me what Prince Aristocles asked you for, and we'll be gone and nobody will be the wiser for it. Of course, there's the third option, which is that I torture it out of you before my young friend eviscerates you. I care not how; but tell us you will, priest.'

The priest saw the fey look in Pheidon's eyes and was swept by terror when Lysander reached under his cape a drew his sword. He stared in trembling fear at the razor-sharp blade. 'He wants an oracle that favours the return of Pleistoanax to the Spartan throne.'

Pheidon's eyes softened in the crepuscule glimmer of the oil lamps. 'There, that wasn't so hard, was it. Give him his oracle, and make it a good one,' he said. 'And have a care you do not disappoint me, priest, or I'll be back and next time, I'll not be so friendly.' Pheidon turned and looked at Lysander, and they left, leaving the terrified priest standing guilelessly in the middle of the room shaking from head to foot.

FORTY-FIVE
Sparta

'Read it again?' Eponymous ephor Sostratidas ordered the messenger.

The messenger looked down at the scroll and read it for the second time: 'Know you better than the fool. In your darkest hours you leave an empty chair beside thee, and calamity shall follow calamity lest Herakles returns–'

'It would be a dangerous move to recall Pleistoanax,' said Autokrates.

'If he can be corrupted once, who's to say he cannot be corrupted twice?' said another Geront.

'It would be unwise to ignore the words of Apollo,' another enjoined.

'Pleistoanax was young when he took Pericles's bribe. The years have matured him.'

'This war is the most serious crisis ever to face us since the Mede,' said Tellis. 'Agis is too young to rule alone, and so is Pausanias, of that none of us are in doubt. Is this really the time to leave Pleistoanax in the wilderness? He has petitioned us many times since the war started to allow him to return, with a promise to pay the fine by instalments over ten years. Our beloved Archidamos is dead, and we quarrel like children among ourselves. Now Apollo himself calls us fools for allowing our pride to stand in the way of sound military sense. We must recall him from exile. We need him.'

'I say leave him out there,' said another Geront.

'We have nothing to lose in bringing him back.'

'He is still king.'

For the next three hours, the old men debated, their opinions divided, but the arguments in favour of Pleistoanax's returned eventually outweighed the arguments against it. But it was the oracle, an oracle Tellis knew came through corruption, that won the vote in favour of bringing Pleistoanax home.

*

The house echoed with Telephassa screams. The agony of it was beyond comparison. She had been in labour for fifteen hours and she was exhausted, her face soaked with sweat and twisted with pain. She panted rapidly as her grandmother had taught her to, and when the contractions came, she pushed with all her strength.

Argileonis was there, tightly holding her hand, comforting her, encouraging her.

The midwife was looking between Telephassa's legs, she could see the crown of the baby's head. 'The child is coming,' she said. 'Not long now.'

Rhea bathed Telephassa's sweat slicked forehead with a cool damp cloth.

Another contraction came and Telephassa sat up and screamed as she pushed.

'Yes!' declared the midwife, holding the baby's head, that was completely out. 'One more push,' she said.

'I can't! I can't!'

'Yes you can,' said Argileonis, stoking her head. 'You have to. It's almost over...'

Telephassa looked at her. She was so tired, so utterly exhausted. Her grandmother smiled reassuringly. 'Just one more push...'

'You must hurry,' said the midwife.

Telephassa's face screwed twisted and contorted with the pure agony – she took a deep breath and pushed again...

The midwife's face was one of delight. The child was born. She bit into the umbilical and clamped it off, then lifted the baby and almost immediately the baby cried...

Telephassa fell back, smiling, relieved, looking at her child cradled in the midwife's arm.

'A daughter,' said the midwife. 'A strong daughter.'

Telephassa looked warily at her grandmother.

Argileonis smiled. 'From strong daughters come strong sons,' she said.

All the same, Telephassa sensed her disappointment. She thought about Lysander, who had told her that he would love a daughter equally as he would a son.

The midwife brought the child to her mother.

Rhea looked at the babe and beamed with such happiness. There will be children in the house. She helped her mistress to sit up as the midwife handed the child to Telephassa.

Argileonis had tears in her eyes. So, it was a daughter instead of a son, but it was still momentous – her first great grandchild and she was still alive to see. Tellis would be happy too, he had always loved Telephassa dearly, he would love her child just as dearly. A son will come – next time perhaps; it was the will of the gods. 'She's beautiful,' she said uncharacteristically.

Telephassa held the child close, wrapped in swaddling cloth, she smiled as only a mother can at her beautiful healthy daughter. If only Lysander was there, she thought.

FORTY-SIX

Ionian Sea, West of Kythera

The Minerva's sails were raised and she sat in the water, forty miles off the coast of Kythera – waiting. This was the third day and Quintius didn't feel at all comfortable. If the Athenians should happen by, and if they should discover his passengers...? Well, he dared not think of what would happen. Then there was the other problem, the bloody Spartans, fickle and unpredictable. If they come, it might be to arrest or even kill those very passengers, and him and his crew along with them. Why in the name of Sacred Vesta, did he ever let Pheidon talk him into this.

Dexius was thinking along similar lines as he paced about the aft quarterdeck like a caged animal. The crew were restless too, from the idleness. Only the promise of extra silver settled their complaining.

It was quiet aboard, every voice subdued. The ship creaked as she rocked gently in the water.

They had picked the exiles up at Patrai, where they boarded incognito.

There was an enormous Egyptian grain ship, the Ma'at two stades off the starboard beam. In her hold were near seven hundred men instead of grain, there were sixty more aboard the Minerva.

'SAILS!' cried a sailor.

'My Lord...' Philocles was pointing to three sails on the horizon. 'Spartans, My Lord.'

'About fucking time,' Quintius sighed.

The cool sea wind blew through Pleistoanax's long braided hair and robes as he stood amidships with several of his officers. He looked at one of his servants. 'Fetch my armour and cloak. I do not wish to be improperly dressed when they get here.'

'Yes, My Kyrios.' The servant hurried along the deck to the King's cabin.

He hid his uncertainty well. They all knew that this was going to go one of three ways. They were either going to welcome him back as their king. Turn them away ... or kill them. Pleistoanax stroked his earlobe thoughtfully with his thumb as he watched the war triremes rowing towards them, growing bigger the nearer they got. He could see hoplites lined up along the decks of the ships, wearing their armour, clasping their spears and shields – no, they're not hoplites, he thought as he took a closer look at the black plumes of their helmets. *Hippeis*! He looked at the others. 'Get to your warlike state, gentlemen. Remember, you're Spartans, now look like Spartans.'

The officers walked away to change out of their civilian robes into their hoplite armour.

The servant returned with two other servants, carrying Pleistoanax's armour, cloak, helmet with its transvers crest, spear, sword and shield, greaves and wrist cuffs. They started to undress the King, removing his fine and colourful robes and clad him in his polished bronze cuirass, war kilt and his crimson war cloak.

He took his sword and looped the baldrick strap over his head and hung the sword under his left arm at his side. He took his helmet and held it under his arm.

The triremes were sailing in a line towards them, less than a minute away and His Majesty stood with his loyal officers and fellow exiles, in their warlike state, their helmets tilted back on their heads so their faces were exposed, spears erect, shields at their sides at the prescribed height, the inner dishes resting on their shoulders, all watching the war triremes approaching in muted silence.

Quintius and Dexius exchanged looks.

Pleistoanax saw a man standing on the prow on the middle ship, flanked by two Dioskouri, their cloaks puffing out in the wind. They were too far away for Pleistoanax to make out who the grey-haired old man standing on the prow was.

The three triremes broke formation, One turned to port and another turned starboard, both ships taking up positions, coming about, prows on the Minerva's amidships.

'Fuck me! They're going to ram us!' Dexius exclaimed.

'Calm yourself,' said Pleistoanax unflustered. 'They're going to do no such thing. That would be very ill mannered,' he added dryly, watching the third ship approaching. 'Tellis,' he murmured, recognising the grey-haired old man standing on the prow.

The third ship drew in her oars and came up alongside the Minerva.

Tellis and Pleistoanax looked at one another. Pleistoanax's officers looked wary and anxious, there were thirty hippeis aboard the ship, standing at attention along the side of the outrigger.

The exiles had been out in the cold for near twenty years and none of them knew what sort of reception they were going to get.

Tellis came aboard the Minerva and stood face to face with Pleistoanax. 'My Lord, the Gerousia has voted. I am sent to escort you to Sparta to resume your place as Agiad King of Lakedaimon.'

There was a collected sigh of relief among the exiles.

'Then I will ask a service of you, Geront Tellis.'

'Name it, My Lord, I am at your command.'

'I should like to sail back with you aboard your ship?'

'My Lord honours us to do so.'

Pleistoanax turned to his body servant. 'Bring that wine I've been saving...' He gave Tellis a smile. 'We'll drink to the gravestones.'

'And to your return, My Lord.'

Pleistoanax smiled. Finally, he was home, where he belonged, and there was a war to fight. A chance to redeem himself...

FORTY-SEVEN
Boeotia
Herasios/October

This was the sixth day Lysander had been patrolling in the densely forested foothills, a lone wolf hunting for Delian infiltrators who had been coming over the mountains, using the ancient shepherd trails in order to spy on the Peloponnesians at Plataea. Just what they hoped to achieve was negligible, the pass was in Theban hands now, and they had a large presence there. They had built temporary fortifications and garrisoned them on the Boeotian side of the pass.

He travelled light, without armour or his helmet, carrying only his shield and spear, his crimson cloak draped diagonally down his body over his tunic, his sword hung under his left arm from a baldric strap over his right shoulder.

It was cold, especially at night, but he lit no fires, lest he alert his prey.

Lysander encountered a party of Thebans a four days ago, who had captives with them, three prisoners, each one a Theban, tied together and under guard, bearing cuts and bruises from a beating, they had staggered heavy footed through the forest. They were deserters, according to the *phylarch** in command. They were looking for a suitable place to hang them as a warning to others. All he had seen since then was a wolf with her cubs drinking at a stream. He watched them from the rocks above them. The wolf was a sacred creature to Lysander. His father and mother told him that when he was born, he was watched over by a wolf who sang its howling laments. That wolf, his father told him was Apollo. Brasidas called him Little Wolf, and Tellis too called him a wolf of Sparta. Thus, the wolf played a significant role in Lysander's life.

The Shewolf knew he was there, but she seemed to know Lysander would bring no harm to her or her playful cubs.

It was late afternoon and the low autumnal sunshine sloped through the forest canopy in dappled rays that glimmered and danced across the forest floor and Lysander's face as he picked his way along the ancient track. He stopped suddenly and stared ahead. There was a pungent smell in the air; the unmistakable smell of death and it made him more cautious. He lowered his spear and advanced soundlessly. The stench grew stronger, and he could hear a distant droning.

A pigeon cooed nearby to his left – he moved his shield into a covering position in front of himself, his spear shaft resting on the rim as he continued on – the stalking wolf of Sparta, light-footed over the dry autumn leaves that had shed from the trees. He could taste the vile stench of carrion in the back of his throat, sickly and pungent.

Then, where the track intersected with another track, he saw them, the same Theban prisoners he had seen four days ago, hanging by their necks from the single bough of an ancient tree, one beside the other swinging gently in the breeze from creaking ropes, crook necked, their bodies stinking, their flesh grey and pecked by birds and swarmed with flies and insects.

He felt easy again and brough his spear up and placed the dished inner of his shield over his shoulder to take the weight and moved on, fleet footed, turning onto the second path, leading up into the mountains, towards the rocky peaks...

*

'We're wasting our time,' said Pantares as the trudged up the steep hill, deeper into the forest.

'Tell that to Simo and see what happens,' replied Koinos. He was much older than Pantares, thirty-five with years of experience. The kid was fresh out of the Rearing and already he thought he was an all-knowing veteran.

'Well, it's a waste of time,' Pantares complained. 'It's like being back at the Rearing. Doing pointless things to no consequence but our own misery,' he went on indolently.

'*Huh*. You young'uns just don't have the stamina,' said Koinos.

'Not even the Athenians are foolish enough to cross over here, where they know only death awaits them...' They stopped at a clearing just off the track. 'No, they would cross further down or further up, where the Thebans and Corinthians are. Besides, I heard there are Dioskouri over on the other side in Attica,' Pantares continued.

Koinos set his shield and spear down, resting them against a fallen tree. 'Who told you that nonsense?'

'I heard the enomotarch* talking to Simo about it. The King ordered them up here.'

Koinos heaved himself up onto the fallen tree and sat on the trunk. 'Them Dioskouri are like ghosts,' he said as he lifted his leg and scratched his shin. 'They learn their skills in the *krypteia*. You don't know they're there until they're slitting your throat.'

Pantares jumped up onto the tree trunk and scanned the darkness, the amorphous shapes of the undergrowth and trees pressed into the night.

'We'll stay here the night,' Koinos said, 'and head back to camp in the morning.'

Pantares nodded his head, standing on the tree trunk at the far end, where the roots splayed out like twisted and gnarled fingers grasping at the night. He pulled his tunic up and made water, aiming high to see how far his stream of piss could reach. 'It's been ten days since anybody reported any Athenian activity near our lines,' he said. 'No...' He shook his head like some wise old warlord, 'they'll cross further down through the Corinthian line. You could march an army passed them Corinthians and they wouldn't notice ... Useless bastards they are...'

'Not as useless as you, hoplite!' Lysander rose up out of the ferns not a stride away from the tree-trunk, startling the both of them out of their wits.

'*Pan's prick*!'

'They can hear you all the way to Athens...'

'*Dioskouros Lysander*!' Pantares exclaimed.

'Who were you expecting? Apollo?' Lysander moved out from the bushes.

Pantares and Koinos both jumped down from the tree-trunk.

Lysander recognised Pantares; he was one of Libys's friends, and he was pleasing to the eye, he thought, affording himself a little pleasure.

'What are you doing here?'

'Phylarch Lamachos ordered us to patrol the forest,' said Koinos. 'There have been reports of Delians.'

Lysander looked at Pantares again and then he walked away, heading up the track towards the peaks. 'Don't just stand there like a couple of cock swingers. Come with me.'

Koinos and Pantares looked glumly at one another, then they hurried on after him.

'May I ask where we're going, Dioskouros?' asked Pantares.

'To see if there are any Athenians camped on the Attican side.'

Koinos and Pantares exchanged another look with one another in bewilderment.

Pantares tripped on a root knuckled out of the ground across the track and lurched forwards stumbling. He knocked into Lysander as he steadied himself.

'*Watch where you're going*!' Lysander gave him a withering stare.

'Apologies, Dioskouros. I tripped.'

Lysander stared at him a moment longer, and then, without another word, he looked forwards and they continued on, picking their way up the mountainside in the near pitch darkness.

'You fool,' Koinos whispered to the clumsy youngster.

They came to a narrow cleft in the mountain, it was so narrow there was barely space for a man to pass through.

Lysander stopped and turned to them. 'We can cross over here,' he said quietly. 'If there are any Athenians over there, we'll take them quietly and by surprise...' He looked at Pantares. 'Try not to trip over yourself, and if you do, better kill yourself, because if you give us away, I'll kill you myself,' he warned sternly. Of course, he didn't mean it, but the naïve young Pantares clearly believed every word. 'We'll leave of shields here,' he said. We go light, we go swift, and above all, we go in silence...' He looked at Pantares and Koinos in turn. Koinos nodded his head, his experience had taught him well enough. But Pantares worried him. He had never killed a man before and that might make him hesitate, and hesitation is usually a fatal condition in situations like this.

They removed their armour and hid them behind some bushes. Stripped to their tunics and armed only with their swords, they followed Lysander into the narrow crevice.

It was so dark in the crevice; they couldn't see their own hands in front of their faces. They sidled through, the ground beneath them uneven and strewn with loose rubble.

Finally, on the other side, they searched through the forest for about an hour, before they spotted the glimmering light of a fire, and smelled the smoke in the air. They crept in for a closer look, crawling through the undergrowth on their bellies, concealed by the impenetrable night.

Athenians! Lysander counted five in the camp and three guards at the perimeter, armed with spears and swords. A patrol, he thought. Not infiltrators, not even Athenian shadow men were that stupid as to light campfires. The Athenians were so certain no Peloponnesians would be lurking around on this side of the mountain, they had fallen into complacency. Even the sentries at the perimeter weren't keeping their wits sharp.

They were so complacent, one of the sentries even called back to the camp: 'Save some of that mutton for us!' he said.

'Yeah, yeah. We'll save you a bone,' one of them laughed back.

Lysander and Koinos looked at one another.

'Easy prey,' Koinos whispered.

'You take the one on the left,' said Lysander to Koinos. He looked at Pantares. 'You take the hungry one. I'll take the one on the right.'

Pantares and Koinos both nodded their heads, and then, they crawled off in different directions.

The Athenian was watching out into the forest, the still silence undisturbed except for the low chatter of the men in the camp, the occasional bark of foxes and wind kissing the lush green fronds.

The men in the camp suddenly broke into laughter at something funny one of them said. The sentry looked round quizzically, smiling and he had no idea why. The distraction was his doom–

Like a dark spirit rising from the earth, Lysander slowly rose up onto his feet behind the sentry, barely a foot away from him, the leaf blade of his sword extended from his fist, and like a striking cobra, he grabbed the sentry from behind, clasping his hand to his mouth before he had a chance to cry out ... a jerk of his right arm and the sentry stiffened like a log of wood as the cold bite of iron thrust upwards into his body under his ribcage; he dropped his spear and it landed in the bushes, too quietly for the others to hear over their constant drivel and laughter. – The sentry went limp and Lysander had all his weight. He lowered him carefully, pulling his sword out, he picked up the sentry's spear and took his place as he watched Koinos and Pantares kill the remaining two sentries, clasping their hands to their mouths, they both slip the sentries' throats.

Lysander signalled them to attack–

Before the five Athenians realised what was going on, the three Spartans, lurched out of the darkness like earthbound phantoms from different directions, wielding the spears of their dead companions, attacking at once, running in towards the shocked Athenians, spears raised to throw, their pointed tips glinting.

The Athenians scrambled to their feet – too late, the Spartans deployed their spears with deadly accuracy, impaling three of the Athenians before they were barely on their feet. All three fell dead, one smashed into the fie sending a column of bright orange sparks up into the air.

Lysander took to his sword as the fourth Athenian spun to him, sword in hand and ready to fight.

Lysander was breath-takingly fast, he leapt at the Athenian, swinging his blade into the Athenians with a resounding crash of iron, and parrying into the Athenian, he drove his blade up under the Athenian's chin, through his mouth and into his brain, killing him instantly.

Behind him, Koinos made fast work of the last Athenian, stabbing him in the belly. The Athenian crumpled to the ground screaming in agony before Koinos pulled a spear from one of the bodies and finished him off.

The Athenians dead, Lysander spied a half-eaten leg of mutton lying in the grass around the carnage. He picked it up and took a hearty bite from it and surveyed the little camp as he chewed.

Koinos searched the bodies for booty. He took two gold rings from two of them and a few coins, and their weapons.

He looked at Pantares, who was looking mightily pleased with himself. He had tamed his first mortal.

Pantares looked back at Lysander and met his stare, filled with libidinous hunger and for a long hot moment, Pantares was trapped in Lysander's spell...

'That's that then,' said Koinos, his voice breaking Cupid's spell. Koinos pulled a gold ring off the figure of the last corpse with some effort.

* ***Commander of a file or rank of men, modern equivalent would be sergeant.***

* ***Commander of an enomotia, a platoon sized unity of the ancient Greek army, approximately 36 men, although this number varied in the Spartan army and could be double that size. Equivalent modern rank would be lieutenant/captain.***

FORTY-EIGHT

The allied camps glowed in the light of their many fires; thousands of soldiers, Corinthians, Spartans, Thebans and other Boeotians, and the beleaguered city beyond the siege walls, doomed, yet stubbornly, it was holding out.

The armies had fallen into relative inactivity as they waited, week on week, month on month for Plataea to surrender. It couldn't be long now, for that city had become a world of misery and terrible suffering as their food supplies dwindled below subsistence, contained as they were within Sparta's siege walls, encircling the city with an inner and outer wall, the outer wall a defensive barricade from any potential Athenian attack, the inner wall to keep the Plataeans penned in. Both rings of the siege walls had palisades accessed by ladders, and there were towers for guards and Boeotian archers evenly spaced around the entire encirclement.

There was a gap of sixteen feet between each wall, with soldiers billeted in long wooden huts built between the walls.

Lysander stalked through the Spartan camp, between huts and tents, his face glowing in the light of the campfires where off-duty Spartans were resting, sitting around eating rations, drinking watery wine from their kothon cups, many of them were playing dice and backgammon, whjich was popular with Spartan soldiers. Some were exercising and line dancing, something that fascinated the allied soldiers who had crowded around to watch and admire the Spartans and their boundless energy.

He had been ordered to report to the King, who had his headquarters in a big log house that also served as the King's residence.

Clearchus was waiting outside just in front of two of Lysander's brother Dioskouri, standing guard either side of the entrance.

There was a Theban light infantryman nearby holding the reins of a magnificent black stallion.

'They're waiting for you, Lysander,' said Clearchus.

Lysander gave him a nod of his head and went into the log house.

Clearchus's father Ramphias was there, acting as Agis's tactical adviser. Pagondas of Thebes and Ephor Leonnatos were seated at a table.

Lysander presented himself at attention in front of them, his eyes roving them.

'Be at ease, Lysander...' Agis gestured to a servant to bring his friend a cup of wine. 'You're invited to dine with us.'

Lysander was flattered. 'You honour me, My Lord.' Despite being a personal friend of Agis's, it wasn't usual for the most junior officers or a hippeus to dine with the King and his generals and senior officers in the theatre of war, and he knew it was a significant gesture on Agis's part.

*

After observing the usual rituals, they took their places at the long tables in the mess, laid out in much the same way as the syssition back in Sparta, with the king seated with his most senior men at the top table.

'Your little escapade into Attica's got everyone talking,' said Ramphias as Lysander took his place half way up the table to Agis's right, sitting between Menedaios and Pagondas.

'It unnerves the enemy, Geront,' said Lysander. 'When they know they're not safe, even in their own territory.'

'Do you think it makes any difference?' asked Pagondas.

'Fear is a powerful weapon, Strategos,' Lysander responded. 'When an enemy is afraid, he becomes unsettled, and that makes him more likely to make mistakes, and his mistakes are our advantages.'

Ramphias nodded his head. 'That it does,' he said.

'You're a student of tactics, Lysander?' said Polymnis of Thebes.

'I'm a student of war,' Lysander replied.

'As are we all,' said Ramphias.

Polymnis raised a brow. 'But not all men are tacticians. Not even Spartans,' he said. 'It is a gift granted to but a few men, would you not agree, Lysander?'

'Lysander's a very good petteia player,' said Agis before Lysander had the chance to respond. 'A game that requires a good deal of tactics.'

'A game you learned from Geront Tellis I understand?' said Pagondas.

'Yes, from the age of ten, Strategos.'

'You must be an impressive gamesman? Perhaps we might have a game sometime?'

'If it please you, Strategos.'

Polymnis took a swallow of wine.

'I wish someone would come up with a tactic to finish this siege,' said Menedaios.

'Patience,' said Lysander. 'That's the best tactic here. Those behind walls always have the greatest advantage, until they run out of food. Putting force to their walls achieved nothing.'

'He's right,' agreed Pagondas. 'They're already at the point of starvation. It can't be much longer now.'

Ramphias agreed with him. But Agis was clearly impatient to finish it, and to declare Nike for Sparta and himself, he was still a king without a reputation.

FORTY-NINE

Daimachus had summoned the Plataeans and Apollodoros along with the other Athenians trapped in the city, to gather at the Altar of Zeus Eleutherios, which was itself a powerful reminder of those solemn oaths taken by the Spartans, Athenians and other Hellenes after the Persian Wars, guaranteeing Plataea's freedom and independence. It was an hour to midnight, and as ordered, everybody came without torches, so as not to alert the enemy of their assembly.

'The situation is dire,' said Daimachus. 'The food is almost gone, and in just a matter of ten or so days, there'll be nothing left.'

'What do you suggest, General?'

Before he could answer, someone spoke out: 'It's time to talk terms with the enemy, Daimachus,' said one of the Plataeans.

'And trust in the Spartan to protect us from the Thebans, who will put us to death and raze Plataea to the ground?' barked an angry young man, extricating himself from the assembly. He was Daimachus's youngest son, Eupompides. His friend, Theaenetus was but a stem behind him, and the two young men strutted to the marble steps of the altar. 'Surrender and we doom ourselves to eternal shame and the death of cowards, in chains...' He climbed the steps so all could see him and hear him. 'We cannot fight them either. And clearly, to stay here is also death to us all.'

'Then what do you suggest, Eupompides?' asked Apollodoros.

'We break out. All of us,' Theaenetus as he came up the steps to join his friend. 'We wait for the right night, and we break through the Spartan wall. There may be a dozen Theban guards, but with stealth and surprise, we can overpower them quickly and quietly and then scramble over the Spartan wall, thence into the mountains and over into Attica and safety.'

'It would be suicide!' someone shouted, and there were a lot of doubtful faces among the Plataeans, Apollodoros and his Athenian brothers, however, seemed to see the merit in it.

Eupompides looked at the citizens. 'Perhaps? But is it not more noble to die in the attempt, than to wait like the condemned for the executioner's pleasure? This,' he went on surveying them all carefully, 'is our best and only hope. It might be that many of us die, but others might not. This is the lottery of our fate. We can use the tunnels we dug to undermine their siege works to get out without the enemy seeing. Then we make for the inner wall with ladders and our best men go over first to kill any Thebans there before they can raise the alarm. When all is clear, we all make our escape.'

'And what if there are Spartans there?'

Theaenetus shook his head. 'There won't be. Eupompides and I have tested the plan by going over every night for the last ten nights. There are only Thebans, and they're complacent and few in number. On these cold nights, they tend to stay in their huts, not expecting us to make an attempt to escape. There are no Spartans there.'

'What did you mean, we wait for the right night, Eumolpids?' asked Daimachus.

Eupompides looked at his father. 'When it rains, there are no guards on the ground or the battlements. Only the towers are manned, we wait for such a night and pray the gods make such a storm for us as will make the enemy entirely blind to our venture.'

'It could work,' said Apollodoros.

Daimachus nodded his head.

'How many of us will go?' asked an old man.

Eupompides looked at him. 'All of us. We'll leave them an empty city. We can escape over the mountains, or to the gulf. To Naupaktos to the Athenians.'

'We'd never make it,' said one of them.

'If we stay here, we die. This way, at least some of us will get to safety, if the gods are with us, we might all make it. But we have to try...'

FIFTY

Daimachus, Eupompides, Theaenetus and Apollodoros of Athens had been watching the storm brewing for over an hour, since dusk, from the parapet of the city's east wall. The dark clouds fermenting over the mountains, flashing with arcs of light and distant rumbles of thunder as the storm rolled towards Boeotia, accompanied by a cold wind that buffeted them, through their hair and their robes.

'What're you think?' asked Apollodoros.

'I think the gods may have answered our prayers,' said Daimachus. He looked at the Theban guards on the palisades of the siege walls, walking up and down with their spears, like shadow people in the dark, their cloaks billowing in the wind. He looked at Apollodoros. 'We should get everyone ready to leave. Are the scaling ladders ready?' He looked at Theaenetus.

'Everything's ready, General,' said the young man.

Daimachus looked at his son, his eyes glimmering in the darkness. 'Break out the weapons and tell everybody to meet at the tunnel. Tell them to bring no baggage. Just enough food for three days and to wear warm clothes. And tell them not to wear anything bright or shiny that would be easily seen by the men in the towers.'

Eupompides nodded his head, about to hurry to his father's orders...

'Once we're through the enemy lines,' Daimachus continued, 'if we can, we'll make for Attica over the mountains. If not, we'll go to Delphi, and claim sanctuary there. The Spartans would not dare pursue or harm us there. Their piety forbids any offense against the gods, and especially Apollo. We'll be safe there. I have friends who will give us accommodation. Apollodoros, you and your companions should come with us?'

'We'll make for Attica, if not over the mountains, then across the Isthmus, or we can make for Naupaktos.'

Daimachus nodded his head. 'We should go in small groups. No more than five, so as to avoid drawing attention, lest we forget that our brother Boeotians are Theban allies.'

Eupompides and Theaenetus ran off to Daimachus's command.

Finally, the heavens opened and hard rain fell down in torrents, reducing visibility even further, like a veil of water to cover their escape. The streets had become rivers, and cascading from the rooftops, turning them into waterfalls; the downpour spattered the roof tiles and pavements with a roaring din.

The streets were as dark as caves, and the citizens, hunched against the rain in their dark robes, hurried along the unlit streets to the mustering place under the city wall.

It was a storm of rare ferocity, even for these parts, as if whipped up by the gods themselves. The heavens boomed with thunder and blinding white hot fingers of lightning streaked across the sky, lighting up the world for a second, into the fearful and anxious rain-slicked faces of the Plataeans.

The sky lit up again with lightning, and the glowing veins of blinding light exploded above with a buzzing crack that made Daimachus look up.

An almighty BOOM of a thunderclap made the air around them shiver, the city's dark angles limned into sharp contrast against the blinding white flashes.

Everybody gathered where they had dug the tunnel under the city wall, out into the no-man's-land between the city wall and the Spartans' inner siege wall.

This was going to be their last chance to escape. One of the militiamen, confirmed that the Theban guards on the palisades of the siege walls had left their posts and headed for their huts, leaving only a few men in the watchtowers, which had open sides under pitched rooves. The ground between the wall was quickly becoming a mire.

Daimachus looked at Eupompides, Theaenetus, Apollodoros in turn, each of them clasping swords tight in their fists at the tunnel entrance in the ground. He looked beyond them, where the citizens were gathered under the city wall, armed with spears, swords, axes, pikes and whatever else was at hand to use as a weapon if it came to a fight.

Another flash of lightning, and he saw the spectre of terror in many faces.

Then, some started to have doubts, now they were faced with the dangers of scaling the siege walls with the ladders and the possibility of encountering Theban hoplites. And what if they did manage to get over both siege walls, how would they get through the Spartans, who were encamped with near three thousand warriors beyond.

The fear spread quickly.

At first, it was just a few who changed their minds. Apollodoros and Daimachus tried to stop them, trying to persuade them to come with them. There was a better chance this way than there was staying here, Daimachus told them, but it was no use. Then more of them decided not to risk it, and before they knew it, over a hundred Plataeans lost their nerve, consumed by fear, too much fear to risk the consequences if they were captured.

They caused considerable confusion as they started turning back and pushing their way through the others, who were determined to escape or die in the attempt. Anything was better than staying here, waiting to starve to death.

Their friends tried to dissuade them from staying to the certain death that awaited them, but none would hear reason.

'Leave them. Let them stay, if that's what they want,' said Eupompides.

Daimachus watched them moving away. It was the greatest disappointment of his life. If they were staying, then he too would have to stay with them. It was his duty. He looked at his son...

Eupompides saw it in his father's eyes. He knew his father wouldn't leave anybody behind. 'If you stay, then so do I.'

'No! No, you have to get out, Eupompides,' said Daimachus firmly. 'You're the only child I have left. You must survive, do you hear me, boy?' He stepped to his son and hugged him. 'Tell your mother I love her.'

Eupompides knew this was the last time he would ever see his father and he was too choked with emotions to speak. He clung to his father, and his father clung to him in the tightest embrace.

'I love you, my son.' He broke his embrace.

There were tears in Eupompides's eyes.

'Go now. This storm can't last much longer. Don't look back.'

Apollodoros gave his old friend and empathic look. He reached out and put his hand over Eupompides's arm. 'Come. We have to go now.'

The storm raged on, the rain unrelenting, and the citizens who had escaped prayed it remained so as they rose up out of the tunnel into the no-man's-land.

It was working by the gods, Daimachus thought as he watched from the city wall, leaning against the parapet, his hands on the cold wet stone, fingers splayed.

The rain pounded him and drizzled down his face. He was soaked to the skin, but he cared nothing of it as he watched the Plataeans hurrying fleet-footed and in muted silence to the siege wall with several ladders carried between them, brandishing their weapons, willing them on, praying to Zeus himself.

They put the ladders to the wall and over they went, into the compound between the walls. They were going to make it out.

FIFTY-ONE

Ionian Sea, west of Kyllene

When revolt broke out at Mytilene on Lesbos, Sparta had agreed to send immediate and powerful help, and promised the Lesbians Attica would be attacked to draw off Athenian forces from their island, and Alkidas, who had been elected Spartan navarch for the year, would command an allied fleet of forty ships with hoplite marines to come to Mytilene's defence. A simple plan that had turned into a costly debacle for Sparta and the allies.

Alkidas's conduct had tainted Sparta with the stink of cowardice and cruelty, bringing into question Sparta's word. Once he reached Lesbos, Alkidas had turned his back and retreated in the face of an enemy fleet. That was just one of a few devastating mistakes, and to address Sparta's concerns, the high command sent Brasidas to Kyllene to await the arrival of Alkidas's fleet.

He was in the villa the Peloponnesians had taken over as their headquarters up in the town.

Two triremes from Alkidas's fleet had arrived at Kyllene alone and the trierarchs were summoned to the villa to explain where Alkidas and the rest of the fleet were.

They were led without ceremony into a large room that opened onto a terrace overlooking the port and the sea beyond. Brasidas was waiting for them, standing between two columns, the late afternoon sunshine sloped in across the terrace behind him casting him into silhouette.

The trierarchs looked tired and haggard, despite their efforts to present themselves in the proper manner to the superior officer, holding their helmets under their arms. Truth was, they had barely slept in days, pursued by Athenians and ravaged by an horrendous storm that may well have sunk the rest of Alkidas's ships for all they knew?

'What happened?' demanded Brasidas lowly. 'Where's Alkidas and the rest of your ships?'

'We became separated in a storm, Syntagmatarkhis,' said one of the trierarchs, squinting into the bright sunlight spilling around Brasidas.

'Near Crete,' said the other. 'We suffered damage to our ships.'

'We were scattered like chaff to the winds,' added the first trierarch who spoke.

'And we were being pursued by Delian ships from Lesbos.'

Brasidas moved into the room and they could see him clearly now.

'And you did not offer battle?'

'The Navarch decided it would be unwise given the number of enemy ships,' said the second trierarch in a quieter, more cautious tone, expecting Brasidas to fly into a rage, but he did not, he simply stared at them for a long time without speaking, emotionless.

Brasidas already knew of Alkidas's conduct, so did the Gerousia and the kings. He had been un-Spartan in his behaviour in enemy territory, behaving like a merciless tyrant on the defenceless, inflicting atrocities and cruelties that had become infamous. As if that wasn't bad enough, Alkidas had flinched before his equals in battle, not simply flinched, he had refused to engage in battle and withdrew from the theatre of war like a coward, slinking away with the enemy giving chase. He had invoked Sparta's anger and on learning that Alkidas had not only let their allies on Lesbos down, he had brought Sparta into disrepute. Sparta's shadow man Salaithos had risked his life and more besides getting passed the Athenians into Mytilene, where he persuaded them to hold out, promising that Sparta was on its way.

Salaithos had been captured and executed by the Athenians along with a good number of Mytileneans.

Alkidas had also turned down several offers from a pro-Spartan delegation of Ionians who pleaded with him to take some towns on Ionia, where Sparta and her allies had many friends who wanted to be free of the shackles of Athens. They offered him secure facilities to set up a base of operations on the island, and Sparta's presence there would be sure to give the Ionians the confidence they needed to revolt against the Athenians and divorce themselves from them. The town the Ionians suggested was on the coast with unbreachable natural defences and a secure natural harbour that could be easily defended, and would have given Sparta and the Peloponnesians a very strong and much needed foothold in the Aegean Sea that would put them within striking distance of Athens' Asian colonies, including the islands under Athens' chokehold. It was a perfect gift, and most certainly would have redeemed him of his earlier bad decisions, but again, Alkidas declined, and with the Athenian fleet on his tail, they sailed into the open sea their course set for the Peloponnese.

The Kings, Agis and Pleistoanax both flew into a rage, even to the point of demanding Alkidas be recalled and executed.

But Alkidas came from a very powerful family with intimate connections to King Pleistoanax, his own father a geront, as well as an uncle.

This wasn't the first time the Peloponnesians had turned away in the face of enemy ships since Rhium and Naupaktos. The disasters had made the allies wary of the Athenian navy. It was a dangerous lack of confidence that might just cost them the war.

Pleistoanax too was furious, if somewhat more reserved about it, and the whispering ephors stooping to Pleistoanax and Agis's ears urging this and advising that, like hissing snakes.

It was decided to send an adviser to Alkidas, someone to encourage him. Someone who could reinforce Alkidas's spine with a little old fashioned Spartan courage. Brasidas was that someone.

A servant went around the room with a lit taper, lighting the lamps as dusk fell.

After hearing the trierarchs' accounts, Brasidas dismissed them and told them to get some decent food and rest.

As the trierarchs left, they passed Xenoklides, who was just arriving. They gave the Corinthian admiral a sideways look as they passed.

Brasidas gestured to the servant to bring Xenoklides a cup of wine. 'Lesbos was a disaster,' said Brasidas. 'And if we keep giving the enemy the advantage of us, we'll lose this war...' He looked narrowly at Xenoklides. 'We have to strike at them in the sea and on the land. We have to be bold, Xenoklides. Take risks, for I tell you, there's no such thing as a risk-free war and the sooner everybody realises that, the sooner we can get this thing done.'

'I'm sure Alkidas had his reasons, Brasidas. Alkidas is no trembler.'

'*Hmm...*' He was unconvinced, the example of his courage thus far displayed, had left little to inspire him.

FIFTY-TWO

Musicians were playing a lively tune on their flutes, drums, lyres, aulos and loops of rattle-bells, while two pairs of naked muscle rippled men with glistening oiled bodies wrestled, or rather tried to wrestle, their bodies were so slippery it was impossible to get a firm hold of each other. Every time they did, they just slipped apart, to the great amusement of the guests, who laughed hysterically at the comedic spectacle.

'They look like slugs fucking,' their host, Leagros billowed out with laughter.

'I can't say I've ever seen slugs fuck,' said one of the Leucadian commanders.

'I don't think they do, do they?' asked one of the city oligarchs.

'Of course, they do! How else d'you think they get here?' Leagros responded, slurring his words. He gulped back another big swallow of wine.

Brasidas did not care for Leagros, or what passed as entertainment, nor did he trust him. Men who drink too much also talk too much. In Brasidas's opinion Leagros, the chief oligarch of Kylene was incapable and incompetent in just about everything he did. Money and aristocratic heritage put him in his high office and nothing more. He showed no restraint, not in what he said, or how much he drank. He was making a show of himself, his tongue was as crude as his eating, gorging on the food like a dog, shoving so much into his mouth, he could hardly chew it.

Kyllene had long been an ally of Sparta and the Peloponnesians maintained a strongly defended base here, with a small garrison of Helot and Dweller light infantry and some local militias from the surrounding countryside. The Peloponnesians utilised the boatyards and shipwrights of the town to carry out repairs and maintenance on their ships. The Peloponnesians also brought security to Kyllene, offering them protection from their enemies, and there were a few, not least of them was Corcyra, who had attacked Kyllene not so long ago and set fire to the town, and the nearby island Zakynthos, also firmly in alliance with Athens.

Leagros was Kylene's most important citizen – at least as far as Leagros was concerned, but then he possessed of himself an air of astounding self-importance.

'The oracle at Olympus told me; I'm loved by the gods,' boasted Leagros.

'She was drunk too then,' said Brasidas cuttingly.

Leagros looked at him and Brasidas met his stare with cold contempt. It was too much for Leagros and he laughed humourlessly. 'I swear, I'll never understand Spartan humour...'

'Clearly,' Brasidas responded quickly.

There were other oligarchs there, reclined on their dining couches further down the table in order of class and rank.

As the evening went on, the oily wrestlers were replaced by a youth who sung the verses of Alkman:

'... *Over the drowsy earth still night prevails; Calm sleep the mountain tops and shady vales, The rugged cliffs and hollow glens; The cattle on the hill. Deep in the sea, The countless finny race and monster brood Tranquil repose. Even the busy bee Forgets her daily toil. The silent wood ... No more with noisy hum of insect rings; And all the feathered tribes, by gentle sleep subdued, Roost in the glade, and hang their drooping wings...*'

Over the boy's song, the polite chatter went on, jarred every now and then by Leagros's grandiloquent interjections.

Brasidas observed how fast Leagros drank his wine and how quick he was to invert his cup to signal the serving boys that he wanted a refill.

Brasidas was his usual talkative self, deep in conversation with Xenoklides of Corinth and the Ambraciot commander, quietly discussing Corcyra.

Leagros tried to listen in on Brasidas's conversation with the two men, straining to hear over the sounds of the chatter and music. '... those damned Corcyraeans need teaching a lesson or two, Brasidas, I can tell you that,' he billowed out drunkenly, his eyes seeming to roll in his head, waving his hand about erratically in the air with his winecup clasped in his talon-like fingers, yet remarkably he didn't spill a drop of wine. He put the cup to his mouth and tilted his head back and downed yet another cup in two big gulps.

Brasidas gave him another contemptuous look. He could smell the wine on Leagros's breath and it revolted him. He turned back to Xenoklides and the Ambraciot commander. 'Sparta would be happy just to have them out of the war,' he said. His gaze settled on Xenoklides. 'But it worries me, Xenoklides, that these prisoners you've freed, might have a change of heart and betray us to the enemy. Are you certain these prisoners will keep their word and persuade their Corcyraean kinsmen to our favour?'

Xenoklides nodded his head. 'They're all in favour of abandoning the alliance with the Athenians and coming over to us and the word coming back from Corcyra is that they've persuaded a good number of citizens to the cause. The only problem that I can see is Peithias, who still holds power on the island and he's still popular. But the Corcyraean oligarchs assure us that he'll be silenced before he can damage the enterprise–'

'They're Peloponnesians after all,' said the Ambraciot commander.

'Dorians, like us,' added Xenoklides.

Brasidas nodded his head. He was still unconvinced, and he did not want to sail into a trap if any of the freed prisoners betrayed them...

FIFTY-THREE

Quintius finally staggered aboard the Minerva at dawn, hungover and dazed looking. He was so unsteady on his feet, he almost fell into the water as he came up the gangplank onto the deck, where Dexius was standing with his arms folded, staring disapprovingly at Quintius.

Quintius looked at him and put his hand out, pulling a face. 'Don't you start. I've no stomach for *your* nagging...' He had no stomach for anything right now, not even the cup of water Boy brought him, waving the cup away with a cringing face as if it were poison.

He had had a heavy drinking session with his old friend Mentor last night, and by Vulcan's hammer, he was paying for it now, carrying the mother of all hangovers, a feeling of nausea in his belly, which wasn't helped by the motion of the ship on the water. 'Mentor's bringing the slaves later today. We got them for a good price.'

Dexius nodded his head. 'Worth Bacchus's revenge then?' he said referring to Quintius's hangover.

'I'm not sure about that,' said Quintius. 'Gods below, I swear, that's the last time I'm drinking with that old wine sponge,' he complained.

Dexius gave him a look. 'You said that last year, and the year before that.'

'Well remind me next year, not to drink with Mentor.'

Dexius merely raised a brow. 'I reminded you yesterday, but it made no difference.'

'Try harder next time...' He massaged his temples and closed his eyes. 'Pluto spare me...'

'You two do rub along nicely together though,' said Dexius. 'I was just this minute thinking how nicely you two rub along.' He scratched his chin. 'Must be the wine you have in common,' he added wryly.

Quintius glared at him. 'Are you suggesting I drink too much, Dexius?'

'I wouldn't dream of it.'

'Oh my ... my head's throbbing like Priapus's prick,' he grunted. 'Kill me and put me out of my misery...'

Dexius pulled a face. 'That's what happens when you have drinking contests with the likes of Mentor. I did warn you. Last year when you two got together, it was three days before anyone got any sense out of you. And to be honest,' he nagged, 'I'm surprised you've managed to stay on your feet. Who passed out first? You or Mentor?'

'I don't remember...'

A Spartan hoplite came aboard. 'I'm looking for Quintius the Roman?' he said without preamble, looking at Dexius and Quintius.

'I'm Quintius.'

'Syntagmatarkhis Brasidas requests you visit him at his quarters. I am sent to bring you to him.'

Quintius and Dexius exchanged a look.

Ten Spartan war triremes were approaching the harbour, and beyond, about a mile out, at least twenty others were sailing towards Kyllene in four small squadrons.

Dexius watched the fleet drawing closer under press of oars...

*

Brasidas was sitting with Xenoklides in the garden courtyard, discussing Corcyra and Brasidas's plan to attack the island in support of the freed prisoners and oligarchs. Alkidas had forty ships, with the thirteen Leucadian and Ambraciot war galleys, and a contingent of hoplites and light infantry, a hundred of them of the deadly Spartiate order, plus Alkidas's marines, it made up a substantial force of men.

'Timing will be everything,' said Brasidas. 'Timing's always everything,' he added as he glanced over at Quintius and the hoplite, now waiting about half way across the courtyard for Brasidas's summons.

Xenoklides sipped his cordial. 'More ships arrived this morning,' he said. 'Alkidas and the others can't be far behind them. You should remove him, Brasidas. He has no stomach for it.'

'That's not in my power, and he's too well protected back home. I can only advise him.'

'Is he likely to listen to you?'

Brasidas flicked his brows at the admiral. 'That, Xenoklides, remains to be seen.'

'Gods help us then, if he has straw knees as I've heard.'

Brasidas nodded his head and raised his hand and gave Quintius a come-hither gesture.

'*Salve*, gentlemen,' said Quintius as he approached.

'Greetings, Roman,' said Xenoklides.

'Quintius, did you deliver our message to Sosthenes without any problems?'

Quintius nodded his head. 'I put it into his hand myself. He told me to tell you, everything is proceeding well.'

'Did you observe any Athenian ships in the port while you were there?' asked Xenoklides.

Quintius shook his head. 'None that I saw.'

Brasidas nodded his head and gestured to a servant.

The servant approached and handed a purse of money to Brasidas and Brasidas handed it to Quintius.

Quintius took the purse. 'As always, I'm glad to be of service to Sparta in her efforts against her enemies.'

'Very rewarding efforts,' said Xenoklides.

'A man has to make a living, Admiral.'

Brasidas smiled. Quintius had risked his life many times in the service of Sparta, he was reliable and above all, trustworthy.

A man wearing a white chiton, out of breath, and accompanied by one of the guards hurried to Brasidas. 'Lord. The rest of the fleet has arrived intact and in good condition. They're coming into port as I speak, Lord.'

*

'... I want all repairs carried out without delay,' Alkidas said snappily to his trierarchs, who were gathered on the dock in a half moon around him. 'Put every available man to the task, gentlemen; I want to be ready to sail within three days.'

'Three days!?' one of the Trierarchs echoed with alarm. 'Impossible, Navarch,' he added firmly. 'We need at least six days to carry out the necessary repairs. We've two ships that are taking on water, six with lost and broken oars and–'

'I don't want your excuses!' Alkidas barked back angrily, 'I want my orders carried out as I've put them to you...' He held his stare on them. 'I want these ships seaworthy and ready to sail in three days, and that's an end to it...!' His voice tapered when he spotted a hoplite approaching from the town, and then he saw there were more hoplites of the Spartiate order in the port, liveried in their crimson and bronze. 'What are they doing here?'

The trierarchs all looked at the Spartans in the port, more than there should have been, and then he saw Brasidas coming across the port towards them.

'*Brasidas...*?' Alkidas turned to the trierarchs. 'You have your orders, now get on with it...' He looked back at Brasidas. 'Well, this is a surprise. And what brings you here, Brasidas?'

'You bring me here, Alkidas...'

FIFTY-FOUR

Corcyra

There had been a feeling of unease in the city for days. Although everything continued as it usually did; the market in the agora was just as busy as ever it was, the fishing boats went out before dawn at the same hour as always, the sea was calm, the gulls circled and screamed in the vaulted heavens over the ports. Nothing seemed out of the ordinary. All the same, the atmosphere had a palpable sense of expectation that reminded Peithias of the quiet that sometimes precedes a great storm, and here, in the Assembly, he could feel the tension hanging in the air like an oppressive and invisible weight that pressed down on all within.

There was a low murmur of voices and shifting bodies as everybody settled onto the benches. Peithias's eyes continually roved them, trying to read their faces, and who had they sat next to, pro-Spartans or pro-Athenians, the Assembly was certainly divided, and however it went, he knew it was going to be close.

Yesterday, two ships arrived, one from Athens and the other from

The question was a simple one: Should Corcyra continue to support Athens? Should Corcyra continue her war against the great powers of the Peloponnese? Should Corcyra fall into anarchy and civil strife? – These were the big gambits upon which the future of Corcyra would be decided.

Peithias, despite his aristocratic ancestry and oligarchic upbringing, wholeheartedly supported the great experiment of *dēmokratiā*,* (democracy). But Corcyra had always been an oligarchy. The people, he reasoned, should have a voice – they should be the only voice, after all, he thought, what is any state without its people. They who contribute to its success. They deserved a say, a voice. But today was about far more than the political ideology. Today was about Corcyra's future position in the war.

The anti-Athenian faction had grown stronger over recent months, stronger still when those prisoners were freed by the Corinthians. Just what were those bloody Corinthians up to? More, there had been rumours going about for months of an uprising. More recently, he heard about a Corinthian financed conspiracy of corruption on a vast scale. Nothing could be proved of course, but his spies were abroad in the city, sniffing around in the oligarchic shadows, but nobody was talking.

There had been more than a dozen murders of prominent pro-Athenians in the city in recent days too, including members of the Assembly, thus weakening Peithias's position, but he still felt confident enough to win the debate.

Peithias wasn't the only one who was confident of winning the day. Iolaos sat with a gloating smile on his face. And well he might too; the freed Corcyraean prisoners had kept their word to Corinth and had begun at once upon their return home to curry support for their cause, using persuasion where they could and corruption where they could not.

Yesterday, two emissary ships arrived at the island, one from Corinth and the other from Athens under an agreement of truce, and the Corinthian emissary spoke one word to Sosthenes. "Pegasus." That was the codeword he had been given before leaving Sparta, that an invasion force was coming.

Sosthenes kept the information to himself – for now.

Iolaos had come to the Assembly with good arguments, and a good deal of money to be used to corrupt the senators of the assembly into supporting the argument to rescind the treaty with the Athenians. Even if it was neutrality, it would still be a good outcome.

The assembly listened carefully to Iolaos's arguments. He was respected as one of Corcyra's most politicians and had the respect of most of the assembly, even among the democrats, who were in diametric opposition, they knew him to be a fair and just man.

'... My brothers,' he began, taking a long spritely stride into the speaker's arena, holding his hands out in an open gesture, 'we are united by country, if not by blood. We are also Peloponnesians. *Dorians*, and our traditions stretch back to the time of the dark ages that followed the war with Troy, and many of us here, had ancestors who fought in that war of wars. They fought for their Dorian blood and they gave their Dorian blood too.

'Our mother country Corinth,' he went on, 'has always been our protector until very recent times. So how can we, with good conscience, stand as the enemy of our own mother, or of our brother Peloponnesians in the favour of this ill-advised alliance we have with the Athenians, who have nothing of the Dorian experience about them. They call those of their empire, their allies, as freely the joined in alliance to rid Greece of the Median scourge...' His eyes seemed to glow with emotion as he went on, impassioned by unflinching belief in his cause: 'But we have seen, even in recent months, how Athens deals with those they call allies, who no longer wish to be hitched to Athens, which demands of them, the greatest cost in men, money, ships and grain to prosecute their war with our Dorian brothers – *With our very mother Corinth*! Look to Samos, look to Lesbos, look to Potidaea and all other places that have wished to separate from Athens. They have been met with such brutality as make the gods themselves blush, and make Athena herself ashamed that they bear her name yet dishonour it so...!' He pointed a stern finger at the Athenian emissary. 'They are no friends of ours. Rather they would master us as we master our slaves...'

The emissary shifted with unease as the Assembly looked at him.

'Aye!' someone called out.

Peithias, the leader of the democrats was alarmed to see so many nodding heads, especially among the moderates, who had always been suspicious of the alliance with Athens, even if they had gone along with it when the island was under threat from Corinth, who could never come to terms with the fact that Corcyra had struck out on her own in independence of them.

'... This war will drag us down,' Iolaos continued. 'It will cost us a price we cannot afford to pay...' He looked at Peithias. 'The gods cannot forgive this treachery until it is put right. We must end this alliance with Athens and her Empire, or, I tell you, we too shall be shackled to Athenian chains. The Alliance is slavery by another name,' he said raising the pitch of his voice, his open hands closed into tight fists, his eyes simmered with anger. 'Ask the Mytileneans what it means to say no to Athens, that city now runs red with their blood at the hands of Athens. Ask the Samians when they wanted to separate from Athens, who had insulted them on the whispers of a whore in Pericles's ear,' he said referring to Pericles's mistress, the hetaerae, Aspasia of Miletos. 'What a dear price they paid, when Pericles ordered the trierarchs of their navy to be crucified in the agora...' He shook his head, looking at the assembly, into their faces – into their hearts. 'I tell you, my Corcyraean brothers; the Athenians are tyrants of the worse sort. They come with pretences of friendship, then they ensnare you in their traps. This is not honourable behaviour and we want no part of it. End this alliance! End it now, for the sake of our children. End it!?'

There was an eruption of supporting shouts and stamping feet in applause. As Iolaos resumed his seat. He had made a strong case for Corcyra to divorce from Athens and their alliance, an alliance that had done a great deal of damage to the peace after the Battle of Sybota, and some would say that was the hammer that shattered the fettering chains of mighty Ares and set him loose on the world with fire and carnage.

After the chamber settled back to silence, Peithias stirred from his bench and rose to his feet. 'And do you speak for all the prisoners also, Iolaos?'

'I do.'

'And do you also speak for the exiled oligarchs, who were driven from Corcyra for their treachery in trying to overthrow the elected government? Do you speak for those as well, Iolaos?'

Iolaos was silent for a long moment. 'I speak for Corcyra, Peithias. We all know who *you* speak for,' he said, casting a leer at the Athenian emissary.

Peithias laughed. 'It is for Corcyra that we made this alliance lest you forget, and it is for Corcyra that we must continue it. Or will power on this island once again fall to Corinth? Rescind this alliance and we bear our naked chests to the enemy's dagger. Do not vote for this, I beseech you all,' he said passionately, his eyes continually panning the assembly. Iolaos makes it sound very simple and matter-of-fact. But he does not tell you, that he has received his orders from the banished oligarchs and the Corinthians, who would have us pledge to them under some misguided loyalty to them because of our ancestry. I tell you. The Spartans are losing this war. It is the act of a fool who deserts the winning side to pledge to the defeated...'

'Sparta isn't defeated yet,' came an angry retort from the assembly. 'You make assumptions, Peithias. We want only truth and facts here.'

Peithias was struck dumb for a moment. He picked out the speaker, a grey-haired old man. 'I make no assumptions. I see the evidence of it. Sparta has never had the stomach for this war. Remember how slow they were coming to it? How Corinth pressed Sparta to it.'

'It's beyond that now,' said Iolaos. 'Far beyond, and you underestimate the nature of the Peloponnesian Dorians to think so, which surprises me, Peithias, given that you're a Peloponnesian Dorian yourself, as are we all, and I know the fire in my belly burns hot enough. I know the will of our nature, the unyielding spirit in our hearts, and I tell you, you underestimate the Spartans at your peril. They are a creed of men like no other on the Earth, and well you know it. Well we all of us know it. Do not make the same mistake Athens have made in underestimating their resolve. And I tell you now, the day will come when Athens will be crushed by Sparta, and wiped from the face of the Earth,' he prophesied.

Again, the Athenian emissary looked decidedly uneasy. Peithias looked worried, Iolaos was a clever political with thirty years on the oligarchic assembly. He was a fine speaker too, as Peithias was learning.

Peithias was always going to be up against it. As the war dragged on, opposition to it had grown, and then there were the moderates, who wanted no involvement in the war whatsoever, and they argued in the same vein as Iolaos, when they said that they, the Corcyraeans were Peloponnesians by geography and by blood, their historical loyalties had been to the Peloponnese, and they shared a common history. They were Dorians, therefore, their friendship belonged equally to their Peloponnesian brothers and this was the crux of it. This war against the Peloponnese was one Corcyra should not partake in, but instead, Corcyra should be on good terms, both Athens and the Peloponnesians.

Neutrality by a different name? Or were the moderates trying to please everyone, or at least push for an honourable compromise? Peithias couldn't decide; neither could Iolaos and his oligarchic compatriots.

'Some of you here today,' said a moderate speaker, 'are connected by strong family ties and property at Corinth and other places on the mainland. Can you, with honour, raise your swords in anger to your kinsmen, to your cousins, to your brothers? And for why? What great advantage is there for Corcyra to kill our kin and lay waste our own property? Corinth will accept our independents from them, the oligarchs have implied as much to us. So who then, do the Athenians protect us from? Where is this invisible enemy who will devour us if we say we're unwilling to kill our own, and lay waste the land of our ancestors, and indeed, our own land? Show him to us?' the speaker shook his head and looked at the Corinthian emissary and then, at the other end of the chamber, he looked at the Athenian emissary. 'Here they are, these scorned lovers, who have come to vie for our love. Well, I say they have it in equal measure. We love Athens and we love Corinth,' he said, looking at each one in turn, expressing love in his face to both. 'How then, my brothers, can we raise our hand to either?' He paused deliberately for them to consider his words with care. The fate of Corcyra hung upon this debate.

Peithias looked anxious and so did Iolaos as both men gave careful study to the senators of the common assembly and it was clear, many liked this middle ground. But it was a compromise neither Iolaos or Peithias could accept.

'... Peithias,' said the moderate, starting up again, 'knows it is uncertain who has Nike's favour in this devastating war, but Athens seems to have the edge, I grant you. But wars are uncertain with unforeseeable consequences and can turn upon the whims of Fate and the daring of generals. To underestimate the nature of the Spartans would be, as Iolaos has said, be an expensive mistake, for they are war's kindred sons. Neither should we overlook or underestimate the resolve of Athens. So, I urge you, vote that we be as friends to Athens and in equal amount be friends to our brother Peloponnesians. We must answer for ourselves and determine our own destiny through free will and the consent of the citizens of our sacred island.'

And then came the vote and it was a surprise to the Athenians and Corinth equally. The Corcyraeans decided to support the moderates, voting to maintain the alliance with Athens, but also to be on friendly terms with the Peloponnesians, which, in effect was a declaration of neutrality without actually saying the words.

Corinth was satisfied. Just having them out of the war was good enough for them and the Spartans. But the Athenian emissary was clearly disappointed. Corcyra was a powerful combatant with a large fleet of warships and experienced trierarchs. It would be a loss keenly felt at Athens – it would unlikely be acceptable either, and suddenly a scenario unfurled where Athenian displeasure might force Corcyra to ally herself militarily to the Spartans. This was going to require some delicate diplomacy, he thought.

Iolaos was furious, so too was Peithias, and after a brief consultation with his people, Iolaos declared that Peithias, as architect of the alliance, had shackled Corcyra to Athens' leash. He levelled the charge of enslaving Corcyra to Athens at him and demanded he be tried immediately to answer the charge.

When the assembly voted in favour of a trial, Peithias became enraged. If found guilty, he could be executed, or exiled.

**** Dēmos (the people) and kratos (might), founded in 508–507 BC at Athens by Kleisthenes of the Alcmaeonids.***

FIFTY-FIVE

The next day, the trial was convened in the common assembly, and the question of Peithias's motives in pressing Corcyra to enter the alliance with Athens?

Peithias's response was quick and confidently delivered. He made no bones about his politics, he was a democratiser, he was opposed to oligarchy and its unfair system which prejudices the rich over the poor, and exploits the poor to enrich the oligarchs even further, and all the while, the ordinary citizen was voiceless. Democracy was a shared responsibility. It rested power into the hands of everybody, rich or poor. He told them, that, despite his love of democracy, he would never have favoured an alliance with Athens, had Corcyra not been under the deadliest threat from Corinth, who wanted to rest back control of Corcyra's independents that was hundreds of years old, and they conspired to do so with some of the oligarchs, now dead or in exile. '... There were but two choices,' he said. 'We enslave ourselves to Corinth, or we make an alliance of friendship and mutual defence with Athens. Iolaos speaks of Athenian shackles and enslavement to Athens. Yet we see or feel none of these shackles. When has Athens ever come here with less than the very best of intentions? Who here must lower his eyes to an Athenian as a slave before his master? These are illusions of Iolaos's mind. There is no case to answer here, this is merely a tactic by the oligarchs to discredit me, because the fear me and the idea of democracy, that would strip them of their power. They'll have you believe I put Athens before Corcyra, or that I'm low and base and give my loyalty to corruption. You'll find no fortunes hidden in my house, nor will you find any love greater than the love I have for Corcyra before any other place...'

It didn't take long for the judgement. The accusation was without foundation, Peithias was not guilty.

Still, Peithias refused to let the matter rest there. He brought counter charges against Iolaos and the freed prisoners and pro-spartan, and accused the oligarchs of sacrilege for cutting stakes for their vines from trees in the sacred grounds of Zeus and Alcinous. Alcinous was the son of Phaeax, himself the son of the god Poseidon and the goddess Corcyra, after who the island was thus named, and so it is that, Alcinous is sacred to the islanders. Peithias called several witnesses who testified that the oligarchs had indeed cut the stakes from the sacred place and they were found guilty by unanimous vote.

The sentence imposed upon the oligarchs was one stater for every stake they had cut, which came to an enormous sum of money that even the oligarchs could not, or would not afford to pay at once. They accepted the judgement, but asked for terms to pay the fine in instalments.

Peithias insisted the fine had to be paid immediately and the court agreed. It was in this moment that the storm clouds of civil war began to gather and darken the hearts of Corcyraeans on every side.

Fearful that the democrats were planning to arrest and execute them for non-payment of the fine, the oligarchs and aristocrats scattered and went into hiding. Some went aboard the Corinthian emissary ship, others went to the temples of the city, others went into the countryside, and others still escaped from the island altogether to the mainland and the other islands around Corcyra, paying over the odds for fisherman and the like to take them.

The long shadow of civil war now cast a baleful light over Corcyra, and the streets would run red with blood before it was done. Citizens on both sides armed themselves with whatever they could use as weapons, and in hot blood, they took to the streets in angry mobs, their minds set on revolution.

Sosthenes, who was posing as a merchant from Argos, watched as the mobs swept through the city in a storm of destruction, lootings and murder.

As the evening went on, the violence increased as the uprising spread across the city in the coruscating glow of flaming torches, the air filled with smoke and screams, and the clatter of bitter hand to hand fighting. It was chaotic and confusing, Corcyraeans killing and maiming one another, neighbours against neighbours, friend against friend, father against son.

Sosthenes was still outside the assembly building, when a man ran towards him, a look of blind terror etched into his face as he ran as fast as he could. A short way behind him, four angry men armed with knives, and one had a sword, were chasing the terrified man. It was Iolaos, and the four men were democratisers.

The four democrats caught up with Iolaos and the one with the sword plunged it into Iolaos's belly and as he doubled over, the other three men stabbed him in the back with their daggers – Iolaos staggered towards the assembly steps, his white robes now crimson with blood. He collapsed onto the concourse half a dozen strides from the assembly building's steps and there he died.

The men turned on Sosthenes, their faces contorted with rage, their eyes glowing with madness. Sosthenes immediately reached under his cape and drew his sword as the men stalked towards him, postured for a fight.

Sosthenes was startling in speed, agility and sublime skill with the sword as he took all four of them on, dancing the dance of death, and with breath-taking speed, he killed two in his first effort. he stabbed one in the chest, and decapitated the second with a single blow as he swung his razor-sharp blade.

The other two, stunned and fearful, backed away from him. Sosthenes stood his ground, his sword dripping blood, postured to kill them. The two men hurried off, towards the distance din of battle...

Time to leave, Sosthenes told himself and hurried away...

The orgy of murder and violence was as none in all Hellas had witnessed before in their living memories. The factions fell upon one another with furious rage. Men, women, even children, oligarchs, democrats, neutrals, appeasers, and the downright innocent were butchered in the streets as the gangs ran about through the darkness with their flaming torches, with bloodlust, brandishing swords, knives, spears, hammers, axes and whatever else was at hand to kill their perceived enemies. Settling old scores, looting and robbing. People were running about in every direction, from every faction looking for enemies to kill, and into the night went the chilling laments and screams, shouts and crash of violence.

The narrow warrens and alleys were littered with corpses, the pavements incarnadined with rivers and lakes of blood.

A large mob of oligarchs and their supporters stormed the assembly building, running past Iolaos's body as the stormed the building, where much of the assembly, including Peithias were taking refuge behind barricaded doors.

The mob pounded on the doors, shoving against them, but they held. Soon, a dozen men arrived with a battering ram fashioned from a long wooden post.

Inside, Peithias and about a hundred senators all stood in the speaker's arena, staring at the doors as they shook with every impact, weakening, the BOOMS of the impacts reverberated like claps of thunder through the chamber. The senators jerked with fear and expectation, they all knew those doors wouldn't take too much more of a pounding before they gave out...

BOOM – the doors shook again, buckled, and the thick oak split with a loud SNAP of cracking wood – beyond the doors, they could hear the baying mob yelling.

Peithias reaffirmed his grip on his sword, his body tensed with every muscle contracted, his eyes didn't move from those doors. He took deep breaths, his heart was throwing itself so hard against the inside of his chest, for a moment he thought it might burst out of his body...

BOOM – dust and shattered masonry fell from the hinges, the wood cracked again. It was the locking beam across the doors, it was splitting.

A senator looked up and said lowly, 'Gods help us...'

BOOM – the brace finally snapped.

Peithias exchanged a look with the man standing next to him. 'Poseidon bless sacred Corcyra,' he said, knowing he was but moments from death.

'Poseidon bless sacred Corcyra many of the senators responded with fearful voices...

BOOM – the doors finally gave way and flew open! More than sixty armed men rushed in and charged towards the senators.

Peithias and the other armed men got ready to die fighting.

The mob suddenly stopped ten strides from the senators in the speaker's arena. for some inexplicable reason, they stood there in muted silence, staring at the senators and democratisers–

And then, something flew through the air – a spear, it hit Peithias in the chest, the iron barb burying itself deep into his body. Peithias dropped his sword and gave out a single gasp before he collapsed to the ground, the pupils of his eyes expanded across his irises until only black remained in the centre of the whites, like holes in ice.

The mob suddenly came to action and charged the remaining senators, hacking and stabbing them.

By the time they were done, sixty-one senators lay dead, sprawled on the assembly floor in an island of corpses in a crimson sea.

Unsatiated and spattered in blood, the oligarchic mob went in search of other democratisers and their belligerent allies to kill.

Some of the democrats escaped aboard the Athenian emissary ship to safety, others ran from the city, but the fighters remained, and across the city, the ports and surrounding countryside, bloody chaos reigned over all.

*

After the night's bloodletting, the following day was relatively peaceful as the warring factions rested and regrouped, and collected their dead, of which there were scores from every faction, including innocent citizens caught up on the maelstrom. But come the following day, fresh and reenergised, the fighting resumed.

Like a fire in a dry forest, the revolution spread to other towns and villages on the island. All day and well into the night the killing went on without pause.

The democratisers had the upper hand and more support, even from women and children who climbed onto the rooves of the buildings and threw roof-tiles, bricks and other missiles down onto the oligarchic faction in a desperate and valiant effort to stop them from taking control, and again, the city was filled with screams and shouts so hideous as to seem bestial and inhuman.

The democrats were pushing back hard against the oligarchs, and they were in sight of victory, driving the oligarchs into the agora, where, in an act of pure desperation, the oligarchs set the buildings on fire, including their own homes and shops in an effort to create a fire-wall between themselves and the democrats, but the fires took on a ferocious nature of their own and roared with godlike anger as the flames leaped into to the night sky, casting a red glow over the city that could be seen even from the mainland, as the fire spread from building to building. The Corcyraeans quickly realised that the entire city was in danger of going up in flames, and for the sake of Corcyra, which they all loved, the factions abandoned fighting each other to fight the fires instead.

The following day twelve Athenian war triremes from Naupaktos sailed slowly into the smoky port, through the rancid stench of charred wood and scorched flesh. A quarter of the city was smouldering from its very heart, columns of acrid black smoke rafting into the azure.

Nikostratos stood on the prow of his ship in muted silence, his lips pressed tightly together, his eyes roving the port, which seemed to be unscathed by the unrest, but eerily quiet.

Nikostratos had come urgently with five hundred Messenian hoplites. But he feared they might be too late. He was also ignorant of the other storm heading their way. The Spartans were coming!

FIFTY-SIX

Ionian Sea, south of Corcyra

Brasidas stood on the aft quarter with Alkidas. He was looking back at the fleet, sailing out in formation, moving under the press of oars and sails...

'It's good weather, Brasidas,' said Alkidas. 'The wind's steady at our backs, if it holds out, we'll make good time.'

'Sosthenes will be meeting us in the cove opposite the islands. We'll have good cover there for the night.'

Alkidas's flagship, the Persephone led the armada of fifty-three warships, sailing close to the shore, following the mainland coast northward. It was an impressive sight, even so, Brasidas knew that the Corcyraeans could match them ship for ship, and if there were Athenians there, they would be in for some real trouble, but Brasidas was unhesitating and determined, even if Alkidas was less enthusiastic about engaging the Athenian navy, Brasidas was determined to see it through, and he had learned valuable lessons at the Battle of Naupaktos. Brasidas does not tun his back to his enemies, he thought, casting a quick glance to Alkidas.

If there were Athenians there, they would engage and fight. Isolating the Athenians and distracting them with a few ships was the plan they decided upon, whilst the bulk of the fleet would engage the Corcyraean fleet, should it decide to come out to fight.

If the Corcyraeans chose not to fight, as Alkidas hoped, they would take the city through its ports, and put hoplite marines ashore at landing sites along the coast.

Brasidas looked round at Alkidas. Could he be trusted to follow through, or would he lose his courage again? This was Brasidas's big concern, and unfortunately, it was Alkidas who was giving the orders, and he had the confidence of his trierarchs and crews too.

They had been at sea together a long time, the Spartans, Ambraciots, Leucadians, Corinthians and others. They had learned to work together as a single entity under Alkidas's command, which went greatly in his favour, but if he wavers – what then? It would be difficult, even with Brasidas's eloquent powers of persuasion, to convince the trierarchs to remove Alkidas from command.

The problem was, the Gerousia, in its wisdom, decided that Brasidas's role was to provide, tactical advice, but Alkidas was navarch, he did not have to follow such advice. So far, Alkidas had approved Brasidas's plan and tactics, and followed his new orders from Sparta to sail for Corcyra in support of the oligarchic revolutionaries.

Brasidas had it in his mind to seize any opportunity that came along to attack, and if possible, capture Corcyra. They could install a governing panel of oligarchs there. He had already discussed the matter with the kings and ephors before he left Lakedaimon, and they were in favour of the plan, but only if circumstances allowed. Athens would fight hard to keep control of Corcyra, its strategic value was incalculable, with unimpeded access to Sicily, Carthage and Libya.* Sparta's important ally Syracuse had already had engagements with the Athenians and the Hellenic colonies of Italy.

For now, Brasidas kept the plan to himself. Alkidas had enough to think about with what lay immediately before them.

*

The Islets of Sybota were sighted as the fleet sailed in from the from the south.

'Asteropos,' Alkidas called and a young Spartan turned to him. 'When we get ashore, send out scouts and men to buy supplies.'

'As you command.'

'I advise you to beach our ships prows out, Alkidas, to be ready to sail at quick notice.'

Alkidas resented Brasidas's advice, even more so because it was good advice, and that stung his pride.

They came into a sheltered bay with a long sandy beach, on which a good number of the ships were grounded, just as Brasidas advised, with their prows pointed out to the sea in a defensive line, ready to cast off at a moment's notice.

Alkidas ordered the dismantling of the masts and removal of excess weight from the fleet in readiness for battle.

Brasidas sent lookouts from his own men up onto the cliffs, while scouts from the ships' crews went off to find supplies in the countryside.

Sosthenes showed up not long after midnight. He told Brasidas and Alkidas about the unrest that was raging in Corcyra City, and about the twelve Athenian warships and the Messenian hoplites with them.

Brasidas smiled. 'The gods are generous in their gift to us...' He looked at Alkidas. 'Only a fool would miss that opportunity, eh, Alkidas?'

Alkidas did not respond.

* ***In Ancient Hellas, Libya referred to Africa.***

FIFTY-SEVEN

Corcyra

Before Nikostratos had time to leave, word came that a Peloponnesian armada was less than an hour away and was de-rigged for battle. This was all they needed in the middle of a civil war...

Gripped by panic, the Corcyraeans ordered their own fleet of sixty ships be made ready immediately to sail to intercept the Spartans. Nikostratos urged calm, and told the Corcyraeans to follow the twelve Athenian ships out in orderly fashion, but the Corcyraeans were too consumed with fear, alarm and rage to heed the Athenians, and the provisional assembly, such as it was, ordered the trierarchs immediately to their ships with orders to engage and destroy the enemy, placing their confidence in the oligarchic trierarchs. Hoping that they would put Corcyra ahead of their own political opposition to the controlling democrats.

Bulis had made a fateful decision, knowing his crew were loyal to him, he decided that at the first opportunity, he would defect with his ship to the Spartans. He wasn't the only commander who had decided on this course.

Down in the naval port, feelings among the crews and officers were running high, with democrats and pro-Athenians sailing under the commands of Oligarchs, who, up until hours ago were trying to brain one another. All the same, the ships were quickly de-rigged of their masts and sails.

There was no command structure, no plan, no communications between the warships, so consequently, it was a free-for-all in the port. The Corcyraean, ignoring Nikostratos's advice, sailed out in a completely disorganised fashion, sailing erratically towards open water. Some of the ships almost collided in their rush to the sea walls.

Aboard the ships, the situation was tense amongst the crews, still reeling from the revolution, the democratisers seething with hatred and shipmates were fast becoming enemies, and insults were exchanged on the rowing decks, some men refused to obey their officers completely, whilst beyond, the Spartan armada was getting closer and closer, but the political enmities were just too deep to be ignored, even in this grave hour.

The ships cut across one another and bumped into each other with shuddering THUDS and THUMPS and creaking of wood. It was utter pandemonium, the trierarchs and crews yelled profanities from one ship to the other...

'EH! WATCH WHERE YOU'RE GOING, YOU DRUNKEN SONS OF WHORES!'

'OUT OF THE FUCKING WAY!'

'MOVE YOURSELVES, YOU COCK SWINGING ARSEHOLES...!'

The unrest continued out into the open sea, and insults quickly turned to physical violence, and to the Athenians' dismay, fighting among the crews on many of the Corcyraean ships had broken out.

The officers took to their swords to defend themselves from the mutineers, but they were quickly overpowered and thrown off their ships into the sea, or murdered on the spot.

Nikostratos watched with speechless incredulity. He just knew there was trouble brewing on some of those ships, they had heard the shouts and profanities being exchanged aboard several of the ships, even from this distance, the Athenians could hear them.

He exchanged a foreboding look with one of his officers. 'If we get through this day alive, nobody'll be more surprised than I, old friend.'

'They've lost their fucking minds.'

Nikostratos put his hand up to his face, sinking his fingered into his grizzled beard as he watched the Corcyraean ships with growing horror. Instead of keeping in a tight formation or battle line, they were all over the place. He feared some might surrender their vessels to the Spartans or even join them in the battle against their own countrymen. Had Corcyra not been such a vital ally for Athens, he might have sailed back to Naupaktos and let them get on with it.

Finally, they spotted the Peloponnesian fleet, like a dark cloud on the glistening water, oars sweeping a steady pace, making no more than six knots by Nikostratos's reckoning as he moved to the prow and grabbed the landing ladder strapped to the side and watched the Peloponnesian fleet with care, judging their seamanship by the beat and synchronicity of their oars and not one was out of time with the others.

The Spartan fleet formed a battle line, again, their manoeuvres were perfectly timed. These were no amateurs, he though, these were professional sailors.

Nikostratos had seen enough. He turned to his second officer. 'Signal the others and order the battle line, and slow our speed. Bring up the archers and boarding parties and stand ready with the grappling irons.'

'As you command.'

Nikostratos looked at the Corcyraeans, who had sailed ahead, keeping wide of them in a random mass of uncoordinated ships on an intercept course with the Spartan fleet.

And then, his worse feared were realised, when two Corcyraean war triremes suddenly broke away from the others and started rowing for their lives towards the Spartan line, and so not to make the Spartans think that they were attacking, the two defecting ships turned across the Spartans' prows, showing them their open sides. A sure indication they intended to defect or surrender to the Spartans.

'What in the name of Hades are those fools doing!?' gasped the second officer.

'Joining the enemy,' said Nikostratos lowly.

Bulis spotted Sosthenes on one of the Spartan ships. He called out and Bulis recognised him immediately and informed Brasidas and Alkidas.

Things went from bad to worse, the fighting aboard other Corcyraean crews intensified.

Rowers on the outriggers abandoned their oars and leapt onto the decks and joined in the fighting.

'May the gods help us this day...'

FIFTY-EIGHT

Aboard the Persephone, Brasidas and Alkidas could see what was happening aboard the Corcyraean ships. Brasidas raised his brows and had an amused look on his face. 'Looks like they've laid on some entertainment for us, Alkidas.'

'Pans prick,' Alkidas muttered, and seeing the advantage, he ordered a signal be sent for twenty ships to intercept and engage the chaotic Corcyraeans.

The two Corcyraean ships were granted permission to join the rear.

Across the fleet, soldiers, boarding parties with grappling hooks, along with Peloponnesian archers and marines took up positions ready for the fight as the twenty ships headed for the Corcyraean fleet.

The remaining thirty-three ships, including the Persephone set a course to intercept Nikostratos's twelve Athenian triremes.

The Corcyraeans moved in towards the twenty Spartan ships in no set order, aboard many of the ships, the fighting between the crew went on. Punching and bludgeoning one another, stabbing and strangling one another – it was impossible to know who was fighting for what cause. Many of the men who were thrown overboard, weight down by their armour sank beneath the calm water without trace. Others, most rowers who were not encumbered with armour flailed about in the water, screaming out for help but no help came and many, unable to swim, simply drowned, their bodies floating like driftwood.

The violence aboard two of the triremes was so widespread, the ships drifted off course, with nobody at the helm, the rowers were fighting each other and some of the oars slipped out from their portholes and floated away.

Some of the Corcyraean ships managed to maintain some semblance of order, but their actions were still reckless and undisciplined, as they moved in to attack the Peloponnesians.

Aboard his flagship, Nikostratos watched the thirty Peloponnesian ships moving towards them.

'Shall we attack, Navarch?' asked Nikostratos's second officer urgently.

'Not yet, we're in prime position to be penned in...' He pointed to the enemy's left wing. 'We'll attack the wing. Bring us into position. Pass the word and have the crews ready for a speedy engagement. If we can break their formation, we may be able to get in amongst them and snap their oars...'

'As you command...'

Aboard the Persephone, Alkidas and Brasidas watched the Corcyraeans and the twenty Peloponnesian ships. At least five of the Corcyraean ships were in no condition to fight, so the Peloponnesians ignored them, and for now they concentrated their force on those ships in fighting condition and wasted no time attacking them, rowing in at ramming speed.

One of the Corcyraeans was rammed amidships by an Ambraciot trireme.

Aboard the Persephone Brasidas was watching the twelve Athenian triremes, manoeuvring into position towards their flank.

'They're trying to get behind us,' said the boatswain.

Brasidas shook his head. 'No, it's a bluff...'

'Maintain course and speed,' ordered Alkidas, before Brasidas had the chance to suggest it.

The Athenians made their move, rowing in fast towards Alkidas's thirty-three ships...

'They're going for the flank!' said Brasidas as the Athenians suddenly changed course, coming about to prowls honed on the Peloponnesian wing.

The Athenian ships speeded towards the line, moving in like waterborne missiles, their prows cleaving the water. One pulled ahead of the others making fifteen knots under fast oars perfectly synchronised, rising, dipping, sweeping, bearing down rapidly on the flanking ship, the Corinthian trireme Neleus. The Athenian ship's bronze *embolon** glowed beneath the waves like a giant tusk ready to take a bite from the Neleus' aft quarter.

Archers aboard the Neleus opened fire with a volley of arrows as the Athenian ship sped towards them...

The crew of the Neleus were yelling and shouting, under fire from the Corinthian archers, two men were hit and fell as the Athenian ship gunned towards them...

There was a terrific CRASH and the entire ship shuddered like a trembler's knees as the Athenian ramming horn smashed into the aft quarter. The great bronze tooth smashed through the bow just below the bottom rowing deck below the waterline.

It was carnage. Rowers were crushed to death, others badly injured, screamed out in pain. Some were trapped in their rowing stations as the snapped ship's timbers buckled in on them. Elsewhere, uninjured rowers scrambled out and headed for the steps up to the upper decks as the sea began pouring in, quickly flooding the lower rowing deck, and soon those terrible screams of trapped and injured men, desperately trying to free themselves, their arms flailing with growing terror as the water rose rapidly around them were silenced as the water covered them.

The Neleus was done, sinking from the rear end, slipping deeper into the water. On her deck men threw themselves into the sea. The Neleus finally died, slipping almost gracefully under the water with a glug of bubbled – the Neleus was gone.

Meanwhile, aboard the Persephone, Alkidas gave the order to circle the Athenian ships.

The Peloponnesian fleet responded quickly, laagering their ships in a big circle around Nikostratos's ships, drumming them in, rowing in a perpetual circle.

The other twenty Peloponnesian ships were making quick work of the Corcyraeans, exchanging arrow fire but the Peloponnesians had a greater number of archers aboard their ships, and the disarray of the Corcyraeans had given the Peloponnesians a clear advantage, sinking and capturing several ships, while the remaining vessels began a retreat.

Across the way, a quarter of a mile away, Alkidas with his thirty-three triremes, was still circling the Athenians like wolves circling prey.

The twenty ships disengaged the Corcyraeans who were now in full retreat back to their homebase, turning about, the Peloponnesian allies speeded towards Alkidas...

Nikostratos, taking advantage of the distances between the Peloponnesian ships that was circling him, gave the order and they Athenian squadron made a dash for it under the fast press of oars out from Alkidas's snare, when Nikostratos gave the command to retreat and they rowed away in a single line, heading south to safe waters.

'What're we waiting for. We have the advantage,' said Brasidas urging Alkidas to give pursuit.

Alkidas refused. They had scored a victory and he did not want to jeopardise it by forcing the Athenians into a fight, when Spartan losses could be high. He ordered their withdrawal back to the cove to collect their rigging, with orders to sail back to Kyllene, taking their prisoners with them, along with the two defector ships and thirteen captured Corcyraean warships.

'We should press the advantage, Alkidas and attack the island directly and take the city by force with my men,' said Brasidas. 'It would be madness to let an opportunity like this pass.'

'It's too risky, Brasidas. Athens is sure to send more ships,' he said.

Brasidas was furious. 'I strongly advise–'

Alkidas spun to him. 'I command here, Brasidas. The decision is mine and I've made it,' he said snappily.

As it turned out, Alkidas wasn't wrong, they received information through signal fires that a large Athenian fleet was sailing urgently towards them.

* Ramming horn.

FIFTY-NINE

Sparta

The low autumnal sun was warm on their faces when the wind dropped, the sky was deep blue with not a cloud to be seen, and the quiet was immense with just the steady hoof-beats from their horses maundering leisurely along the road back to Sparta. They had been to Geronthrai to visit the sacred Grove and Temple of Ares, where Lysander made a sacrifice and left three coins in thanksgiving.

After, they rode to Therapne, where the dwellers and Helots watched the warrior and the youth trotting along the trade road. The two Spartans took no notice of them.

Agesilaos had something on his mind, something he wanted to do so badly, it was almost consuming him, the trouble was, he had no idea where or how to start.

'The weather's been kind to us today, Agesilaos.'

'It has. And I don't want to go back yet.'

'We don't have to. This day is ours.'

Agesilaos smiled. 'I'm so glad you're back, Lysander. It's been the worse time since you left. I worried and fretted, and my heart was empty without you. Truly I tell you, Lysander, you are the joy in my life.'

'You flatter me, Agesilaos.'

'Spartans do not flatter, Lysander and well you know it. We always speak with truth on our tongues.'

Lysander reined his horse closer to Agesilaos and reached to his hand and clasped it in his. 'And you're the light in my heart, Agesilaos.'

'I wish I could go with you when you go to war.'

'Your time will come, and when it does, then we shall go to war together.'

'The war might end before then, Lysander.'

'It might. And if it does, there'll be other wars for us to fight. There are always wars; it's in the nature of men and it'll always be that way until we destroy ourselves.'

'My father always said that this war was the most important war we've ever had to fight since the Trojan War.'

'He was right. This is a war of freedom, a war to tame the imperialist Athenians who would make slaves of all men. This is a war to preserve our way of life.'

Agesilaos huffed. 'That's why I don't want to miss it.'

Lysander chuckled amusedly to himself. 'I've a feeling you won't. Brasidas thinks it's going to go on for another ten years. You're just three years from the crimson and the bronze, so be patient, and learn all you can in those short years, because you're going to need to be a warrior in your heart as well as your head. You also have to be a prince of Sparta, a leader of armies. There's no point having an army if you don't know how to lead them.'

Agesilaos patted his horse's neck and looked thoughtfully at the Eurotas River glinting in the late afternoon sunshine. 'And what if the Athenians win, Lysander?'

'They won't win, not while we have breath in our bodies,' said Lysander. 'Athens will have her day of reckoning, and when she does, I pray the gods I'm there to see them cowed by Spartan might.'

Agesilaos had grown into a fine young man. He was shorter than most youths his age, but he was powerfully strong and he had a keen mind, curious and hungry to learn and in a hurry to come of age, when he could become the warrior he longed to be.

They stopped at the Menelaion, the tomb of King Menelaos and his beloved wife Helen of Sparta, daughter of Leder, sister of Castor and Pollux, who have their own sanctuary nearby at the Phoebeon. In centuries past, they sacrificed youths there to honour the Dioscouri, but that was no longer practiced.

The Menelaion is a far cheerier place, as much dedicated to love as to Menelaos and Helen. It was peaceful with just the sounds of the wind through the trees and birdsong and the smell of wild lavender and damp earth.

They dismounted their horses and sat together on the grassy bank close to the Menelaion with its pleasing architecture and statues of King Menelaos and his beautiful queen. In the apex above the columned porch, magnificently carved marble reliefs depict the rescue of Helen from the Trojans, and the mighty fleet of warships from a united Hellas, who, with a thousand ships, went to bring Helen home.

Agesilaos reclined on his side and propped his head up in his hand and looked deeply at Lysander, sitting on the grass next to him, gazing at the sanctuary. 'I enjoy days like this,' he said.

'As do I.'

Agesilaos shuffled himself round and laid back resting his head in Lysander's lap.

'It seems this is not a war for battles,' said Lysander as he stroked Agesilaos's short cropped hair.

Agesilaos rolled his eyes up and looked at Lysander. 'They cannot beat us on land.'

'So, they fight us in the sea, where we cannot beat them. But that's going to change. But for now, we're in a war of attrition. They're trying to wear us down and run our war chests dry to diminish our ability to fight and our morale. They believe that's how they can defeat us.'

'Then how little they know of us,' said Agesilaos.

'And that's their gravest mistake. Never underestimate your enemy, Agesilaos.'

SIXTY

Eponymous year of Hagesistratos Phliastos/June, 426 BC

Little Eupolia tottered to her father, a big bright smile on her face. 'Papa,' she said and it delighted Lysander to hear it.

He stooped and swooped her up in his hands and held her aloft over his head and spun her around. Eupolia chuckled.

Telephassa watched with a smiling face and bright happy eyes. 'Our daughter learns quickly, husband,' she said.

Lysander smiled at her. 'Like her mother,' he said and gave Eupolia a big silly smile and kissed her as he put her down. 'She grows a little more every time I see her,' he said.

Telephassa gestured to Rhea, who brought a jug of cooling cordial to them and set it onto the table. 'Come, Lysander, put your hand on my belly and feel our son move within.'

Lysander reached and put his hand on her bloated belly. She was near her time. He felt it, the child moving and he smiled. 'It may be a daughter.'

'No. It's a boy. And he's strong even now, and in such a hurry to get out. Only boys are thus inclined.'

'Then I pray our son will be born soon, before I have to go away again. But I tell you, Telephassa, boy or girl, I will love him or her no less than I love our beautiful Eupolia...' He watched the little girl, playing with a servant.

'Grandmother said you would feel that way.'

'She knows me well.' He poured the cordial in the horn cups and handed one to his wife.

He was fond of her, very fond; she supposed that he even loved her in his way. She knew that he would always be good to her and he would love their children, and he would be a good husband everywhere but her bed, because she also knew that his heart; his nature, belonged elsewhere. He had always been honest with her about that and she accepted him for it. One cannot change nature any more than one can change the direction of the wind.

'You would be punished if they discovered that you're here,' she said. Men rarely visit their wives socially at Sparta, but Lysander enjoyed her company, and he adored his daughter greater than life itself.

'Not if my reason is an official. Such as seeing Father Telis.'

She smiled. 'Grandfather is as devious as you are.' She took a swallow of the apple and honey cordial. 'Your mother comes to visit us often,' she said. 'She made me a beautiful winter cape.'

'She said as much when I saw her the day before yesterday. Do you need for anything, Telephassa, before I leave for the war?'

'We have all we need, Lysander. 'Your mother and my grandmother see that we're never without.'

Eupolia escaped the maid and came over. 'Papa, Papa...' She wanted him to pick her up again and hold her aloft and spin her in the air.

Lysander picked her up and sat her on his knee and bounced her up and down instead, which was just as much fun to her. She reached for his face with a big cheeky smile. 'Papa...'

'That's right, Eupolia. Papa,' said Telephassa. She fanned herself with her hand. Even in the shade, it was a hot and airless day. It seemed even worse, being heavy with child, every movement took the greatest effort.

'You spoil that child, Lysander,' came Argileonis's sharp voice from behind him.

Lysander looked round at Argileonis, standing under the shady porch. 'I fear I always will, Mother Argileonis.'

She gave him a haughty look and came out from the shade of the porch into the courtyard and sat with them. 'I fear you're right. But a father has a right to indulge his daughters. But not his sons,' she warned. 'Sparta indulges our sons,' she added, referring to the brutal Rearing. 'If you're here to see Telis, you may have a long wait. He is with the kings,' she said.

'I don't mind waiting. If that's well with you, Mother Argileonis?'

'Lysander,' she said, looking into his eyes. 'You are always welcome here. Now, hand the child to me and pour me a cup of that cordial. It's barely summer, and already the heat is uncomfortable.'

Lysander smiled and handed Eupolia over, and it was clear from the way Eupolia put out her arms, that she was fond of her great grandmother. It seemed that he wasn't the only one who overindulged her. 'It is unseasonably hot,' he said as he poured a cup of cordial into a cup for her.

'Telis says that you're to join Brasidas at Kyllene?' she said as Lysander handed her the cup.

'I am. My ship leaves in three days.'

'You did not say, husband?'

'I didn't think it necessary to say. I belong at Brasidas's side. Now I'm no longer a hippeus, I'm joining him in his next campaign.'

'Achilles and Patroclus,' Argileonis quipped amusedly – proudly, as she put the cup gently to Eupolia's lips for her to have a taste. 'Is that nice?' She smiled at Eupolia, who apparently wanted more. She looked at Eupolia. 'She has a taste for it. We must ask cook to make some more.'

Lysander reached down and picked up a carved wooden doll of a Hellenic woman with articulated arms and legs and held it out in front of Eupolia and made its arms and legs swing.

'Pero,' Eupolia said, wriggling on Argileonis's lap, reaching out for the doll.

'Pero?'

'The doll's name, husband,' said Telephassa.

Lysander smiled and gave the doll to Eupolia, who cuddled it.

Telephassa stood up slowly and carefully. 'Excuse me a moment,' she said and went effortfully into the house with a sudden need to empty her bladder.

'It will come any time now,' said Argileonis.

Lysander nodded his head.

SIXTY-ONE

Ionian Sea, South of Kyllene

Hecatombeus/July

There were four ships in the squadron, two old galleys and two of the captured Corcyraean triremes, renamed the Achilles and the Memnon.

The wind was at their backs as he and Narkissos stood on the forward quarter watching the rocky coast as they sailed around the Kyllene promontory to their right. The oars were rowing at a steady rate, the ships making barely three knots as they made their turn. The sails were drawn up to the crossbeams and tied off, the deck crew were about their duties, preparing the ships for port.

'We've made good time, Lysander,' said Narkissos.

'We had favourable winds, Trierarch,' said Lysander, 'and a good crew.'

The wind blew through Narkissos's long grey streaked hair; the late afternoon sun glimmered across his shiny bronze-skinned muscled cuirass. 'Take us in, Enomotarch.'

Lysander was pleasantly surprised. 'As you command...' He went to the aft quarter and watched their course carefully as they came in close to the coast as they turned towards Kyllene harbour. On the mount, the city loomed on the precipitous summit.

Lysander counted sixteen Peloponnesian war triremes at anchor in the bay, including two of the Gorgons, Euryale and Medusa. About six of them had dismantled their masts and rigging in readiness for immediate action, should Kyllene be caught in a surprise attack. In consequence, these ships were constantly crewed. Tomorrow, six more ships will be de-masted to take a turn. This was a Brasadian tactic, Lysander had discussed this very sort of thing over the years, so a portion of his forces are constantly ready for battle and surprise attacks. It was the same at the garrison, with half the soldiers on constant full battle readiness on a rotating system of shifts. Brasidas also took his turns, so the men knew he wasn't asking them to do anything he wasn't willing to do himself. It was one of his greatest qualities and it earned him an undivided loyalty among his men and junior officers, Spartan or otherwise.

Narkissos stood back wordless, watching everything Lysander did without interfering.

'There's no docking room in the port...' Lysander looked over his shoulder at the men on the rudder oars. 'Put us ashore on the beach, prow on,' he ordered.

Lysander looked at the boatswain. 'Signal the Memnon to follow us in. Prow on. The galleys will have to anchor until births become free.'

'As you command.' He picked up yellow and blue flags and signalled to the Memnon and then he signalled the galleys.

Narkissos nodded to himself. Lysander was competent and confident.

The town of Kyllene overlooks the bay from where it stands on a high mount that rises from the low flat land stretching off on three sides, with the sea on the fourth. It was a strategic place, easily defensible and lookouts could see for miles in every direction. It was a vital stronghold for the Peloponnesian allies to re-supply, rest and carry out repairs to their vessels, as well as a busy merchant port and fishing fleet.

Lysander stepped to the open deck down into the rowing decks below, he could feel the stinking heat rising up in his face. 'Raise oars!' he commanded.

The trièraulès stopped playing his flute and the oars lifted up out of the water like either side.

Lysander monitored their speed as they maneuvered under their own inertia into the port towards the stretch of beach, they were still moving too fast.

Narkissos grabbed hold of the side rail in anticipation grounding on the beach.

'Backwater!' Lysander called at the right moment as they steered towards the beach.

The oars dipped into the water and backstroked, slowing them down to a near stop.

'Raise oars!'

The ship barely jerked as they hit the soft sandy beach, the prow rising onto land, the solid bronze embolon ramming tusk shining like gold in the sun, dripping water.

Narkissos was impressed.

Once the ship was secured, Lysander and Narkissos jumped down from amidships, landing knee deep in water and waded onto the beach.

Phylarch Ephoros marched up to Lysander, the thirty-six hoplites who disembarked from the Memnon, formed in four ranks on the beach behind him.

'Take the men up to the garrison,' Lysander ordered.

'As you command.' Ephoros turned back to the men and ordered them to march.

Above, Brasidas was standing out on the terrace of his headquarters watching the new arrivals. '*Little Wolf*,' he said quietly to himself, his lips curling into a smile.

'Sir?'

Brasidas turned to the young officer standing behind him. 'What?' He frowned. 'Why are you still here, Libys?'

Libys cleared his throat. 'The Eleans are pressing for a reply, sir. Regarding the Achaians?'

Brasidas huffed. '*Pan's prick*! Not this again?'

'They've made several fresh incursions into Elis over the past two months and stolen livestock and other chattel. They've killed at least four Eleans and wounded many others.'

'Achaia is neutral.'

Libys wasn't sure if that was a statement or a question, all the same, he said guilelessly, 'Yes, but the Eleans are allies, sir.'

'Yes, thank you, I think I know that already, Libys.'

'Apologies, sir–'

'Why would we want to go stirring up hornets to sting our arses, boy? We attack Achaia, they pledge to Athens, and suddenly we have fifty thousand more enemies to fight. Are you with me, Libys...?' He waited for an answer.

'Yes, sir,' said Libys.

'Then the answer's no. The Eleans will have to sort it out for themselves. We're not here to become embroiled in domestic disputes with their neighbours. Besides, we don't have the manpower to launch military operations into that shithole.'

'No, sir,' said Libys, lowering his tone. 'And the deserters, sir?'

Brasidas raised a brow. 'I forgot about them. Have them taken to the place of execution at sunset to await my arrival. Now go away, Libys, you're giving me a headache. And when Trierarch Narkissos and your brother Lysander arrive, send them out and tell that lazy bastard Bellerophon to bring us some of the good wine. Not that dog's piss we give to everyone else. That sweet stuff the Roman brings me.'

Lysander was here? Libys's heart skipped a beat. He strode away back to the house.

It was good to see his brother again, and Lysander looked just as pleased to see Libys. They embraced and kissed and kissed each other on the cheek.

'Where's Brasidas?' asked Narkissos.

'Waiting for you on the terrace, Trierarch...'

A servant brought water in a jug and poured it into a wash basin for the officers to bathe their hands and faces.

Narkissos marched off without bathing.

Lysander bathed his hands and face unhurried.

'I'm glad you're here, Lysander,' said Libys. 'He's been in a dark mood these past months. If anyone can bring him out of his melancholy, it's you.'

'I'll do my best.'

Libys patted Lysander on his arm. 'He's already cheered up since seeing you down on the beach. And he ordered his best wine for you.'

Lysander took a drying cloth from a servant and dried his hands and face.

*

'... *Thirty-six men*!?' Brasidas barked at Narkissos. 'And four ships? That's it, is it? My reinforcements, four ships and an enomotia of hoplites? And with this I'm supposed to take on the might of the Athenian navy, am I?' he ranted at Narkissos.

Narkissos shifted his weight.

'What else have you brought with you?' he said sarcastically. 'The plague perhaps?'

'That's unfair, Brasidas. Like you, I'm just carrying out my orders.'

Brasidas calmed and nodded his head. 'Yes. You're right. Forgive me, Narkissos.'

Narkissos nodded his head. 'A cup of wine and all's forgotten.'

Brasidas smiled. He gestured to the bench and they sat down. 'How's my Little Wolf? Where is he?'

Narkissos looked back to the villa. 'He was with me just now.'

'Probably talking to his brother.'

'He's got the makings of a good officer,' said Narkissos as Bellerophon arrived with the wine.

Brasidas looked narrowly at his faithful mothon. 'You took your time getting here.'

Bellerophon set the jug and cups down on a stone table. 'Had to press the grapes,' he said sarcastically.

Narkissos raised his brows at the servant's insolence.

It was water off a duck's back to Brasidas, he and Bellerophon were like an old married couple, and it was well known they bickered like hens, but Brasidas never punished him. If a hoplite or junior officer spoke thus to him, Narkissos had no doubt that Brasidas would have that man flogged to within a fraction of his life.

Just then, Lysander came out into the garden and approached them, looking smart liveried in his armour and cloak, his helmet under his arm.

'Welcome to Medusa's arsehole, Little Wolf,' said Brasidas.

'Greetings.'

'Sit down and have a drink.'

'Gladly.' He sat on a stone seat and took a cup of wine from Bellerophon.

'He's in one of his moods,' Bellerophon whispered.

Lysander smiled to himself.

'So, they've sent you here to rot with me, have they? Sorry about that, boy.'

'I'd not want to be anywhere else, but here with you, Brasidas.'

Brasidas appreciated the sentiment, even if he didn't say so.

'They've not sent you here to rot,' said Narkissos.

'I should be in Attica, or at sea, taking the war to the enemy, not scratching my arse doing nothing here. This is Alkidas's doing. He's a bloody rat as well as a trembler!' Brasidas shook his head lowly. They either expected miracles from him, he told them, or they expected him to fail, to give his enemies back in Sparta the opportunity to clip his wings, or worse still, ruin him?

Lysander and Narkissos looked at one another.

'The war's going badly, Brasidas.'

Brasidas wheeled on Narkissos. '*Well, that's hardly a surprise is it, Narkissos*? With procrastinators on every front making the wrong decisions.'

'Have a care, old friend,' said Narkissos. 'Now you speak among your friends who love you. But there are those who fear and despise you. They'll use anything they can against you.'

After they drank to the gravestones, Brasidas ordered Libys to have accommodation made ready for Narkissos and Lysander.

Once Lysander and Brasidas were alone, Lysander reached under his cuirass and pulled out a cypher strip and handed it to Brasidas. 'From your father,' he said as Brasidas took the cypher from him.

Brasidas pulled a thong up from around his neck, upon which hung his scytale and wrapped the cypher around it and read the message. It was intelligence regarding Sicily and the possibility that the Athenians might be contemplating dispatching a significant fleet against Syracuse and other Spartan allies on the island and mainland Italy, such as the Spartan colony of Taranto. His orders were to monitor the seaways and report on any large-scale enemy movements north or westward beyond Corcyra.

Lysander watched him and sipped his wine, as sweet as honey. Gulls screeched overhead, their screams echoing in the sky.

Brasidas finally looked at Lysander. 'We're to watch for enemy ships heading for Sicily and Italy,' he said. 'And conducting secret operations around Corcyra isn't going to be easy. You can't fart around here without the neighbours knowing of it,' he said, referring to the island of Zakynthos. 'The Athenians will know you're here. Their lookouts on Zakynthos would've spotted you. They stay quiet over there, thinking we'll forget about them. But they report everything back to the Athenians.'

'We could try taking the island. The Athenians rely on Zakynthian tar for waterproofing their ships.'

'Forget it,' said Brasidas. 'Knemos tried taking the island a few years ago and failed, and he had more men with him than I do. I've sailed right around Zakynthos. I've even been over there a few times disguised as a merchant to take a look around. The city's well-fortified, so's the port, and the tar pits are inaccessible...' He poured himself a fresh cup of wine. He looked at Lysander. What a fine young officer he had turned into. 'It seems like yesterday when you surrendered to me in the mountains.'

Lysander gave him a sharp look. 'As I recall, I didn't surrender to you. We negotiated a truce.'

Brasidas chuckled. 'Bound with a sprig of sweet root.' He laughed, but it soon petered away to another thoughtful silence, the scytale clenched tightly in his fist.

Lysander sensed despair in Brasidas, something he had never seen in him before and it unsettled him.

'They say I'm reckless, and I fraternise too much with the allies, who they think are trying to influence me.'

'That's what your enemies say. It's not what your friends say, Brasidas, and you have a lot of friends back home. Powerful friends like Ramphias, your father, and even the kings. Especially Agis.'

'Then why have they left me here, Lysander? Where I'm as useless as a eunuch in a fuckhouse.'

Lysander had no answer to give him. All he knew, was that his posting was considered tactical. His guess was, they might be planning an invasion of Corcyra, or another attempt at taking Naupaktos and Stratos? Or they were expecting trouble here at Kyllene and Brasidas was good at dealing with trouble.

SIXTY-TWO

Athens

Eponymous year of Angenidas

Gamelion/January, 425 BC

It was an auspicious time of the year to marry, Gamelion being the month that honours Hera, the goddess of marriage, and it was the High Priestess of Hera herself who blessed the marriage at the sacrifices on the first day of the wedding. Today was the third and last day of the wedding, the day of receiving gifts, when the family and guests bring gifts, for the bride and groom to the marital home, which was one of the finest houses in Athens, in Alcibiades's ancestral demos of Skambonidai, one of the wealthiest districts in the city.

Everyone was gathered in front of the house, nestled in large and beautifully maintained gardens. Alcibiades, with his beautiful bride Hipparete, daughter of Hipponikos, stood either side of the threshold, receiving their generous tributes and thanking their guests wholeheartedly for their generosity.

The gifts were varied. Furniture from Hipponikos, blankets from an uncle, exquisite cloth, perfumes, oils, pots and pans, jugs of wine, jars of rare spices, even a marital bed, which was scattered in flower petals.

The guests had come from far and wide, the great and the good of Athenian aristocracy were there, political friends and enemies too.

Hipponikos smiled joyously, opening his arms to the guests as he addressed them 'What a joyous occasion this is,' he said. 'I cannot remember an occasion when I was prouder or happier than today, when I welcome Alcibiades into my family, and truly I say, I love him as mine own son...'

Alcibiades surveyed the guests, some of them shivering in the cold, willing the old man to finish his speech so they could get inside, into the warmth and enjoy the celebratory feast.

Not everyone was pleased to see Socrates among the guests, Cleon utterly detested the unkempt conscience of Athens. But he was the groom's friend, not only that, he had saved the groom's life at Potidaea.

Finally, Hipponikos's long and rambling speech was over and Alcibiades formerly invited the honoured guests into the house to feast.

Socrates was perfectly at home amongst the lofty and powerful men of Athens. He was seated between Nicias and Hyperbolos, an ardent imperialist, who believed Athenians to be superior in intellect to all other Hellenes, and it was the right of Athens to impose her political will on her allies and expand Athenian territories by planting colonies in places like Macedon and Thrace, and any defeated Peloponnesian territories. Socrates listened to him and his rabble-rousing views about the ruling democratic party and its ineptitude towards fighting the Peloponnesians "*man-to-man*", as he put it as he ranted on with Cleon. Who was in complete agreement with him.

'The Boule is far too lenient with dissenters in the alliance,' said Hyperbolos. He was referring to the back-tracking of the order to execute the Lesbian revolutionaries.

'Too damned soft,' said Cleon. 'We have to set the examples that we'll not tolerate such behaviour from our tributary allies, no more than we would our Peloponnesian enemies. War's a very dirty business, Hyperbolos, and sometimes, we have to show that we can be ruthless to the extreme.'

Socrates, stared at them with icy disapproval.

Hyperbolos stared back at him with equal contempt. 'Something to say, Socrates?'

Socrates smiled at him. 'To you, Hyperbolos...?' He shook his head. 'I can't think of anything I would ever want to say to you...'

Hyperbolos winced, and before he could respond to Socrates's insult, Socrates started a conversation with a servant, who delivered the wine, just to add injury to the insult, preferring the opinions of a slave over a powerful aristocrat. Hyperbolos was furious, and he was about to bark something at him, when Cleon put his hand over Hyperbolos's wrist and shook his head. They were guests at Alcibiades's wedding feast, this was not the place to begin a shouting match.

Alcibiades knew everyone it seemed, Theramenes thought as he looked along the long tables set either side of the dining room, like a Spartan dining mess. There were about fifty guests, with Alcibiades sat at the top table with Hipponikos and his young son Callias and two of Alcibiades's cousins.* Alcibiades's brother, Ariphron, who had the curse of the Maniai, was not invited for fear of him having one of his violent outbursts.

Everyone seemed to be enjoying themselves as they feasted on fish, pork, venison, beef, mutton, squid, stuffed vines and sweet fruits. The wine was of the very best quality; Alcibiades had spared no expense, and there were minstrels playing music, and the room echoed to the chatter and laughter of the guests.

Nicias and Diodoros were talking politics as usual, and every so often, they cast their sour looks at Cleon and Hyperbolos; incredulous that they were among the guests, given they were among Pericles's most vociferous rivals.

* ***Women did not dine with men at wedding feasts at Athens, a highly misogynistic society, especially in the aristocratic and merchant classes. In fact, they did not eat at all until the men had finished dining.***

SIXTY-THREE

Sparta

Pleistoanax called the Gerousia into urgent assembly. King Agis was away, invading Attica with the main body of the Spartan army and the host of the allies ravaging the Attican countryside as usual, so it was just Pleistoanax and three of the ephors who remained to tend the administration of the kingdom.

The chamber was filled with whispering voices and shuffling bodies as the twenty-eight elders settled onto the benches, wondering what was going on? Had Agis been wounded? Killed? Had there been a battle? What was it that had brought the King's urgent summons? The whispering voices were loaded with worrying speculations.

'We've received disturbing news from Messene,' said Pleistoanax once the gerontes fell silent. 'An enemy fleet has put in at Pylos and they've put men ashore who are building defences there...'

His words hung in the air for a long moment.

'How large is this force, My Lord?' asked a geront.

'Five triremes and an unknown number of hoplites,' said Tellis.

'It was part of a larger force that has now departed from the area,' Pleistoanax added.

'Witnesses tell us that the ships put into Pylos to shelter from a storm,' said Eponymous Ephor Angenidas. 'When the main body departed, they left behind the five triremes with hoplites. We believe the larger fleet is on its way to Corcyra and then on to Sicily.'

'Five ships and a handful of hoplites are hardly cause for great concern, My Lord,' said Autokrates.

'I disagree,' Ramphias put in. 'We've already underestimated the Delians on at least three occasions, each one has left Lakedaimonia bruised and tarnished–'

'Do we know who commands these Athenians?' asked Autokrates.

'Demosthenes of Athens,' said Tellis.

Archias frowned. 'I feel that I know this name?'

'Demosthenes commanded the attack on the Aetolians last autumn,' said Tellis. 'He was routed by the Aetolians, who killed a hundred and twenty of his hoplites. Not long after, he engaged our forces at Olpae, where Eurylochus was killed in a land battle with a good number of his men.'

It was yet another example of the Athenians outwitting the Spartans and their allies with ambushes and surprise attacks, inflicting a devastating defeat on Sparta, and a humiliation. After Eurylochus was killed, his colleague, Brasidas's boyhood friend Menedaios negotiated a truce with Demosthenes, but Demosthenes would only allow the Spartans and their officers to leave, but not their allies. What followed, was nothing short of murder. When the Spartans moved out to return to their ships, their Ambraciot allies tried to follow them out. Demosthenes with his Acarnanian allies cut the Ambraciots off and slaughtered two-hundred of their hoplites.

'... We should send a strong contingent from the Fifth Mora, My Lord,' a geront suggested.

Tellis nodded his head. 'I would advise that word be sent at once to King Agis for his immediate return to Sparta with the army. Further, a message should also be dispatched immediately by fast ship to Navarch Thrasymelidas and Brasidas with orders to go with their fleet to Pylos under sail and oar without delay–'

Archias stepped out, coarsely chuckling, putting out his hands, shaking his head. 'My Lord, this is an overreaction. We deal here with a few Athenians helped by a few treacherous Helots...' He shook his head. 'Really, I see no urgency here that commands us recall the armies from Attica...' He chuckled again. 'Nor is there any justification in recalling the fleet...' He shook his head again and looked almost clownishly at Tellis and Ramphias. 'No, no, My Lord. Let all be and do as was originally suggested and send some good men from the Fifth. They'll have these recreants taking to their ships soon enough. The cost of recalling the armies and the fleet, will not simply weigh upon the treasury, but upon our standing, that we should respond with such haste and alarm over what is a minor incursion.'

'Caution must always be our wisest adviser,' said Tellis. 'We must inform them, or we put ourselves at risk. 'This Demosthenes has already proved himself a capable strategos, and we cannot risk them fermenting rebellion among the Helots. We ignore this incursion at our peril.'

'I agree with Tellis,' said Pleistoanax, nodding his head. 'We must send to Agis and Eurylochus. This might be just the first of many incursions. Possibly the beginning of an encirclement.'

SIXTY-FOUR

Ionian Sea

This was a war in which fowl deeds had become fair game, Brasidas told him, where honour sat beside disgrace, and righteousness went hand in hand with murder and atrocity. This was a new sort of war altogether, alien to everybody who was fighting it.

Before, Brasidas had said, in the old days, wars were settled on battlefields, one army pitched against another, and whoever was left standing at the end, had Nike's love. But not this war, this was a protracted war of attrition, fought from behind high walls and ideological politics and avaricious greed. Even the gods were lost in the carnage as the hearts of men grew darker and darker, and became as granite mountains before the wind, immoveable and unchangeable.

It was like some colossal living creature, visceral and sinuous, a monster that came as an unstoppable storm that had neither beginning nor end; it ravaged everything it touched in one way of another. This was what Brasidas understood so clearly, even if others did not.

For keen young officers like Lysander, the war offered many opportunities for his own advancement. He was an elite warrior, a natural tactician, a chance-taker like Brasidas. He knew that if he continued to make a good show of himself, he would rise quickly in the ranks. It was his ambition to achieve that drove him, it was that same raw ambition that drove him through the Rearing to become an elite of elites, a kryptes and then ten years a Dioskouros of the Three Hundred. He was ready for command. He was ready to fight this war by all means he could – he was ready to go to the Beautiful Death.

He was now thirty years old, an equal among equals, a Spartiate and a junior officer marked for greater things. He had started to grow his hair long, and his thick black wavy mop was already below his ears almost to his shoulders with several platted braids that hung like slumbering snakes from his head, studded with coloured clay beads. He had also grown a beard on his chin and along his jawline that he kept neatly trimmed in his own distinctive fashion, which was entirely different from the beards of his older colleagues and it made him stand out, which was exactly what he wanted.

Lysander was amidships aboard the Spartan War Trireme Medusa, with Brasidas who was in command of the hoplite marines and twenty of the ships that made up the fleet, massed just off the coast of Epirus five miles from Corcyra.

Navarch Thrasymelidas was aboard the Euryale.

They were sailing passed the Ambracian Gulf in three squadrons of twenty ships, like dark wooden islands, their sailes bloated to the wind, on a northerly course to Corcyra, where the civil war still continued, added to that famine had broken out and there was desperation, butchery and hunger besieging that island and the oligarchic faction sent an emissary to Sparta to ask for help, and they jumped on the opportunity and so did Brasidas, who wanted to finish what was started the last time he was at Corcyra, and so, with sixty Peloponnesian warships under the command of Navarch Thrasymelidas to capture the island and install the oligarchs.

The fleet of ships were as graceful as they were impressive, a powerful fleet of predators, their shimmering bronze tusks below the waterline made the trireme the deadliest engine of war ever created, swift and filled with the spirit of Nemesis, the goddess of carnage who dances upon the gouged corpses of the fallen, bringing merciless death and destruction wherever she goes. The apotropaic eyes leered from the prows just above the waves, warding off evil sea spirits and monsters, gave the ships the look of living creatures as they moved steadily in their menacing packs, their prows parting the water.

Brasidas wanted to change everything; he wanted to reintroduce a mounted cavalry; to incorporate Spartan archer divisions into the morai, expand the navy and more recently, he suggested training Helots to be hoplites, which was met with shock and ridicule.

Not everyone was opposed to the reforms. Pleistoanax was open to modernising the morai, so was Brasidas's father and Ramphias. Younger officers too, where his innovative ideas were more popular, especially among officers with frontline experience, who grasped the need for change, and not just militarily. There was a growing call for social changes too, to allow for fresh blood in the Spartiate order, which had been declining ever since the war with the Persians. Radical thinking was afoot, that even the Helots should be given a form of free status, including the rights to conduct commerce, and to introduce the best of their sons into the Rearing. The idea was immediately dismissed and the matter was to be a forbidden subject.

The Spartans did not hate the Helots, they feared them. And as the Helot saying goes, *they would eat the Spartans raw given the chance.*

Since Methone, Brasidas had come more and more to prominence, a maverick hero, the un-Spartan Spartan as some were calling him, and that made those old warlords in the Gerousia uncomfortable, or envious, probably both was Lysander's thoughts on it.

The wind thundered in Brasidas's ears as he stood on the aft quarter, the big sail bloated in the wind, giving them two and a half knots.

Lysander came up onto the quarter.

'We're harbouring the night at Elaias Limen,' said Brasidas.

SIXTY-FIVE

Elaias Limen, Thesprotia, Epirus

They sat in the sulphurous glow of braziers and cressets, music and feasting and pretty girls danced in the smoky hall, where the Spartan and allied commanders were treated to a feast worthy of a king, put on by the local Thesprotian prince, Alexander. He was apparently happy to have the Peloponnesian fleet in his port, and he expressed pro-Spartan views and had nothing good to say about the Athenians, who had accused them of piracy and called them barbarians.

Alexander was a big man with a deep booming voice and bore many battle scars on his face and arms from fighting many local wars that had plagued the region for centuries.

The Epirotes considered themselves Hellenes, but most Hellenes considered them as half Hellenic and half barbarian, or completely barbarian, but never did they say they were completely Hellenic, even if their language was almost the same and they worshipped the same Hellenic gods. So did the Macedonians, and they were considered completely barbarian by most Hellenes.

They ate more red meat than they did fish, despite being on the sea. They drank undiluted wine like the Macedonians, and they were crude in their manner, but Brasidas couldn't fault them for their hospitality, and he dominated the feast with funny stories and tales of adventure.

It was quite extraordinary, even Thrasymelidas had to admit, how easily Brasidas seemed to be able to get along with just about anybody, from the lowest to the highest; barbarian or civilised.

Alexander reached for a leg of mutton. 'What're you think, Brasidas of Sparta? Are they as beautiful as Spartan girls?' he started up, looking at the four naked young dancing women, their bodies painted like serpents in bright yellow and dark green, and long snakes slithered over their arms and around their necks and down their bodies as they danced with slow eroticism, their painted bodies undulating smoothly like their snakes, with a saurian grace. Quickly shaken tambourines emulated the hissing of snakes, accompanied by the slow and hauntingly melodic song of a lone flute. 'They are the maidens of Echidna.' He took a swallow of wine to wash the mutton down.

Brasidas watched the dancing girls for a while; the light from fiery braziers set around the big stone hall rippled subaqueously over their oily bodies, their tongues poked out and they hissed at the guests with wide rapturous eyes that seemed possessed by the serpent goddess as their dance grew faster and more energetic, holding the writhing snakes out at arm's length.

Alexander was pleased to see his guests captivated by the dancers. He gave Brasidas a hard clap on his back. 'You want to take them to your bed no doubt? Fuck them until the dawn breaks?'

'Is that an offer, Prince?' Brasidas came back quickly.

Alexander leaned back and roared with laughter. 'I like you, Brasidas of Sparta. Yes indeed,' he boomed out, nodding his head broadly, pausing to take a swallow of wine, he gave out another loud laugh. 'You want girls? I have girls. You want boys? I have boys too.'

Thrasymelidas gave Brasidas a disapproving look. Around the long tables, the trierarchs were all having a good time, eating their fill, drinking the strong wine, enjoying the entertainment. Corinthians, Ambraciots, Spartans, Eleans – it seemed that only he, Thrasymelidas was not enjoying himself.

'They're as succulent as ripe peaches, Prince,' Brasidas said with a big grin on his face and a sparkle in his eyes as he watched the maidens of Echidna, now in a frenzied state, the music was faster, the hissing was louder. Sweat ran from their painted bodies as they flew about the hall, spinning and jumping with their snakes, casting shadows in the gloaming hue of firelight...

Alexander clapped his hands and the music stopped. He flicked the back of his hand, and the maidens of Echidna, hurried away. He clapped his hands again and two naked men ran into the hall and stood between the tables, and they started to wrestle.

Lysander watched them, their moves. They were both lean and strong, evenly matched...

One of Alexander's nobles came into the hall and went to his prince and whispered something in his ear.

Alexander looked at Thrasymelidas. 'A Spartan trireme has just arrived in the port,' he said.

Thrasymelidas frowned. 'A Spartan ship? Are you certain?' he looked at the old man who brought the message.

'Yes. There are red cloaks on the deck.'

Thrasymelidas looked at Lysander. 'Go and see.'

Lysander rose to his feet, still chewing a mouthful of mutton, he marched out of the great hall and was led through the citadel by a warrior holding a torch aloft as they walked to the port.

The trireme was just tying up when Lysander arrived, and sure enough, it was one of the new Spartan triremes, the Tisiphone, and Lysander recognised her trierarch, is was Clearchus's boyhood friend Homer, whose leg Lysander broke at the Rearing when he knocked Homer out of Old Herakles.

'Greetings, Lysander,' he said as he disembarked, carrying his helmet under his arm. 'I need to see the Navarch urgently. I've a message from the Gerousia.'

Lysander nodded his head. 'This way...' They started walking away, following the same warrior carrying his torch. 'It must be urgent to risk sending out one of the Furies on its own?'

'It is. The Athenians have invaded Messene and captured Pylos.'

Lysander shot him a look.

'I know nothing more than that,' Homer said.

Back at Prince Alexander's lavish banquet, Lysander went to Thrasymelidas and told him the news about Pylos, and added, 'The herald awaits you outside with a dispatch, sir.'

Thrasymelidas nodded his head and rose to his feet. 'You will please excuse us. An urgent message has come from Sparta...' He looked at Brasidas. 'Brasidas...'

Outside, Homer gave Thrasymelidas the sealed dispatch from the Gerousia and Thrasymelidas...

'What's going on?' asked Brasidas.

'Athenians have captured Pylos,' said Thrasymelidas. 'We've been ordered to break off from Corcyra and make haste back to Messene to the relief of Pylos,' he continued as he read the dispatch.

One of Brasidas's marines came out from the banquet. He came over and stood next to Lysander, curious to know what was going on.

Brasidas looked at him. 'Epitadas, muster the men and crews and be ready to sail within the hour.'

'As you command...' Epitadas marched back into the great hall.

SIXTY-SIX

Kephissos River, Attica

It was more like autumn than spring; the weather was utterly miserable with strong cold winds and heavy rainstorms hampering them every step of the way, slowing the mighty Peloponnesian armies down as they pressed on along roads of mud, practically impossible for their supply and baggage wagons. The river was high too, and in places, it had burst its banks and turned fields into lakes. As for ravaging the grain crops with fire, that was completely out of the question.

They had had some skirmishes with the Athenian cavalry and taken a few casualties.

The annual invasions of Attica were a Sisyphean effort, even in the best of weather, but this, this was exceptionally bad weather, and Agis had attempted to dissuade the Gerousia from the waste of resources, time and men on conducting their unproductive torching of grain fields and burning of olive and fruit groves and vineyards, of which there were many hundreds across Attica. The invasions did not tempt the Athenians to come rashly from behind their walls with their hoplites hot for battle. And the damage inflicted was but temporary. Crops regrow, and olive trees are hard to destroy. At best they could destroy a single harvest, but come the next season, those fire blackened olive trees spring back into fruitful life again. Chopping the trees down, and they did chop trees down by the hundred, was a labour-intensive task, and again, it achieved little if anything at all; there are millions of olive and fruit trees in Attica, and if they came every day for a hundred years, they'd not cut even a tenth of them down. And those they did chop down, simply sprouted saplings again the following spring, like the dead rising from the pit. Pointless, all of it, Agis thought, and he didn't care who knew it. His father before him had known it too. The Corinthians and the Thebans had come to the same conclusion.

It did nothing for morale. The vast amounts of food and supplies entering the Piraeus was ample to feed the population of Athens and those sheltering there. Destroying their estates and farms made no difference to the war, except possibly to the morale of owners of the land they destroyed. Hardly enough to force the enemy's capitulation, or to entice them into battle.

'What do the scouts report on enemy activity in the area?' He looked at Gylippos.

'They've sighted no enemy soldiers this side of Panakton, My Lord,' Gylippos replied. 'I think the weather's deterring them from leaving their garrison.'

'And who can blame them,' Agis said quietly. 'Besides, they've no need to,' he added in a louder voice. 'We're as useless as eunuchs in a fuckhouse, as Brasidas would say.'

Some of the officers chuckled.

Gylippos looked at the King; one side of his face was in darkness, the other was almost iridescent in the flickering lamplights hanging from a tall standard beside him.

'They know we'll not achieve much in weather like this,' Agis said, looking at the polemarchs and allied commanders.

A servant stepped to his side with a cup of wine and handed it to him. Once Agis took the cup, the servant stepped away, back into the shadows. 'If this rain continues, we'll be sailing across the Isthmus,' he said in an effort at humour.

'Indeed, My Lord,' said one of the Corinthians.

Agis cast a cold stare at the two ephors. By the gods, how he despised them. Like a couple of Hadean daemons that haunted him night and day. Humourless bastards, both of them, he thought.

Outside, it was cold, muddy and everybody was soaked through to the skin after days of rain, and they were utterly miserable, not least among them, their young general, King Agis. The sound of the rain pattered on the tent constantly, but at least it was relatively dry and relatively warm in here.

'We should reconsider our situation,' Agis said.

The two ephors both raised their brows as if by a symbiotic thought.

'In what way, My Lord?' asked the older of the two ephors, who was about fifty; he was a lean and gaunt man with a sallow cadaveric face and a bushy grey briar for a beard that hid his mouth.

'Well, we can't burn their crops, can we? And we need food, so either we go home, or we'll have to think of some other mischief.'

'What sort of mischief, My Lord?' asked the other ephor, who was about ten years younger than his colleague. He had no left eye, just a big open crater that looked black in the flickering light of the oil lamps' shadowy glow. 'The scouts report that there are minimal forces at Eleusis. There are several villages in the area. I suggest we attack them and destroy as much as we can.'

The ephors hoisted their brows again.

'My Lord. This is a rash decision,' cautioned the older ephor. 'And one you have not told us about.'

Agis did not respond.

'Eleusis is walled, My Lord,' said the other ephor.

Agis looked guilelessly at him. 'I'm not proposing an attack on the town. But the villages around it, and there are some fine houses there too, especially in the Rharian plain.'

Polymnis of Thebes who commanded the Theban hippeis and Alexarchus of Corinth, both agreed with the plan. There would be booty to be had, something to cheer the men up at least.

Agis raised his cup. 'To the gravestones,' he said.

'To the gravestones,' they replied.

'To victory,' Polymnis added. 'And to our kinship in this great endeavour.'

'To Victory! *Hoi-hoi-hoi*!' they responded and finally drank.

The tent flap opened and a hippeus, caked entered, holding a scroll. 'My Lord, an urgent message from Sparta...' He stepped forwards and handed Agis the sealed scroll.

The commanders exchanged curious looks. The two ephors, as miserable as widows, moved close to the King as he snapped the seal and unfurled the message. He turned to a lamp standard and read the short message under the light.

After he had finished reading, he kept the uncoded dispatch in front of his face, to give him a few moments to think.

Menedaios and Polymnis, standing directly opposite one another, exchanged a look, they could see it was serious.

Eventually, Agis lowered the letter and looked up. 'King Pleistoanax advises that an Athenian force has landed at Pylos and have installed fortifications and hoplites there. A Spartan force has engaged the enemy, but has been unable to overcome them. The Spartan Morai are ordered to move at once to Messene...' He looked at the allies. 'Eleusis will have to wait. Menedaios, give the order to muster the morai, we march as soon as they're ready.'

'As you command.' Menedaios left the tent.

SIXTY-SEVEN

Pylos, Spartan territory of Messene

Seven days later

The small band of Athenians had placed themselves in a defensible position on the promontory. They had constructed stone walls, using primitive methods of dry-walling, built from rocks and anything else they could find, creating strong defences to the landward and seaward side of the cliffs to defend from an amphibious attack. Demosthenes posted archers and light infantry to protect the seaward defences, where they could react quickly and kill from a distance.

Demosthenes, had around six hundred men with him, ninety of them were hoplites, fifty from Athens and forty Messenian exiles, who were on their way to Naupaktos when they spotted the Athenian ships, they pulled into Pylos Bay.

Demosthenes told them his plan, he had already corrupted and persuaded some of the local Helots into joining them, keeping them supplied with provisions. He asked the Messenians, who were the sons of the Helots who left Messene in exile twenty some years ago, bringing the Helot revolt to an end. That was then and this was now, and when Demosthenes asked them to stay, they refused, but in a gesture of alliance, goodwill and patriotism to their motherland Messene, they agreed to leave forty of their hoplite marines, all of who had volunteered to a man without being asked.

They were tough, battle hardened, Spartan hating warriors of the first order, and they had a lot of old scores to settle with their ancient enemy, who had subjugated their people for hundreds of years.

The Spartan slaughter of the Helots during the uprising was beyond barbarity, tens of thousands of Helots had been butchered by the merciless red cloaks, turning the Pamisos River crimson with Messenian blood; men, women – children, many were trying to reach Mount Ithome, where the main Helot rebel army had dug in deep, ready to make their last stand, fighting for their very lives and their homeland, they denied the Spartan's a single toe's length of ground on that sacred mountain. This was a perfect opportunity to unleash their long-awaited vengeance on the red cloaks, and they seized upon it.

Demosthenes's force had little in the way of tools and there was a scarcity of weapons to issue to the sailors of his triremes, who were pressed into manning the seaward defences with the light infantry, armed with grappling hooks, slingshots and clubs.

Even with the assistance of those local Helots Demosthenes managed to entice into helping, gave the bold Athenian very little help, especially as six thousand Lakedaimonian hoplites, two and a half thousand of them elite Spartans were now encamped at the end of the promontory, and they were watching every move being made by both the invaders and the local Helots, who dream of eating Spartans raw.

Demosthenes wavered as he looked at their campfires glowing, the innumerable assembly of the deadliest warriors upon the earth. If they managed to break through his makeshift defences, the Spartans would tear them to pieces.

Last night, under the cover of darkness, Demosthenes dispatched two of his five ships to row with all speed and urgency to intercept Eurymedon's fleet, now on its way to Corcyra, still in the grip of civil war, to reinforce the Democratisers, and then the plan was to sail on to Sicily and a mount an attack on pro-Spartan allies such as Syracuse with his thirty-five war triremes.

It had been an accident, or perhaps a twist of fate, that the Athenian fleet ever came to Pylos at all. The fleet had been hit by a severe storm, forcing them to seek shelter in the bay between the

Island of Sphacteria and the mainland. Demosthenes, who was no longer in office, but a private citizen, had requested to accompany Eurymedon as a volunteer. He quickly realised the potential wound Athens could inflict on Sparta by seizing Pylos, not simply for its tactical advantage, but for the psychological impact it would have on the Spartans, having an enemy squatting in their home territory. He quickly identified the defensive position he now occupied, and laid a plan before Eurymedon and Sophokles to occupy the promontory and fortify it. He asked them to give him men and some of his ships from the forty strong fleet.

Sophokles and Eurymedon both refused outright, but Demosthenes, like a petulant child, pressed them hard, putting good arguments to them, but they remained reluctant.

In the end, the decision was taken out of their hands, when the Athenian marines and sailors spontaneously started building the defensive walls and palisades upon which Demosthenes now stood. It was only then that Eurymedon and Sophokles relented and agreed to leave Demosthenes behind with five Triremes and fifty hoplites and some light infantry.

From the top parapet of his makeshift fortress, Demosthenes surveyed the Spartan encampment in the baleful light of dusk, seeing the campfires burning and hearing the songs of the Lakedaimonian warriors drifting disembodied up the steep hill that separated them unsettled his nerves, and as he looked at his hoplites positioned along the parapet, he could see the unease in them too.

'Good of them to sing to us,' he said in an attempt to ease their fear with some humour.

The men gave out a laugh, but there was no joy in it.

'They won't be singing after running up that hill,' said one of the men. 'I can tell you that. They'll be too exhausted to sing, carrying all that armour. Easy meat for our spears...'

'That's the way of it, soldier,' said Demosthenes. 'They won't scale these walls. We won't let them. They may out number us, but we hold a solid position and all the advantages, just as their beloved Leonidas did at the Fiery Gates. Trust me, men, it should us who are singing. And once the reinforcements arrive, well, we'll hold out for as long as the war lasts if necessary.'

There was a murmur of agreement and nodding heads. These men were ready to fight – ready to die.

It wasn't Eurymedon's fleet that came sailing over the horizon at dawn the next morning, it was the Spartan fleet, and they came ready for a fight.

SIXTY-EIGHT

'*They do know how to build a wall those Athenians, do they not?*' Brasidas quipped dryly as they looked at Demosthenes's position from the forward quarterdeck of the Medusa. The small Athenian force, he observed, had made his positions on and beneath the promontory cliffs.

'They've had a lot of practice,' said Lysander.

Brasidas laughed as his eyes roved the coastline. There he was, he Athenian in command, standing on the rocks looking back at him, his dark blue cloak billowed by the wind, clad in his hoplite armour, his helmet tilted back on his head. He made eye contact with Brasidas. 'Bring us in a little closer, let's see how jumpy these rabbits are,' he ordered.

'As you command,' said the boatswain without hesitation. He ordered the men at the rudders to bring the Medusa closer to shore.

Brasidas stood as bold as Zeus himself, his legs apart, his hands on his hips, there for all to see. 'Closer,' he ordered.

'Lord, there are rocks in these waters,' the boatswain cautioned.

'Noted. Bring us closer.'

The boatswain gave a nod of his head with a reluctant look in his eyes, he ordered the steersmen to come in closer.

They sailed in provocatively close to the enemy position and to where the deadly rocks met the sea and sat like teeth beneath the water, causing the coxswain a few nervous moments when Brasidas ordered him to get even closer.

The Athenians were getting nervous behind their barricades.

'Hold your nerve, men!' Demosthenes called. 'They're just looking at us...!'

Aboard the gorgon trireme Stheno, which was a thousand yards away with the rest of the Spartan fleet, Thrasymelidas was also looking uneasy as he watched Brasidas's daring sail-by. 'There's no caution in that man,' he said.

'Fortunate it is that the gods love him, then,' Kallikratidas responded.

Thrasymelidas looked at his young adjutant. 'The gods always love the bold...'

Demosthenes's three ships had been drawn up onto the beach prows out, jutting like giant spears into the bay against attack, their masts sails and rigging lying on the sandbank.

'I've seen enough,' said Brasidas. He ordered the ship to re-join the fleet.

*

Thrasymelidas, Brasidas, Kallikratidas, Lysander and several other officers went ashore and were conveyed by perioikoi hoplites to the sprawling Spartan camp.

Lysander looked along the bay to the sandbank, where Demosthenes's three ships were beached. He observed the sailors aboard them, who were poorly armed with clubs, scythes grappling hooks, knives and anything else they could lay their hands on to use as weapons, and they had made flimsy shields from reeds and birch. He could see the Athenian warriors in their positions just beyond the narrow stretch of beach below, behind their hastily built palisades. Archers and peltasts. He saw heavy hoplites too, further up, also behind the dry-stone walls and the natural defences offered by the rocky terrain. Few in number, but he recognised the difficulty they would have in assailing Demosthenes's position.

At the Spartan camp, they met with King Agis, who had marched the Lakedaimonian divisions directly from Attica.

There was a smell of stale mildew in the big tent, being hastily packed up in rainy Attica when they left, and after a few hot days on the road, the mildew had fermented. Even with a burner billowing sweet smelling resins did little to diminish the unpleasant odour, added to that the number of sweaty officers in the tent adding their own rancid smells as the hot midmorning sun pounding down on them. But these were the smells of war, just as surely as the air fettering stink of blood, meat, shit and piss in the battle field, or the rotting corpses upon it. To the seasoned warrior, these were the lurid perfumes of their creed.

It was cramped in the big tent; besides Thrasymelidas, Brasidas, Epitadas and Lysander, there were two ephors, King Agis and four senior commanders from Sparta, Skiritis and Tegea shifting their weight.

'... We have little time,' Agis went on as he looked at his commanders. 'News has arrived minutes ago that Athenian ships under the joint command Eurymedon and Sophokles have turned about and are on their way to reinforce their friends.'

'Do we know who's commanding the interlopers on the promontory?' asked Brasidas.

'Demosthenes,' said the Skiritan general.

Brasidas nodded his head. He knew this name. Last year, Demosthenes had been elected a strategos, and made a play for the new Spartan colony Herakleia, which commanded a controlling position at Boeotia's flank, and the road to Thessaly. The fortress colony is located on a rocky plateau overlooking the left bank of the Asopos River in a tactically prominent position in the shadow of Mount Oeta northwest of Thermopylae, where Leonidas and the Three Hundred Dioskouri stood so valiantly against the might of Xerxes and the Median invaders. From a tactical point of view, Herakleia's position is vital to counter any rear-guard actions against Boeotia from the enemy.

Fortunately, Demosthenes met with disaster, and was routed from the territory by Sparta's Trachian allies. Demosthenes's Messenian and Acarnanian allies also suffered heavy losses inflicted on them, and they didn't get anywhere near Herakleia. Brasidas had a measure of respect for him, his attempt was bold and brave.

'We have to act quickly, My Lord,' said Thrasymelidas. 'We've looked at the situation from the coast,' he went on, 'and it's vital that we deny Eurymedon the harbour,' he said.

'What do you suggest?' asked Agis.

'There's only two channels into the harbour...' Thrasymelidas turned to the crude map outlined on a stretched tanned cow skin showing the bay and the island of Sphacteria that sheltered the bay from the sea. 'At each end of this island,' he said.

They looked at the map.

'Does the island have a name?' asked Brasidas.

'Sphacteria,' said Lysander, recalling the name from when he was posted here when he was a first-year hippeus. 'As memory serves, there are remnants from an ancient fortress at the northern end,' he said. 'From King Nestor's time.'

'Have you been over there, Lysander?' asked Agis.

'No, My Lord.'

Brasidas looked at the map. Also painted on it was the location of Demosthenes's position in the cliffs on the promontory, in a difficult place to reach by land and by sea with just a narrow strip of beach, occupied and defended by the Athenians, deadly and jagged rocks everywhere else, making a sea landing almost impossible. An assault by land was uphill all the way, and Demosthenes had positioned his hoplites and crack-shot archers along his landward wall, making the Lakedaimonians easy prey, as the soldiers who first arrived found out when they tried taking the Athenians in a charge up to the walls before the main army arrived.

Agis looked back at Thrasymelidas. 'Continue.'

'My Lord...' He pointed to Sphacteria. 'Here at the northern end of the island, it's wide enough for two ships abreast to pass. And here...' He pointed to the southern end of Sphacteria, 'it's wide enough for several ships to pass abreast of one another. Here is our most vulnerable point. The narrow channel between Sphacteria and the promontory can be easily blockaded to deny the Athenian fleet entry into the bay. The southern end won't be so easy–'

'We must blockade and defend these sea lanes to deny them,' said Polymnis.

Thrasymelidas nodded his head. 'we'll need to put men onto the island,' he said.

There was a brief discussion and it was agreed to put men onto the island.

'We should mount a simultaneous attack by land and by sea, My Lord...' He looked at Agis and then at the others. 'And overwhelm them.'

'It won't be easy,' said Thrasymelidas. 'Getting our ships in close enough to mount an amphibious attack.'

*

Four hundred and twenty Lakedaimonian hoplites, including fifty crack Spartans were chosen by lot from across the divisions, with the Spartans went their servants, who were themselves armed with swords and spears, adding another fifty more combatants to their ranks.*

Lysander was down at the beach at dusk, when the hoplites marched down with Epitadas. He spotted Pantares was among them. Once Epitadas stood them down, Lysander came over.

Pantares extricated himself from the other men, beaming at Lysander.

'Greetings, Pantares.'

'Greetings. I saw you earlier, when you were with the Navarch and Syntagmatarkhis Brasidas.'

They walked up into the tall grass beyond the beach and sat down.

'Your friend Kromios is in the camp too,' said Pantares.

Lysander nodded his head, glancing into the bay, where several of their shops were guarding the channels either side of Sphacteria.

A phylarch shouted for the hoplites to board the waiting ship.

'Our time is to be brief it seems,' said Lysander. 'Gods watch over you, Pantares.'

'And may they watch over you. 'No more than a few days, the lochagos said. I hope we get an opportunity to meet properly again then,' he said.

Lysander nodded his head. 'we'll share a jug.'

'And a bed I hope.'

Lysander smiled. 'That too.'

Pantares rose to his feet and hurried back to the others, who were already boarding the ship that was to carry them over to the island on Demosthenes's blindside.

Lysander watched the ship sail across the bay, little knowing the terrible fate that awaited them. A fate that would altar the course of the war, and put an end to the legend of Spartan invincibility forever after.

* ***Ambiguous. History does not tell us how many servants went over to Sphacteria with Epitadas, only that their servants went with them. Nor do we know the fate of these servants after the battle.***

SIXTY-NINE

The attack began at dawn the next day as the landward charge on the Athenians began, so too did the naval assault with several Peloponnesian ships, two of them Spartan.

Brasidas was commanding the lead ship. He knew he had to set the example to his nervous compatriots on the other ships, to demonstrate that courage is measured in bold but calculated risks, and what needed to be done without hesitation.

Lysander could see Epitadas's hoplites up on the island, armed with their shields and spears, moving into position at the north end of the island opposite Demosthenes's fort; one of them was his friend Pantares, but he was unable to distinguish one Spartan from the other, their faces hidden behind tempered bronze.

'There!' Brasidas pointed to the rocky spit of land, the jagged rocks stuck out like teeth, ready to rip their hull open. 'Ground us!'

The coxswain and boatswain were horrified.

'Greater, more noble, more terrible,' Brasidas said, invoking the warrior chant to the gods before battle as they anoint themselves with funereal oils and comb their long hair to make them presentable to the afterlife, knowing they went to their deaths as honourable men – as Spartans. 'Run us aground!'

The coxswain nodded his head. 'As you command.'

Brasidas ordered Lysander to muster the men, then he ordered the boatswain to signal the two Corinthian ships following behind them. Brasidas boomed out: 'RAMMING SPEED!'

At once in synchronisation, the oars rose from the water, thrust forwards-dipped and heaved back over and over, the ship speeded to fourteen knots, the prow splitting the clear green-blue water with a swoosh, sending out wavelets either side, the embolon horn glinting in the morning sunshine sloping across the water

The shore grew ever closer, the deadly rocks ever bigger and more threatening – the Athenian defenders sheltered nervously behind their walls, looking incredulous as the Spartan trireme speeded towards the rocky strip on land in front of their palisades.

Demosthenes, wearing a brown leather skinned torso cuirass and clasping a hoplon shield and his spear stared in near disbelief at the lone Spartan ship speeding head on towards the deadly rocks. He looked on the deck and saw the Spartans liveried in their bronze, draped in crimson mustering at the forward end of the ship in readiness to jump onto the land, ready to fight – ready to kill. 'The mad bastard's going to run his ship aground,' he mumbled to himself, and then he shouted to the lower wall: 'ARCHERS AT THE READY!'

Above, in the main fort, he could hear the shouts and clashes of battle as the Peloponnesians charged up the promontory from the landward side, just north of the ruins of Nestor's palace. But here, from the sea was there most vulnerable point.

Their best hope was to strike quickly and get ashore in number to overrun the enemy positions behind their cowardly walls of rock and stone, Brasidas had told his men as the oars swept the water, below them, propelling them ever onwards, they were but seconds from the inevitable impact of the ship hitting the spit of rocky beach, the cockswain doing his best to put them between the hungry rocks rather than on them. Fortunate it was, that he was an experienced seaman.

Brasidas, Lysander and fifty crack Spartan hoplites held onto whatever was available, waiting for the imminent crash, the promontory now looming above them.

Lysander looked up and he could see men charging Demosthenes's wall, men fell, shot with arrows. Some fell from the cliff and smashed onto the rocks or into the water, their screams filling the air.

Suddenly – startlingly, even if expected, there was a tremendous grating as the hold scraped along the rocks beneath the water – then a terrific CRASH and everybody jerked forwards violently as the ship grounded onto the rocks.

'VICTORY OR DEATH!' Brasidas called.

The Athenian archers let fly their arrows, whistling as they cut the air–

'NEEDLES!'

The Spartans raised their shields to cover and a rain of arrows thumped into their shields, bouncing off the bronze, only a few them pierced it...

All at once, Demosthenes's light infantry and peltasts leaped over the wall and charged at the ship, launching their javelins at the Spartans–

'GIVE THEM DEATH!' cried Brasidas, leaping forwards to jump ashore at the head of his men – in the same moment a javelin struck Brasidas and pierced his cuirass at the abdomen – Brasidas staggered back and swayed, but he was still on his feet, the spears sticking out of him, he could feel something warm running down his legs and for a terrifying moment, he thought he had pissed himself, and that would not be a good look in the afterlife, but then he realised it was blood – THUMP, he was hit again, by an arrow this time, in the side where his armour was weakest.

The world suddenly made no sense, voices shouting all at once and he didn't understand a single one of them, the world around him spun at incredible speed with flashes of light – he could feel himself falling into a dark bottomless pit–

'BRASIDAS!' Lysander called in horror and utter panic as Brasidas dropped to his knees, an arrow and spear sticking out of him; Lysander leaped to him–

Brasidas felt all the strength leaving his body – *is this death*? Then came the blackness–

Brasidas toppled, hanging limply over the gangway, his arms dangling over the side, all around the Athenians were charging at the ship with a roar of voices, trying to board, but the Spartan hoplites and crew fought for all they were worth.

Brasidas's shield slipped from his arm and landed on the beach, washed by waves. The Athenians scrambled for it, to retrieve it as trophy, and to deny Brasidas the honour of going to his grave laid upon his precious shield.

Lysander struggled along the deck to reach Brasidas, relentlessly jabbing his spear and smashing his shield into to Athenians scrambling to get aboard as he fought his way through the roaring chaos to get to Brasidas.

Finally, he reached Brasidas's apparently lifeless body, fearing the worse. He and several hoplites pulled Brasidas's bloody body onto the deck, dragging him to safety...

'He's still alive!' said one of the men.

'BACKWATER! BACKWATER!' came a panicked shout.

Brasidas's hand moved.

Lysander pulled Brasidas's helmet off and tossed it to one side and it clattered on the deck. He pulled his own helmet off and did likewise.

'I don't know how long for,' said one of the hoplites, watching the blood leaking onto the deck from under Brasidas's armour. 'He's losing a lot of blood...'

All around the din and clatter of battle went on. Hoplites were thrusting their spears into the Athenians trying to board the ship. The oars backstroked frantically.

One of the Corinthian ships came in and threw them a line to toe them off the beach, and hope for the best that their hull wasn't smashed open.

The second Corinthian and the Euryale speeded in, side on to the shore, with archers on their decks, and they opened fire to drive the Athenians back.

Lysander refused to accept that Brasidas was dying. He simply refused to believe it, and he refused to leave his side. *He can't die, gods save him! Gods save him...*!

THE END

To follow: Gods of Men, AMPHIPOLIS

CHRONOLOGY of KEY EVENTS

*** All years are BCE.**

*** I refer to the Peloponnesian War as the Delian War, which indeed it was from the Peloponnesian perspective.**

464 (?) **A devastating earthquake in Lakedaimon**, sparks a Helot revolt, primarily in Messene.

464 First Peloponnesian (Delian) war begins.

455 (?) **Approximate year of Lysander's birth**. He is the son of Aristokleitos, an impoverished noble from the Herakleidai (Forebearer of Herakles/Hercules).

448 (?) **Aged 7, Lysander** enters the Rearing (Agōgē).

445 Helot revolt ends.

445 The Thirty Years Peace (peace of Nicias) between Sparta and Athens is sworn to, bringing an end to the First Peloponnesian (Delian) War.

441 Revolt of Samos against Athens.

439 The Samian revolt is crushed by Pericles. Pericles orders the crucifixions of the Samian trierarchs (ships' captains), who are crucified in the Agora of Samos. The act is widely condemned by the Hellenic (Greek) states, especially Sparta. This event is arguably one of the catalysts towards the Peloponnesian (Delian) War, and a sign of the "un-Hellenic brutality to come".

436 (?) **Lysander graduates the Rearing (Agōgē)**. He was probably inducted into the Three Hundred Hippeis (cavalry). Note: The Three Hundred aka **Dioskouri** were elite heavy infantry and not mounted cavalry.

435 The outbreak of war between Corcyra (mod. Corfu) and Corinth.

433 Corcyra asks Athens for an alliance, and puts her large navy at Athens's disposal. Athens ratifies the treaty.

433 The Battle of Sybota was a naval engagement off the Sybota Islets near Corcyra. The Corcyraeans put 110 warships commanded by Miciades, Aisimides and Eurybatos, plus 10 Athenian warships commanded by Lakedaimonios, Diotimos, and Proteas (who have strict orders <u>not</u> to engage Corinth unless Corinth attempt to land Marines on Corcyra, but in war even the best laid plans go awry) against 150 Corinthian and Megarian warships under the command of Xenoklides of Corinth. The battle is intense and violent, with the belligerent ships coming close together, allowing armed boarding parties. The fighting is at close quarters, more like a land battle than a naval engagement. The ten Athenian warships disobey orders and engage the Corinthians, a violation of the Thirty Years Peace. Indecisive outcome, although both sides claim victory, and raise Trophies to the goddess Nike (Victory). This is the event that triggers the Pan-Hellenic war we call the Peloponnesian War (Delian War).

433 (?) possibly 432, Athens, under Pericles enacts the Megarian Decree, effectively cutting Sparta's ally Megara, a merchant city state on the Isthmus of Corinth off from all Delian ports. Sale of all Megarian goods are barred from Delian markets, the excuse used is an accusation that Megara had committed sacrilege against Demeter. This is one of the first state imposed sanctions and embargoes in recorded history.

433 After pressure from Corinth, Corcyra and other aggrieved allies, the Spartans reluctantly summon the allies to the first of two congresses in Sparta, to debate if Athens had broken the peace treaty. The issue is hotly debated. The Eurypontid King of Sparta, is reluctant to declare war on the Athenian Empire and delivers an impassioned speech to the congress, not to go rashly into war in hot blood.

433 Second congress of the Spartan allies. A vote is taken by the Spartan Gerousia (assembly of elders). The vote favours war by a majority.

433 Still hopeful for peace, Archidamos of Sparta dispatches the first of several embassies to Athens, to appeal for bi-lateral talks. Athens reject the requests, insisting on arbitration, which Sparta cannot accept. A phony war begins.

431 The Thebans launch a daring attack on their neighbouring city of Plataea, an Athenian ally, through means of treachery. Eurymakhos (Lat. Eurymachus) sneaked 118 Theban soldiers into the city. The assault fails, Eurymakhos and his men are captured by the Plataeans. Some days later, the Plataeans executed all of them, the Phony War ends and the long and bloody fighting war begins.

431 The first annual invasion of Attica by the Spartans and their allies, who try to entice the Athenian army out from behind Athens' impenetrable walls for pitched battle by burning their estates. The Athenians refuse to engage the Spartans in a pitched battle. This is the first real indication that this war would not be fought in the traditional hoplite way; instead the war will be a protracted and bloody affair, and would change the nature of warfare in Europe that resounds to this very day.

431 Siege/Battle of Methone. An Athenian fleet of 100 warships under the commands of Carcinus, Proteas and Socrates, with 1,000 hoplite marines and 400 archers besiege the Messenian city of Methone. The siege is broken by Brasidas with 100 hoplites and most likely their Mothones (servants) another 100 men, being lightly armed and placed in the ranks to strengthen Brasidas's number. Brasidas, vastly outnumbered, breaks the siege with a bold and daring attack on the 800 Athenians commanded by Socrates, who were besieging the city from the land, while the Athenian fleet blockaded the city from the seaward. The attack by Brasidas became legendary, as did the man himself.

430 Outbreak of plague in Athens. The city and beyond are ravaged by the plague, that decimates the population.

429 Battle of Rhium, Gulf of Corinth, takes place between 47 Peloponnesian ships under the commands of Machaon, Isocrates, Agatharchidas. (The ships were on their way with troops in support of the Spartan Navarch Knemos who is mounting an amphibious attack against the Acarnanian fortified city of Stratos) and 20 Athenian triremes under the command of Phormio. The battle was an Athenian victory.

429 Battle of Naupaktos. Following the Battle of Rhium, Sparta sends 3 senior officers to Knemos as "advisers". They are Brasidas, Timokrates and Lycophron. It is decided to attack Naupaktos to drive the small Athenian force led by Phormio out of the gulf. The operation starts well but turns into a debacle. Athenian victory, although the Corinthian contingent claim the day. (Timokrates is killed).

428 The plague abates, but it does not completely vanish, with sporadic outbreaks throughout much of the war.

428 Mytilene, an ally/subject of Athens, secretly send Emissaries to Sparta asking for assistance in a planned revolt against Athens who refuse to allow them to divorce from the alliance. The Spartans agree to send ships and hoplite marines, and one of their spies, Salaethos.

427 Civil War erupts on Corcyra, with oligarchic pro-Spartans who want to end the alliance with Athens.

427 Mytilene rises up in revolt. Athens crushed the revolt ruthlessly. A Spartan fleet with hoplite marines, dispatched to assist the Mytileneans refuses to engage the Athenian fleet at Lesbos and retreats. The hard-line Athenian politician Cleon pushes for the extermination of all Mytilenean men and boys and the enslavement of the women and girls. Initially, the Athenian Bouleuterion (senate) agree and a ship is dispatched with the order. But the following day, the decree is overturned, and only the ringleaders of the revolt are executed along with the Spartan spy Salaithos.

427 (?) King Archidamos dies. He is replace by his son, Agis II.

426 Demosthenes of Athens is elected as a general. He takes a fleet of ships and marines into western Hellas.

426 the exiled Agiad king, Pleistoanax is recalled back to Sparta following a Delphic oracle obtained by corruption through the exiled Agiad king, King Pleistoanax's younger broth Aristocles.

425 Battle of Pylos. A small Athenian force under the command of Demosthenes, occupies the promontory. King Agis who is in Attica with the army returns home urgently, marching the Lakedaimonian army to Messene. Word is also sent to Navarch Eurymedon and Brasidas, on their way to Corcyra with a fleet of ships and marines to support the Oligarchic faction. Brasidas attempts a heroic landing on a narrow strip of rocky land at the foot of the promontory to oust the Athenians. Brasidas is seriously wounded as he rallies his men to jump ashore and take the Athenian positions.

425 Battle of Sphacteria. Lakedaimonian soldiers, exceeding 400 in number including some Spartans are landed on the small island of Sphacteria under the command of Epitadas. The Athenians cut the soldiers off from their Lakedaimonian brethren, try to starve the Spartans on Sphacteria into surrendering, but they are unable to blockade the island tightly enough, and loyal Helots and Spartans manage to keep the soldiers supplied. In Athens the government is worried is concern that the approaching winter will necessitate abandoning the blockade, unless the stalemate is broken. The politician Cleon sails reinforcements from Athens and joins forces with Demosthenes, and the Athenians launched an assault on Sphacteria. Landing on a poorly defended point, the Athenians overrun the Spartan beachfront defences and advance inland, harassing the Spartans by using bows and spears, whenever they attempt to push the Athenians back. The Spartans retreat to the northern end of the island, where they dig in behind their fortifications, but when the Athenian Messenian allies succeeds in bringing his soldiers into the Spartan rear, the Spartans surrender.

The Athenians capture 292 hoplites 120 of who are Spartans. This surrender of Spartan hoplites delivers a deep a wounding blow to Sparta and emboldens the enemy, who make a great deal of propaganda from the Spartan surrender. The prisoners are taken back to Athens, and the Athenians threaten to execute its prisoners if Sparta invades Attica. Consequently, the annual invasions were halted.

423 a one-year truce is agreed between Sparta and Athens.

422 Brasidas of Sparta and Cleon of Athens are killed at the battle of Amphipolis. A Spartan victory.

421 (?) the Peace of Nicias ends the first part of the war, often referred to as the Archidamian War. A fifty-years alliance between the two superpowers is agreed, but it does not last. Within 5 years, the war will rekindle.

419 Athens makes an alliance with Sparta's neighbour and old enemy Argos. This does not sit easily with the Spartans.

415/14 Athens sends a fleet to Sicily. Assault and capture of Sparta's ally, Syracuse.

413 Athens is defeated in Sicily.

413 Sparta declares war on Athens. Sparta sends a fleet under Gylippos to Sicily.

411/10 Oligarchic coup at Athens, the democracy is overthrown. 400 oligarchs now rule Athens.

410 Democratic counter-revolution at Athens. Oligarchs are overthrown, democracy is restored.

406 Athens defeats the Spartan fleet at the Battle of Arginusae.

406 Athens rejects Spartan offer of peace.

405 Lysander is placed in de-facto command of Peloponnesian Aegean forces.

405 Lysander wipes out the Delian naval forces at the Battle of Aegospotami.

404 Athens is besieged by Lysander's forces on land and sea.

404 Athens capitulates.

404 Lysander installs the Thirty Tyrants to rule over Athens.

404/03 Athens formerly becomes a member of the Spartan/ Peloponnesian League. Sparta is now the most powerful state in Europe for the next 30 years, until they're defeated by Thebes.

A

Agathoergoi:

"Good service men." Five former hippeis, selected or elected annually to serve as diplomats, foreign emissaries and unofficial spies, but they were not Sparta's only spies.

Apella:

The citizen assembly of Sparta, to which every Spartiate belonged. (at Sparta a man did not become a citizen until he reached the age of 30). The Apella ratified laws made in the Gerousia (see below) and were responsible for electing the Ephors every year, and the elders (gerontai) of the Gerousia, who were elected for life.

B

Bouleuterion:

The representative citizen assembly/senate house of democratic city states such as Athens, which had an elected council of 500 men.

D

Dioskouri:

Mythology. The twins Castor and Pollux were the Dioskouri - 'The sons of Zeus sometimes translated as Sons of God.' They were the sons of Leda, Queen of Sparta, their conception being both human and god, one 'Castor' being sired by King Tyndareus, the other, 'Pollux' being sired by are said to have been hatched from an egg, and were most associated with equestrianism in Greco/Roman mythology. At Sparta, they were elite warriors, and the 300 hippeis (cavalry) of Sparta were colloquially known as Dioskouri. There are many stories and legends regarding Castor and Pollux, many contradicting one another, so I'll not dwell on them here.

E

Enomotarch:

Commander of an enomotia. 25 to 36 men.

Enomotia:

"Sworn band." Approximately 36 men sometimes more.

Ephor:

'Overseer' were annually elected magistrates at Sparta, and consisted of 5 members, one an Eponymous Ephor, after whom the year was named. The Ephors had a lot of power, and oversaw the kings of Sparta and curtailed their monarchic powers. Upon their election to office (the Ephorate) they declared war upon the helots, and bands of youths, possibly candidates for the Krypteia (see Krypteia below) roamed the countryside to murder helot men.

Eponymous Ephor:

Each year, one man was elected Eponymous Ephor, usually in recognition of some service or notable deed, after whom the Spartan year was named.

Erastês:

'Lover.' Usually pertains to the young adult male in an ephebophilic relationship with a youth. (see eispnelas above)

Erômenos:

'Beloved.' Usually pertains to the youth in an ephebophilic relationship with an older young man. (see aitas above)

G

Gerontes:

Member of the Gerousia, the council of elders at Sparta. There were 30 members of the Gerousia, the two kings from the Eurypontid and the Agiad dynasties, and 28 elected elders over age 60. The gerontai (plural), were elected for life by the Apella. (see Apella above)

H

Harmost:

Military governor of a Spartan province such as Kynouria or Messene. He was responsible for maintaining law, civic order and military deployments.

Hebóntés:

A young warrior aged between 20 to 30. It was not until men reached age 30 that they achieved citizenship, became Homoioi (the equals) and could call themselves Spartiates.

Helot:

The indigenous non Spartan population of conquered territories. Helots were not quite slaves, but not quite free either. They farmed Spartan estates (see kleroi below). Disenfranchised and brutally subjected, the helots were a constant threat to Spartan hegemony.

Hetaerae:

Pl. high class female escorts. Singular **Hetaira.** *Usually very beautiful and highly educated. Although their purpose undoubtedly involved sex, they were not considered to be prostitutes.*

Hippeis/Dioskouri:

Hippeis were cavalry in ancient Greece, except Sparta, which only periodically deployed its own cavalry. At Sparta, the hippeis were elite heavy infantry. They were the fabled 300 of Thermopylae. They made up a royal guard for the king and were selected by the Ephors from the elites hebóntai, 20-30 year olds, probably from the aristocracy. The 300 hippeis of Sparta were colloquially known as Dioskouri, the sons of Zeus. singular.

Hippagretas:

Commander of a wing of cavalry (hippeis).

Hoplite:

Infantryman.

Hoplon:

The large circular bronze armoured shield from which the hoplite takes his name.

Hypomeiones:

Spartan outcasts, either through transgression, failure at the Agōgē (Upbringing), or from poverty, being unable to afford to go through the Upbringing.

K

Kaddichos:

Lat. Caddichus was a large jar used to collect votes at the Spartan syssitia when voting for new members.

Krypteia:

"Hidden things" was a Spartan secret police made up of elite Spartan youths considered to be potential officer material. It was also a right-of-passage, the initiation into the Krypteia was by murdering a helot during the annual declaration of war against the helots by the incumbent Ephors for that year.

L

Lochos:

An infantry brigade of a minimum of 720 men. Contemporary sources such as Xenoklides puts the number at over one thousand men, but this is very unlikely.

Lochagos:

Military rank. Commander of a lochos.

M

Morai:

Unique to Sparta, the Morai were infantry divisions not including the Hippeis. There were 5 morae, representing the five villages of Sparta. The fourth and fifth morae usually tended home defense in times of war, while the first, second and third were crack frontline heavy infantry.

Mothax:

A mothax was of mixed race, through the union of a Spartan male and a perioikoi (see below) or helot woman, or from an impoverished family. Spartans could not legally marry perioikoi or helots, thus their offspring were mothakes (plural). It is also likely that very poor Spartans were also classed as mothakes.

Mothon:

Steward/servant. Mothones (plural) served Spartan warriors, usually from childhood at the Upbringing until one or the other died. Only the sons of rich Spartiates, or hearers of rich indulgent inspirers, could afford to pay for a personal mothon for a boy. The relationship between mothon and his master is uncertain, but it is likely in many instances that there were sexual and loving relationships between them. The mothones carried their masters' armor and went to war with them. They would probably have been taught how to fight and were likely as tough as their masters.

N

Navarch:

Naval rank. US/UK equivalent is Admiral.

P

Paidonomos:

'Boy-herder.' The Paidonomos was a magistrate rank, and he was basically the head teacher/principal of the Upbringing.

Palaestra:

Wrestling arena/school. There was a palaestra within the ephebeion. Wrestling, boxing, pankration (see below) were important parts of the curriculum.

Pankration:

A violent form of martial arts that combined boxing, wrestling, kickboxing and a sort of judo. It is still popular in Greece today.

Parasang:

Unit of measurement of Persian origin. Approximately 4 miles (6 kilometers).

Pentekostys:

A unit of the Spartan army consisting of approximately 180 men or more. (Not to be confused with Penteconter alt. spelling pentekonter, a 50 oared ship).

Phauaxir:

Fox-time. The right-of-passage of Spartan boys, living off their wits alone in the wilderness. This may have had a duration of months or possibly up to a year?

Phyle:

File. Unit of the Spartan army. Usually consisting of 12 men, sometimes more.

Phylarch:

NCO rank. The commander of a phyle/phyloi (file/files).

Polemarch:

Warlord. Spartan infantry rank. 'Warlord' commanded a mora (see above). The Spartan Polemarch was also in charge of a number of civil offices, and in war, abroad, their rank was equal to that of the kings. There were 6 polemarchs (polemarchoi) at Sparta. Athens also had an Archon Polemarchos, who was the senior general (strategos) at the Athenian High Command (strategoi).

Psiloi:

Soldiers without armour.

Pythia:

The oracle at Delphi.

S

Side-flasher:

Spartan colloquialism referring to the girls who underwent the girls version of the Upbringing, whose institutional name is lost to history. I refer to these girls as the Spartan Sisterhood. – It is worth noting here, that ancient societies were in the main misogynistic. Middle class and aristocratic women were often shut away by their menfolk and veiled in public. Forbidden to engage in commerce and disenfranchised from politics and owning property in their own right. Sparta was a very notable exception to these traditions. – Although disenfranchised from politics, Spartan women could and did maintain commercial interests, they could go about the streets as they pleased and could say more or less what they wanted. Women were held with special status at Sparta, for they are the mothers of Sparta's sons, and women who had given Sparta a son were held in very high regard. Looking at Sparta with contemporaneous eyes, one realizes that it was probably the most liberal and open society towards women until the advent of the 20th Century.

Stade (stadeion/stadion):

Unit of measurement. 184.9 meters or 202.2 yards, the size of an ancient Greek stadium.

Strategoi:

Athens and other city states, military high command.

Strategos:

Military rank at Athens and other city states. Equivalent Spartan rank of Polemarch. (At Sparta the rank held more authority and thus was very rarely used, as it, in effect, gave to one man the authority of the kings as supreme commander of ground and naval forces in theatres where the kings were not present. Lysander was one of the few Spartans in history to hold the rank of Strategos).

Syssition:

The syssition was the common dining mess. There were different messes which were inclusive for members of all ranks and positions. At 21, a young man was elected to a syssition by its members, who rolled pellets of bread and placed them in a jar. He could only be accepted to a syssition if the vote was unanimous.

T

Trierarch:

Captain of a Trireme, (see below).

Trièraulès:

Flutė player aboard a ship to pace the oarsmen's' rowing speeds.

Trireme:

Warship with three rowing decks. Commanded by a trierarch (see above).

X

Xeno:

Foreigner, outsider.

Lakonian Calendar

1. ***Herasios – October***
2. ***Apellaios – November***
3. ***Diosthyos – December***
4. ***January is Unknown, so I have used the Attican calendar to denote January***
5. ***Eleusinios – February***
6. ***Gerastios - March***
7. ***Artemisios – April***
8. ***Delphinios – May***
9. ***Phliastos – June***
10. ***Hecatombeus – July***
11. ***Carneios – August***
12. ***Panamos – September***

Attican Calendar

1. ***Hekatombaeon – July/august***
2. ***Metageitnion – August/September***
3. ***Boedromion – September/October***
4. ***Pyanepsion – October/November***
5. ***Maimakterion – November/December***
6. ***Poseideon – December/January***
7. ***Gamelion – January/February***
8. ***Anthesterion – February/March***
9. ***Elaphebolion – March/April***
10. ***Mounychion – April/May***
11. ***Thargelion – May/June***
12. ***Skirophorion – June/July***

Dear reader.

Thank you for reading my novel and I hope you enjoyed it! If you found this book useful, I'd be very grateful if you'd post a short review or rating on the retail site you purchased your book from. Your support really does go a very long way and makes a big difference and I read all the reviews so I can get your feedback and make future books even better. Thanks again for your support!

Remus.

Books by PHILIP REMUS include:

Gods of Men, Where the Spartans are Made (I)

Gods of Men, The Delian War (II)

Gods of Men, Rise of the Wolf (III)

Gods of Men, Amphipolis (IV)

Collegium, Brotherhood of Rogues (I)

Collegium, Blood of Fire (II)

Collegium, in the Shadow of Eagles (III)

www.philipremus.com[1]

1. *http://www.philipremus.com*

Also by Philip Remus

Collegium

Collegiüm, Blood of Fire
Collegium, Brotherhood of Rogues

Gods of Men

The Delian War
Gods of Men, Where the Spartans are Made
Rise of the Wolf
Gods of Men, Amphipolis

Watch for more at https://www.philipremus.com/.

About the Author

I have two great passions in my life, history and writing, which is an irony, considering that I'm also dyslexic. I was educated at an Inner London state high school and graduated with above average grades in English, English Lit and History. I grew in South East London, the son of a truck driver and a bookkeeper. I lived for four years in France and travelled extensively throughout Europe.

Read more at https://www.philipremus.com/.

www.ingramcontent.com/pod-product-compliance
Lightning Source LLC
LaVergne TN
LVHW041010150826
845672LV00001B/38

* 9 7 9 8 2 3 0 9 3 3 7 0 0 *